Powder Keg

A personal memoir of growing up a Knickerbocker
and the family history of how they came to be

Barbara Knickerbocker

Powder Keg

A personal memoir of growing up a Knickerbocker
and the family history of how they came to be

To Bridget-
You will recognize first hand
much of the story- content in Part I, and
the writing styles and techniques I
brought from days writing in your classes,
to bring sparkle to the content here-
and a "first-hand- observer" to history
of the distant past. Many thanks, Barb

Barbara Knickerbocker

BKB Press
New London, New Hampshire

Powder Keg
A personal memoir of growing up a Knickerbocker
and the family history of how they came to be

Barbara Knickerbocker Beskind

Published by the BKB Press
103 Hilltop Place
New London, New Hampshire 03257

Cover design: Kitty Werner, RSBPress
Book Design: Kitty Werner, RSBPress

ISBN 978-0-9817768-1-1

First U.S. Edition May 2008

Printed and bound in the United States

9 8 7 6 5 4 3 2 1

Dedications

I wish to dedicate this book, *Powder Keg*, to my father, Harrie Doughty Knickerbocker, and my mother, Mary Ham Knickerbocker. They withstood inordinate household stress—with unswerving devotion to each other, and to me.

I am deeply indebted—

To my father for imparting his strong sense of organization and attention to the date and detail, and his ability to analyze data for useful conceptual constructs;

To my mother for her love of research and curiosity to get to the roots of family history;

To my Grandmother Knickerbocker who inadvertently contributed to this book being written; and

To Isabel Knickerbocker Jordan, R.N., for her dedicated and positive influence during the early formative years of my life. Although she was not directly related, she was closer to us than some of those in our family who were next of kin.

Powder Keg also provides my stepsons, Mark and Daniel Beskind, and their children a window of little-known history. Surprising threads of history run parallel in the diaspora of the Jews and the Walloons. Their experiences in Europe and in the earliest days of our country intertwine and overlap.

Acknowledgments

The following individuals have made a significant contribution which they can each identify. They have either enriched or clarified the book or provided certain illustrations or other inclusions in it:

James Andrews
Roberta Andrews
Dorothy Burdick
James Coffin
Barbara Cooper, Ph. D.
Carol Fryer
Pauline Freer
Jeanne Gurin, MD
Roberta (Bobbi) Hohman
Reilly Hohman
Stana Iseman
Gloria Kamen
Paul Knickerbocker
Janet Le Brecht
Erna Laing
Catherine (Cathy) Lees
Roberta (Robin) Lees
Anne Mausolff
William Nash, Ph. D.
Judith Nierenberg
Rev. Charlotte Spencer
Mark Stern
Jon Stevens
Amy Wetzel

I wish to give my special appreciation to Mr. William Price of Sunapee, New Hampshire, who screened much of this manuscript for factual accuracy and clarity of presentation.

Mr. Peter Allen of the Evans Map Room, Baker-Berry Library, Dartmouth College, Hanover, New Hampshire, has been an invaluable asset. He has located and professionally prepared the series of 16th and 17th century maps of Europe and those of America.

I am especially appreciative to my friends, Bill and Carole Moody, of Pinehurst, North Carolina, for our travels in the spring of 2004 throughout the lowlands and the terrain of my distant ancestors. We visited Tournai of the Hainaut Province of Belgium, traveled through the Rhinephalz, also called the Palatinate in Germany, then along the IJssel River of the Overijssel Province to Wijhe, and to Amsterdam, Leiden, and The Hague.

I am appreciative to Jeremy D. Bangs, Ph D., curator of the Pilgrim Museum in Leiden, Holland, for his contribution to my research.

I appreciate the help from the staff of the Library of the Jewish Historical Museum in Amsterdam for their help in uncovering material about the original Portuguese Jewish congregation and their synagogue built in 1671, and information about Recife.

I am indebted to the Archaeological Department of the South Street Seaport Museum, 17 State Street, New York City, New York, 10004, for their excellent lectures throughout a one-week course there, the fall of 1995. Of particular relevance to my area of interest were the lectures entitled "Archaeological Excavations at Pearl and Whitehall Streets in 1984" and "New York Unearthed."

I wish to thank Michael Saddis, historian and librarian, Georgia Rehabilitation Institute, formerly Georgia Warm Springs Foundation, Warm Springs, Georgia, for his valuable assistance regarding information about Franklin Delano Roosevelt and his personal physical therapist, Alice Lou Plastridge (Converse), RPT.

I am grateful to Bridget Ahrens for nurturing my love of writing and her insightful guidance throughout this long process.

I extend my sincere appreciation to the following facilities and to their tireless staffs who have willingly enabled me to research areas of specific interest:

Adriance Library, Poughkeepsie, New York
Baker-Berry Library, Dartmouth College, Hanover, New Hampshire
Connecticut State Library, Hartford, Connecticut
Crossett Library, Bennington College, Bennington, Vermont
Dutchess County Historical Society Library and Archives, Poughkeepsie, New York
Family History Library, Church of Jesus Christ of the Latter Day Saints, Salt Lake City, Utah
Franklin Delano Roosevelt Library, Hyde Park, New York
Huguenot Historical Society Library and Archives, New Paltz, New York
Knickerbocker Historical Society, Schaghticoke, New York
New Hampshire State Historical Library, Concord, New Hampshire
New York State Library and Archives, Albany, New York
Pleasant Valley Free Library, Pleasant Valley, New York
Rauner Special Collections Library, Dartmouth College, Hanover, New Hampshire
Speer Library, Princeton Theological Seminary, Princeton, New Jersey

My appreciation goes to June Morgan Cole of Lady Lake, Florida, and to Ellen Perry Berkeley of Shaftsbury, Vermont, for their work in editing Part I, and to Sue Publicover of Castleton, Vermont for her work on the manuscript.

My special thanks goes to Kitty Werner of RSBPress of Waitsfield, Vermont, for her talented graphic design and expertise in preparing this book for publication.

Contents

Part II

Part III

Introduction
Glimpses through the Windows of History

P*owder Keg* is a multi-layered personal history of my extended family and an historical account of two ancestors.

Part I portrays my adult recollection of childhood in a house where three generations lived under one roof at my Grandmother Knickerbocker's home in Bangall, New York. I grew up in this matriarchal setting during the Great Depression when my father was unemployed and depressed.

The story relates how members of the household interacted, and impacted each other in powerful ways—there being limited alternatives. It focuses on the many aspects of history that touched my life and helped to shape it.

My grandmother's house firmly molded our lives. It contained sufficient stress that the whole household seemed at times likely to erupt. As a child, I learned that keeping my silence, or moving quietly, helped to keep the fragile peace.

As much as I appreciated the stresses on my mother then, my adult reflections of these circumstances confirm an even more profound respect. I am in awe of her dignity and grace in coping with difficult times over which she—had no control.

My mother had a deep interest in family genealogy, but my interest is marginal. Fortunately for me, this line of genealogy on each side of the family had been compiled by earlier generations. What is more relevant is that I share my mother's curiosity over the challenges, concerns, and conflicts of our early Walloon ancestors, circumstances over which they—had no control.

Events in history clearly directed the course of my professional career. This offered me opportunities to observe events that were unknown to the public then, and are little-known still. I have developed insights in retrospect, about those aspects of history as they related to my military service and professional life as an occupational therapist. These include insights about Franklin Delano Roosevelt, whom I had seen occasionally as a child, since we lived within 20 miles of his Hyde Park home.

Our house had been sold in 1971, long after I was grown. It was on a September afternoon in 1991, when I returned for the first time. As my foot touched the bottom step of the front porch I was shocked into a distant reality: I had left for college exactly 50 years before; it was the September before Pearl Harbor. During my four years at college, I had returned to visit over Christmas and summer vacations; after graduation, I left permanently to embark on a far-flung career.

The story opens when the current owners uncover a mysterious finding on the third floor. Since they were putting their house on the market, they invited a journalist from the *Poughkeepsie Courier* to meet me there in hopes I could confirm their speculation. A feature story about the possible historic link might stimulate interest and market value.

This obscure discovery was puzzling for them and a jolting experience for me. It unlocked long-buried memories, distressing questions, and now, new mysteries to be solved.

This book offers my perception of the family history filtered through the eyes and ears of childhood. I often heard words, or concepts, I did not understand, but I was on my own to discern their meaning. Frequently I developed unique misconceptions. Some were sad, some were humorous, but my interpretation was usually very different from what the adults in my grandmother's Victorian household would have given.

Part II cites relevant European history of the Walloons in the Belgic Lands of The Netherlands, dating back to the early days of the Protestant Reformation in the mid-1500's.

It provides a context of American history about the original Walloon settlers of Manhattan Island, the Dutch West India Company, and Nieuw Amsterdam prior to the time it bore that name. This is further depicted in Chapter 2 of Part III, entitled, 1630: A Benchmark Year in Nova Belgica and Beyond.

In order to convey the sense of time and place, I have used the spellings of that are consistent with the time being depicted. These may be at variance with today's usage. These include: Noordt, Jssel, Leyden (Leiden), Mechlin (Michelin), Macherel, and others: Hainaut is spelled Hainault by early historians Lamb, Wasseneur and de Laet.

Part III illuminates this history through the lives of two ancestors.

Adrian Vincent, an ancestor on my mother's side, arrived in 1634, a decade after the first settlers, eight Walloon families, landed on Manhattan Island. Drawing first on family genealogy, and then on historians' accounts, I have tried to construct a background that is presumed to be feasible.

It would appear that the Vincent family had been flax growers on the banks of the River Scheldt near Tournai, perhaps for generations. It would have put them at the heart of the Hainaut Province of the Belgic Lands during the early, contentious days of the Protestant Reformation.

Harmon Jansen (van Wye) Knickerbakker on my father's side, had a colorful career in the Dutch navy before departing for America in 1674. His family can be traced back to 1245 in the Oberyssel Province of The Netherlands.

Harmon settled north of Albany, in Half Moon, now Mechanicville, New York. It can be said that his endeavors led other courageous settlers to protect the northern end of the Hudson River from invasion by the French-armed Indians. Such an incursion could have split the tenuous hold of the emerging colonies the length of the river.

My grandmother Knickerbocker's lengthy monologues of family history fell on the disinterested, rejecting ears of childhood. However, this imposed heritage unwittingly became one of the forces behind writing *Powder Keg*. Having no direct descendants, and being the 25th generation traceable on my father's side, I felt this history should not be lost.

Of greater interest to me was the Walloon history already lost: (1) the Walloons' fierce fight for a reformed religion, (2) forging a settlement in the wilds of the Nieuw Nederlandt territory, and (3) planting the early seeds of our representative form of government.

In attempt to envision the personal experiences of my Walloon ancestor, I found benchmarks of early religious history in Nieuw Nederlandt that converged, and quite remarkably so between the Walloons and the Jews.

After years of research and writing, my exploration of this history came to an abrupt halt. In 1997, a new and compelling focus of interest arose in my life and for the next six years I devoted my time to abstract art. I became intrigued by creating it and studying its history and development. I was fascinated by the parallels and juxtapositions, of line and form in abstract art.

I was surprised, however, to discover how this could provide a unique perspective with which to recognize, and to analyze, the parallels and junctures that arise in life. In identifying what shaped the lives and character of my ancestors, I found parallels that seem enmeshed in me. For instance, their inventive traits and problem-solving skills appear to be the powerful roots that have influenced my own creativity, even though the time-frame is separated by centuries.

In trying to derive a better understanding of their distant past, I often traveled in the lowlands during the two years I was stationed with the army in Europe. A trip through Belgium and The Netherlands in 2004 helped me envision specific areas where these ancestors had lived their lives and fought their battles.[1]

Another trip in 2007 gave me a glimpse of the Dutch West India Company headquarters and the original Jewish Synagogue in Amsterdam that figure in this history.

This book has had a lengthy period of development, starting in 1992, soon after my return visit to Bangall. I did much of the early writing and Hudson River research, during three summers at the Bennington College Writing Program. This study served to support, or refute, findings by generations past on each side of the family. Most of the childhood stories in Part I were composed within the first five years. After a lapse of six years to focus on my art, I resumed concentrated work in 2003.

Many times during the research, writing, or revision phases, there have been surprising junctures in the process, which helped propel the manuscript. Three are cited:

First, was to learn from Jon Stevens at Schaghticoke, New York of the lineage on my father's side going back to 1245 which Paul Knickerbocker of Pittsford, New York had discovered in the New York State Library in Albany, New York around 1960.

1 One unfortunate habit of Americans is to use the term Holland and The Netherlands interchangeably. I have used the term Holland only when it refers to the single province, not to the collective term for the provinces of The Netherlands.

Second, has been to uncover the parallels in experience between that of the Sephardic Jews during the Spanish Inquisition with that of the Walloons of the Spanish-controlled Netherlands at the time of the Reformation.

In Europe, and in this country, their cultural and religious experiences have overlapped. Most notably, the location of the first services of the Dutch Reformed church by the French-language Walloons and their first celebration of The Lord's Supper in 1626, was the place where the first Jewish congregation worshipped after their arrival in 1654. It also became the site of the first Synagogue in North America, built in 1730.

Third, and surely serendipitous, were *The New York Times Book Review* of Russell Shorto's book, *The Island at the Center of the World* and an interview of the author by Terry Gross on National Public Radio in April of 2004. I was able to obtain a copy of this history of early Manhattan just days prior to leaving for my trip to Belgium and The Netherlands that spring.

I am indebted to Russell Shorto for citing the renowned Dutch historian of the period, and curator of the Pilgrim Museum in Leiden by the name of Jeremy D. Bangs, Ph.D., who has assisted me in further research.

My research has been drawn from literature of the present, and back to the long-distant past. I first looked to a cluster of authors and historians of the early 1900s, then to those of the mid-1800s, who were closer to the actual events, and finally, to those accounts from early Dutch historians Wassenaer and de Laet. Their writing is contemporaneous with an overview of the management of the Dutch West India Company from the Amsterdam Chamber, in the 1620's.

The most fascinating aspect of this endeavor has been to explore the little-known history about early Manhattan and the Walloons who came to settle it first. Collecting obscure facts from disparate sources often shapes a new significance to those times, when seen as a whole. This becomes the joy of discovery and ignites the driving force for further research.

There were also times throughout my writing that I felt it was not I, but the influence of a higher hand, helping me to craft, and create, this multi-layered manuscript. Such was the case when composing the final pages of *Powder Keg.* The insight about the unintended consequences of Washington Irving's writing came as a complete surprise to me, as it may to the reader.

Part I

This is the west side of my grandmother's house, the powder keg that becomes a character in the book, molding our lives and shaping our actions.

Seated: Thaddeus and Jerusha Ella Knickerbocker, my grandparents.

Standing: May K. Card, my aunt and Harrie D. Knickerbocker, my father photographed in 1920, a year after my parents married.

1

The Front Doorbell

I stood before the double front doors and pulled the tarnished brass knob that had been our doorbell. Its sound had not changed since I left—that same flat, tinny ring like a piano badly out of tune. When I lived here, its harsh clang aroused great expectations, ever hopeful someone would be coming to call. Sometimes it was a salesman for Hoover vacuum cleaners, Fuller brushes, or the *Encyclopedia Britannica*.

Had the doorbell ever rung for me? I could not remember that it had. Occasionally it was a visitor of Grandma's, one of those old ladies who shed their dreaded, spitty kisses on me. More often it was for Emma, the housekeeper.

Emma's minister at the Methodist Church in Bangall, New York, made annual pastoral calls. Even though Grandma never came down to greet him, he may have considered he had ministered to her as well, perhaps padding his record of contacts for the Lord just as he might have during the week while he peddled vacuum cleaners to supplement his paltry income. Never had I seen Jerusha Ella, my paternal grandmother, attend church even for a funeral or wedding, although it may have been different when she was younger.

Seldom did the bell ring for my mother, unless it was Miss Jordan, the district health nurse. Now, I realize how regularly she came. It was not that Miss Jordan came just to attend to Emma's minor ills and chronic pains, one bitter cold winter she came every day to see to Grandma, then in her mid-eighties, when she had pneumonia.

Miss Jordan's empathy extended throughout our family. She was compassionate for my mother's plight, as well as watchful of my growth and development in this household of black lace, corset stays, and rippled hairpins. She also shared my mother's concern over my father. He was fighting his depression the best way he could, head in his hands, staring at his well-polished, ten-year-old shoes.

I left for college in 1941. Now I faced this same front door 50 years later. I shifted my weight to the other foot. It seemed like endless minutes since I had rung the bell. I knew this shrill sound had been heard from cellar to third floor. No need to ring again. I knew precisely how the interior of that dark hall looked to anyone descending the carpeted front stairs. The muffled rhythm of right foot and opposite hand, shifting at regular intervals down the glossy, walnut banister sounded no different than when my grandmother lived here. Closer and closer. Fingers of the left hand must now be curling around the carved newel post.

As the key turned in the lock, the worn "tumblers" caught with a distinctly resistive sound. That old lock did not work any better when I was growing up. Maybe it had not worked for a lot longer. Did it work when Grandpa bought the house? It had been in the Knickerbocker family 87 years when I sold it in 1971. Even when I lived here, this old lock often resisted in an unwelcoming manner. My father and my grandmother knew best how to coax it into action.

If the person who was waiting on the other side of the door offered to help, or, heaven forbid, nudged it with the knee, each of us inside knew that spelled a prolonged delay. Narrow, frosted windows beside the doors allowed no view and only a vague guess as to the visitor's size.

Waiting on the porch that day, I finally saw the east half of the double-doors open. I was greeted warmly by the current owners. Suddenly it was as though they were not even there. Light from the south flooded the dark hall. I stepped in and looked through the open door to my right. With a measure of hesitation, I moved across the doorsill. The still, the static, the same scene of my grandmother's living room rushed in from the recesses of my mind. I could see each chair drawn up in its usual place around her square reading table. This was the house where I grew up. It was home only to my grandmother.

2

Under the Living Room Table

I remember as a child how I clutched Alice, my biggest doll, in my left arm and scooted under the square oak reading table. From there, I watched each adult draw up a chair to its designated position each evening. Grandma pivoted her brown wicker armchair away from the bay window with practiced precision. Neither her grip nor her arms ever faltered. As she sat down, she adjusted the lumpy pillow at her back. The scent of varnish passed my nose. My grandmother sat as erect as a queen, her chair facing the road. The two 40-watt bulbs burned in the brass reading lamp, throwing light over her right shoulder. Her Tiffany lampshade of barnyard brown and bile green cast a limited amount of light to each side.

Grandma weighed less than 90 pounds. She stood erect but still was no more than five feet in height. Her frail appearance belied the fact she was as sturdy physically as she was firm of mind and temperament. Her straight, white hair was combed back in military precision, twisted in a tiny bun at the back and held securely with hairpins. These aluminum wire pins, no longer than an inch and a half, were wavy near the rounded end and meant to suggest a softening look. None developed.

Her face was delicate, wrinkle-free, and powdered. Her cheeks were like the thin tissue paper she used to store fragile lace in a dresser drawer upstairs in her bedroom. Unlike my mother who suffered dreadfully on hot days, Grandma never felt the heat. She always looked cool. In fact, when she came downstairs on a hot summer afternoon in a long, white, dimity dress, petticoats, white shoes, and stockings, she looked like one of my expressionless dolls. But I loved my dolls.

In winter, a heavy knit sweater and black onyx beads covered her high-necked wool dress. Its hem reached to mid-calf when she stood up in her tiny, size five black Oxfords. She could wear the same pair of shoes for afternoons and Sunday best for a decade and still appear as presentable as a queen.

Emma, on the other hand, was a picture in contrast. Within weeks, a new pair of shoes would be curved like cashew nuts at the instep. Often they were decorated with flour, cake frosting, or egg yolks.

Emma arrived in the living room after her chores in the kitchen were finished. I watched her drag a small, caned rocker from the front window to the reading table. My parents registered a silent alarm when she jostled the table enough to rock the heavy lamp and its antique shade. She had assumed the ranking position years ago, while working for my grandparents. She sat with Grandma to her back and right, and faced Grandpa's chair. His chair, now occupied by my father, faced the front windows and the road beyond.

Emma had the warmest spot for winter. Her rocker was parallel to the long radiator between the two front windows. Above this aluminum-painted radiator was the mantel on which sat the gold-faced, antique marble clock. This was one of Grandma's treasured wedding presents, its strike more melodious than that of the three other clocks on the first floor.

Emma's hair was as unruly and scattered as Grandma's was pristine. Her hunched back attested to 50 years of washboard laundry, beating the rugs for spring cleaning, and trudging up the hill past the Catholic church. Without fail, she attended Methodist church services twice on Sunday and prayer meetings on Wednesdays. The Methodist Church Board and the social events of the church were the centerpiece of her life. Just as Grandma was queen of this house, Emma was queen of the Board. Whether she represented the views of the congregation mattered little to her, but this reigning monarch grew tiresome, even to the faithful.

Just before my father was born, Grandpa Knickerbocker hired Emma as the family's domestic, as servants were called. Grandpa's promise of home and lifetime employment extended for 56 years.

"Mommy, why is Aunt Em so bow-legged?" I asked in too loud a voice, as she was taking me upstairs to bed. Although no relation, I was expected to call her Aunt Em. When I went to school, I soon discovered none of my classmates had a 75-year-old "aunt."

"She must have had rickets as a child," she whispered. A rubber ball the size of my doll's head could be bounced between her knees and she would not have felt it.

Emma's sweater was thinner than Grandma's and had holes here and there, which she never noticed unless she caught her fingers in the sleeve. She was a dedicated servant. She cooked and maintained the household, saw to my grandmother's personal upkeep, and met her various daily requests. After all that, Emma was too tired to tend to her own needs.

As I watched from under the table I noticed how differently each of them moved. Grandma kept a steady grip on her reading glass; she folded and refolded her newspaper smoothly into quarters. She was no less precise in her crocheting, her needlepoint, or her fine tatting. She spent the daylight hours upstairs, sitting in her black Boston rocker in the sunny front window. On rare occasions, I was invited to watch while she did her tatting. I saw tiny rosettes form along the edge of a white linen handkerchief. Her oval shuttle of tortoiseshell darted in and out to create a fancy border for our next year's Christmas presents.

I remember as a young child, I was programmed to follow a lifetime of thread and needle skills, given my mother's daily training in sewing, Grandma's tatting expertise, and a print of Vermeer's Dutch-capped *Lacemaker* hanging on the wall.

Unlike Grandma, Emma handled the newspaper with the reckless abandon of an eggbeater. Pages slid out of her grasp without notice. My father's silent disdain implied heaven would be to have a newspaper all to himself. This was my grandmother's newspaper shared four ways. Of course, she had priority over the front section.

Emma concentrated on the obituary page, her sole focus of discussion. Who was left? What was left? Who were their ancestors? Where were they buried? All of this might inspire more comments of scandal than merit about the deceased. With her wealth of gossip and her unquestioned belief in it all, she could have written the Heavenly Gates Social Column.

Besides the obituaries, Emma's curiosity was drawn to the back pages where wills of those earlier deceased might be found, after probate. This added to her repertoire of information. What she could not read, she made up. In time, I discovered this often provided a source of amusement for my parents, but laughs would have to be suppressed until they retired to their third-floor bedroom.

Emma was never at a loss for information, which she gathered by her ill-disguised questions. She updated gossip over the telephone, at the store, at church, and during the monthly meetings of the Methodist Ladies' Aid Society. In addition, using her own rich imagination, she could embellish anything she heard, often slanted by what she wanted our family to hear or do. Emma could have published encyclopedias of misinformation and sold them door-to-door.

As each new pastor arrived, Emma became the self-appointed church representative charged with indoctrinating him as to "who was who" in the church and what he should know about the woodpile relations of this community of 200 souls. The pastor never had to select the hymns—Emma did that. He never had to count the collection plate—Emma did that. As to pronouncing his suitability, or lack of same for their pulpit—Emma did that, too. Perhaps dismissal came as a relief to the steady march of newly ordained pastors eager to escape this "on-the-job" training.

With elbows propped on the leather arms of his oak chair, my father held his newspaper high and wide open, his neck hinged at the back to read with his bifocals. The newspaper shielded his view of Emma as she tried to engage him with her one-track focus on the dead. He tolerated it in silence or an occasional "un-huh" or a rare comment such as, "I haven't gotten to that section yet. Here, do you want the cartoon page?" Emma read the funnies but seldom saw humor in them.

From my grandmother's chair, I could hear a puff of disgust as she read an editorial cast in the Republican's point of view, especially anti-New Deal. Franklin D. Roosevelt's Hyde Park home was located in Dutchess County, a Republican stronghold.

She and my father might exchange a sentence or two on the topic at hand, but any attempt to counter her idealized view of the president, would have been fruitless. Grandma never had high blood pressure, but in a flash, her face would suddenly be transformed from powdery white to beet red when anyone voiced a negative opinion about President Roosevelt. My father, while being a loyal

Democrat, was not always a New Deal advocate. I realize now, years would pass before I sorted out all these loyalties.

My father's interests in the paper were driven primarily by the stock market where he had lost most of our family's savings and in the business page looking for a sign of hope in the job market. Before he had finished his last year of high school, he left home to work out of town. Like the parade of pastors, possibly he, too, sought to escape Emma's grasp.

My father's shoes, like my grandmother's, were immaculate. They were trimly laced and pointed straight ahead. His well-tended, leather high tops could outlast multiple replacements of soles and heels. Black rubbers in summer and high black arctics in winter protected them during routine chores. In the morning, he hauled wood for the kitchen stove and emptied the slop pails from each bedroom. Never did their residue or a drop of rinse water, ever touch his shoes. His three-piece suit, pince-nez glasses, and the leather watch fob holding his gold pocket watch were so much a part of him that as a child I pictured everyone's father dressed like him. He looked as if he were ready for a day at the office, except there was no longer an office to go to. It would be years before the longing for his job and their life in Washington faded.

In 1919, my father, who had worked for years in the Department of Justice, was among the first hundred men selected by J. Edgar Hoover to start the FBI. Six years later, and soon after I was born, two unexpected incidents coincided that brought us back to Bangall. In reorganizing the FBI with his "G" men, Mr. Hoover added a degree in law or accounting as a requirement for continued employment. My father had neither and found himself slowly being "eased out" of the organization. Secondly, before he was able to determine what other government jobs he was qualified for, my grandfather died.

Langdon, Grandma's only grandson, brought my grandmother and Emma to Washington for a trial visit. It was clear they could never adjust to living there. Nor could they, at their advanced ages, manage a big house without my grandfather. The decision was made at the strong urging of my father's sister, that we all move to Bangall.

I remember there was always an unspoken, unsolved mystery in our house I never understood, "We moved back to stay a year." This statement was never explained, and in this household, questions were not invited. But here, in a rural farming community, a former FBI man had few opportunities for employment, and indeed, there was some air of suspicion toward this identity. It would be seven years before my father held a regular job. Depression, both economic and psychological, reigned in our house years before the Crash of '29.

My father's suits were never sent to the cleaners, but in summer or winter, they were kept with impeccable neatness. He might jump up from reading the financial page or international news to clean off a rare spot he had overlooked from supper. On a regular basis, my father would put up the rickety wooden ironing board, the same one he had watched Emma use as he crawled around her feet in infancy. As a child, I watched him dampen a clean cloth at the hand pump and reach with a potholder to lift a hand iron from the woodstove. Minutes later, he exchanged the cooled one for another, pressing his clothes as carefully as a tailor. Even knee patches held a crease.

My mother was last in line for the evening news, not that it mattered to her. Mending, knitting, or embroidery came first. If she were restoring a delicate piece of linen, as she often did for a little income, it would be carefully wrapped in a white towel and placed on top of her workbasket before she touched any newsprint. She had already heard some of the news from the comments around the reading table. Occasionally my father held up a page, and made an oblique remark: "Mary, there's something on this page you'll be interested in." Discussion about it would be on hold until they went to bed.

My mother was no less concerned about local or world news than my father. In Washington, the hub of the nation, they shared a deep interest in the national and world events transpiring around them. As a diligent student of history, she made a well-informed guide for the many relatives and friends who came to visit. The Visitors' Gallery of the House of Representatives, the Library of Congress, and the Smithsonian Institution ranked at the top of her list for first-time visitors. All were within walking distance of their apartment at 456 Massachusetts Avenue. An apartment of their own, furniture of their own, a life of their own, was now a distant memory. Throughout childhood, the very word apartment became the epitome of happiness, embellished to mean both "haven" and "heaven." I craved a home just for us, like the one we left when I was only a year old.

Moving back to Dutchess County must have sent this happy, devoted, and energized couple into a state of cultural shock. My mother had enjoyed reading Pearl Buck, a local Dutchess County author and distant relative, and Willa Cather, as well as stacks of historical novels, but now there was no library within 12 miles. A local book club was my mother's single luxury, isolated as she was here in rural America, without a car, without money, and without a library. That meant a house virtually without books for both of us.

From under the living room table, I recall seeing my mother's ill-fitting shoes were rarely polished. They carried layers of dust from the vegetable garden and the chicken house. In our farming community, raising chickens was a traditional way to provide food and a little revenue for the family.

My parents occupied a "one-room home" on the third floor. Their tiny closet under the sloping mansard roof held all the clothes they owned. The big cardboard box on the floor held cloth and remnants of other people's garments from which most of my clothes were created.

Because there was no room in the closet for shoes, the floor around my mother's wicker chair was "seeded" with hers. These took on new seasons of dust between wearings. My mother was neither disorganized nor unkempt, but these cramped circumstances, and perhaps the depressing atmosphere in general, offered neither incentive nor opportunity to do otherwise.

They fit all the furniture from their bedroom in Washington that this one room would hold; her wicker chair, their bird's eye maple bed, matching dressers, and washstand. The handsome mahogany drop-leaf table, pride of their Washington living room, was squeezed into a corner. It was rarely visible, covered by a protective bed sheet and piled high with her sewing. On top of this heap were remnants, such as pieces of old Mrs. Dickson's black coat. These had been carefully ripped and washed so my mother could reverse them and cut around the moth holes to make a winter coat for me.

Even as a child I realized that her shoes were bought on sale, whether they fitted her or not. Meager funds were saved for the shoes I had needed, bought new, worn hard, and outgrown fast. But these new shoes never offered me the thrill I wished for.

My most anguished recollections were my shoes. Summer shoes were high-top Keds from Sears. Winter shoes were the embarrassment of all time. Year after year, I was fitted with those dreadful, brown, high-top leather shoes. Laced high above my anklebone, they caused blisters in the fall, converted to calluses by winter, but that was the least of the pain. My protest fell on unhearing ears. I was so humiliated at being different from everyone else at Sunday school, I lied. I said I had to wear these high-laced, "grandmother-type" shoes because of an orthopedic problem I had heard about someone else. In hopes of preserving some degree of self-respect, I lied in Sunday school, where fear of God was real, and the lies so visible.

My mother was not insensitive to my pleas, so it must have intensified her own pain. Virtually in solitary confinement, she was surrounded by disapproving old ladies. Who else had not one, but the likes of two mothers-in-law to cast doubt on one's child-rearing skills? She knew issues still to come would be more crucial to my welfare than high-top shoes.

My parents' room, the attic, and the landing where I slept were all without insulation under this sloping slate roof, hot as a frying pan in summer, cold as an icebox in winter. The ceiling was too low for my mother to stand erect on the landing where she set up a pine blanket chest for me. Topped with folded quilts, it served as a bed by night, and my toy chest by day.

Watching my lanky body grow, my mother knew the big request to Grandma loomed before us. She dreaded that day when she would have to face Grandma and ask her for a bed and a room for me. She feared that this request could freeze the air around the living room table into crystals, the floor below it to tundra.

A six-year-old in those dreadful shoes, I lied about in Sunday school, and a fur coat Mom made, from one that Grandma's city relatives gave to the poor.

"Proud Momma" at 42, with a baby she can hold at last.

Two years earlier she lost a little boy at birth. My parents were energized by the culturally enriched atmosphere at the hub of the nation, and now they had their baby to enjoy as well.

"Proud Poppa" bringing home their baby for the grandparents to meet.

In less than a year, everything would change. The loss of his father, his job and their home would throw him into a deep depression.

3

Two Shorts and a Long

I recall that throughout much of my childhood the telephone often rang two or three times in the evening. We shared a party line with someone in the village, someone of dubious character, I once heard my father say. Her ring was two longs and a short. At the very first sound, all ears focused on the shiny oak box that hung on the wall in the dining room. At the top were two nickel-coated bells with a clapper between, striking in a distinct pattern that seemed like magic to me. Rarely did it strike our number, two shorts and a long, but when it did, we were on instant alert. So it was this evening.

My mother's chair was closest to the dining room door. She leaned forward, placed her knitting needles parallel to each other and pushed the stitches of my winter sweater away from the points. One continuous motion followed another. She laid this half-knit sleeve on top of her knitting bag with the grace of one accustomed to changing tasks without dropping a stitch. Stepping into the dark room, she leaned against the warm radiator behind Grandma's vacant chair. Before our number finished ringing the third time, she had lifted the black receiver, big as a tumbler. I heard her adjust the squeaky stem of the mouthpiece upward from the position Emma had used that afternoon. She took a deep breath. Anxiety pitched her voice higher than usual. She did not notice remnants of jelly Emma had left on the receiver.

"Hello." Neighbors only chatted in the daytime. An evening phone call predictably spelled alarm.

"Harrie, it's for you," she called with the brevity of a telegram.

Newspapers dropped into the laps of the old folks. Every ear was on edge as she stretched the short black cord out toward him, whispering, "It's your sister." Then, she pulled the dining room door, to close it as much as possible. That made listening harder for me.

As he stepped into place, my father found the radiator as warm as the message was chilling. His response was terse. Through that crack in the doorway, my sharp ears heard him say: "What? What do you mean? My God! Where is Langdon? I'll be there in the morning as early as I can get a ride." There was no good-bye. The sound of the receiver dropping into its hanger said it all.

We waited, but my father did not return to the living room. I heard his footsteps as he walked away through the length of the dining room and into the kitchen. He yanked the light cord, then turned toward the east door. I listened as he lifted the long, stainless steel flashlight from its hook. He pulled the inside door behind him, while his other hand tried to open the heavy, shuttered storm door. It needed a gentle nudge at the bottom; this nudge was far from gentle. I could no longer hear his footsteps, but I knew his feet were following the stone path to the outhouse.

From under the table, I could see that Grandma and Aunt Em had resumed their reading, but my mother held her knitting needles tightly in her left hand and stared against the distant wall. Perhaps she knew my father was stalling for time, time to cope with whatever news he, and he alone in this house, knew.

In a few minutes my father had composed himself. He had constructed a response that would satisfy his mother when she asked, as she surely would. I heard him step onto the covered porch and stomp snow from his shoes. It was the first time I had ever heard him go out without rubbers or arctics. He opened the kitchen door, yanking the heavy storm door behind him with enough force to jar the floor beneath me.

After jamming the bail of the flashlight over its hook, he walked to the sink and washed his hands. At the first sound of his feet, my mother jumped up from her low chair. As she opened the door that separated the long back hall from the kitchen, she saw him shove the pump handle so hard that water spewed out, not on the fourth wallop as usual, but the second. He kept pumping. The sound of the pump handle and the rush of the water protected the whispers they exchanged. I knew better than to interrupt their privacy, but my ears caught the end of what he said: "The whole damn thing stinks!"

Her steps were slow along the bare boards of the narrow back hall. My father wiped his hands longer than usual on the grayed linen towel, then paced back and forth a few minutes in the kitchen. After pulling the light off, his heavy footsteps brought him to the living room to face the questions that were certain to arise. He sat down, relit his pipe in slow motion, and thrust out a screen of smoke before turning toward his mother.

"That was May. She said the postal inspector came last week and will return tomorrow. Hasn't been there in almost a year. Could be there all week. Said she needs me to help out at the window."

With untarnished trust, my grandmother accepted the explanation as my father had hoped. He was grateful at the sound of her newspaper rustling back into position for her reading silence. As my father resumed reading, I recall that his pipe hung from the side of his mouth toward the table on the chance it alone might shield him against further conversation. No worry here; Grandma soon took off on a well-worn path of memory. She reveled in the days when a far corner of her husband's store housed the Bangall Post Office. Later he moved it to a little building up the street, closer to the railroad track.

Grandpa, whose name was Thaddeus, and Grandma, whose name was Jerusha Ella Doughty, before marriage, had moved to Bangall from Lafayetteville, some 20 miles away. In the mid-1700s, both her family and his had settled in Lafayetteville. He was a descendent of Lourens Knickerbakker, as the name was spelled then, second son of the first-born generation of the original family by that name.

Bullis Hall in Bangall, New York, is currently a destination inn. The left-hand end is where Grandpa Knickerbocker had his store on the ground floor; their apartment was above. It was here my father climbed over the second-floor railing following the "Blizzard of '88" to walk across the road on top of the hard-packed snow drift to meet his six-year-old chum. (To the far right is the Catholic Church, and beyond it, down the hill, is the rectory on the left, and further along, our house on the right.)

After they were married, they took up residence in a second-floor apartment of a long white clapboard building in Bangall. A front porch with decorative railing the length of the building protected children, pets, and belongings from falling onto the street. Below their apartment was Grandpa's store, located in the east end of this long building; the town hall occupied the opposite end.

I had been to this store to buy Tootsie Rolls for a penny when it was run by another grocer, perhaps Grandpa's fourth or fifth successor. Built against an earthen bank, it always smelled musty and damp. The floor was never dry, covered as it was with oily sawdust. I could imagine how my grandfather's store too might have smelled, with gunnysacks filled with dirt-coated potatoes, bags of glossy white onions, and a barrel of salt herring in the back room.

What is curious is that Grandma chose to espouse the singular distinctions of her husband's family origins to the exclusion of her own *Mayflower* ancestors by the name of Doty, now spelled Doughty. These *Mayflower* passengers, known originally as Separatists, left England for the town of Leyden in Holland to preserve their religious beliefs. But when they saw their children adopting the Dutch language and their more liberal ways, these Separatists sought refuge again, this time in the New World. The year was 1620. We call them pilgrims. Given Grandma's natural rigidity and cold aloofness, it seemed that Separatist blood might still be coursing through her veins three centuries later.

The story I liked best was Grandma's description of the Blizzard of 1888. It was remarkable not only for the amount of snow, but because the dry crystals pushed by the heavy winds piled it into hardened hills to create drifts 12 to 14 feet high. Such was the case in the front of the store and their second-floor apartment. What thrilled me most was to hear about my father having climbed out their living room window, over the porch railing, and across the road to the second-floor home of his six-year-old playmate. So severe was the storm that it took two days to open a tunnel to the store and a week before sleighs could get through from Poughkeepsie, 20 miles away.

As a youngster, I daydreamed of all that fun in the snow, which was much more than we ever saw. Only a few days each winter did the Willig boys and others who lived on farms along dirt roads ride to school on the sleighs that were carrying milk cans to the milk factory. These farmers let us jump on to ride to school. Sleigh bells and all, it was a real treat

This time, Grandma focused not on the blizzard, but on her memory of the exalted importance of the post office in their plodding lives. She said, "I remember when the postal inspector came, always unannounced."

My father held his breath, worried about the dramatic contrast of this prideful image and the alarming news he had just learned. Grandma was right about the postal inspector arriving unannounced. It had been an unannounced appearance this week at the Amenia Post Office as well. He exhaled another cloud of bluish smoke in relief, as Grandma continued. I'd heard these stories so often I could recite every one without missing a syllable.

"He must have thought he could get a room next door anytime he pleased!" she exhorted, as if the hotel in our tiny town ever turned guests away.

Even the night when this hotel had burned two years before, few people lost their belongings, and none lost a life.

I was told how frightened I was by the sound of the siren. My father looked up from his plate to see the sky toward town ablaze. He pushed back his chair, dropped his napkin on the seat and rushed up the hill behind the fire truck. I ran to Grandma's bay window and saw the steeple of the Catholic church outlined against the orange sky. They said I was afraid that he might be caught in the flames or they would roll down the hill and engulf us. But that was when I was only four. Now that I was six, I had grown up and no longer afraid.

My father could be grateful for Grandma's extended discourse. It gave him time to think over the news he had just heard, time to consider what could be done, what should be done. He took the pipe from his mouth and turned toward my mother, passing her the section of paper he had just finished. His face looked more relaxed now.

Grandma's monologue droned on. Then, with ardent emphasis, she leaned forward, straightened the lumpy pillow behind her and said, "Well, I can tell you, when you are dealing with government money, your books better balance right to the penny."

Seated: From left, Uncle Clayton Card, my grandparents and Emma on the right.
Standing: Aunt May and Langdon, age 14, and my mother on the right, four years before I was born.

It was eerie. Had she read his mind, just when he thought he had pulled off an effective cover-up to the real news? It was unnerving. He got up for a glass of water, something he never did at night.

"Of course, May and Clayton operate on a much larger scale," said Grandma. Could he accept this last comment as a positive sign? He hoped she was satisfied with this explanation, as he had presented it.

Grandma spoke with the pride of a strutting peacock. She bragged about her daughter's well-established post office career, and by extension, so to speak, of the family tradition. Grandma continued, "After all, Amenia is a town of a 1000 people and has several flourishing businesses. That helps with the annual receipts. Perhaps May's post office will move up to second class next year, now that there are two trains a day out of New York. That's good for business."

Silence settled at last. My father drank the rest of the water, set the glass on the reading table and turned to engage my mother's eyes.

"My throat is very dry," he said. Looking up, I caught her silent, knowing glance. I saw her slowly shake her head and I wondered what it all meant. I was not old enough to understand what was happening around the reading table, nor over the hills in Amenia. It was so confusing.

From what I had heard over the phone, there was hope. Someone needed my father. He would have work. According to Grandma, Aunt May's career was clearly headed up. Now that my father has work, maybe Grandma can be proud of him, too.

In my limited understanding, I thought we had never had such great news. He would be away working in a job, a real job. Maybe he would bring me a present when he came home. What excitement. I was baffled by the look on my mother's face. Her expression did not return to the one I was accustomed to. She tried to act as if nothing were amiss, but she was not a good actress.

Under the reading table, I created my evening playhouse and imaginary home. This was a godsend for my mother who needed to keep me quiet and contained in the evenings so the adults could read. Such was the case this evening and I knew better than to ask questions.

I, too, played my designated role, watching quietly as she resumed her knitting. Her needles flew. The last sleeve might be done sooner than she predicted. I hoped my sweater would be ready to wear to Sunday school that weekend.

Given their advanced ages and rigid living patterns, life with the old folks was hard enough for us under even the most predictable circumstances. My parents tried to protect them from needless worry and themselves from excess stress. Such was the case this evening. Even then I could see that Aunt May, seven years older than my father, was the apple of Grandma's eye. Casting doubt could cause chaos.

Upstairs, my mother tucked the warm quilt around me more firmly than usual. She leaned over to kiss me, her knees tight against the front of the old pine chest originally used to store grain for the animals. There was only enough room for this chest and an old dresser on the landing where a flimsy wooden guardrail protected me against the deep, dark canyon of steps.

My mother had already heard my prayers, but I was not to be dismissed easily. So little ever happened in our house, and here it was! Why couldn't everybody be as happy as I was? I wanted to know.

As she said, "Good night, sleep tight," she pulled the overhead cord to turn off the transparent 25-watt light bulb. There, directly below the light bulb, this cord ran through several screw eyes to the bottom of the stairs weighted there by a brown wooden ring.

Fighting to stay awake, I listened to sounds throughout the house. An hour or so later, I heard my father go down to the cellar to shake the furnace and stoke it for the night. Then he came up to the kitchen, threw a few logs into the firebox and closed the damper of the cook stove. I listened as each old lady pulled an overhead light cord in her room before retiring behind closed doors.

I heard familiar footsteps climb the bare back stairs, walk the length of the second-floor hall before pulling open the door at the bottom of our stairs. He grabbed the old wooden ring to pull on the distant light. As he trudged up the steep stairs, his footsteps sounded like those of old Charlie, the hulky laborer who lived behind the neighbor's house.

I kept still, knowing he would look over to see if I was asleep. A teddy bear under the curve of my arm convinced him. He opened the door to their bedroom, turning the heavy, brass key as he closed it firmly behind him. Visible space narrowed between my parents; emotionally there was no distance.

Quietly, I knelt at the keyhole. I heard the name Langdon. I knew who that was, but I could barely remember what he looked like. As a cousin, he failed my expectations of someone to play with. I heard only a few words, but it was the tone of their voices that revealed the most. None of it carried the joy and excitement I hoped for. My mother's voice was lower than usual, maybe fearful that Grandma, in her room below, might overhear. She sounded solemn and worried when she said, "Will he have to go to jail?" I had never heard that word before. What did this new word mean? It was such a puzzling time.

Whatever was wrong, I knew my father could fix it, even if it were serious. Someone needed him. It never happened before. His luck had come at last. My mother packed his clothes for the week, and he was gone before I awoke.

My father caught a ride at daybreak on a delivery truck going his way, one that sold Yale & Towne locks and keys, handcuffs and security equipment to the State Prison at Wassaic, a few miles south of Amenia. The driver obligingly detoured several miles to "deliver" him in front of the Amenia Post Office.

Aunt May and Uncle Clayton were at their accustomed places when he walked in. She was serving a customer at the "STAMP and DELIVERY" window and he was attached to his swivel-based oak chair in front of the dark roll top desk. Everything appeared as it always had, to the outside world of Amenia.

As soon as Aunt May finished serving her customer, she unlocked the side door. The postal inspector sat glumly at a tiny, ill-lit table near the wide back door where the mail was delivered twice a day from the Harlem Division of the New York Central Railroad in locked, limp, dirty gray canvas bags. He barely looked up when my father arrived. Langdon was nowhere to be seen, but his presence, or lack of it, fell on the whole back room.

Langdon had worked for several years at a bank in Newark. Then came the crash of '29. He had watched from behind the vertical bars in front of the cashier's window as the mob of people outside pounded the glass doors.

Years later I heard about the long lines of men and women winding down the steps and around the block, standing patiently in that cold October drizzle. Some held savings account books in their hands, the size and shade of a blue passport, no longer their passport to security. Loss of their jobs, loss of their life savings spelled eminent poverty, family starvation, soup lines, and despair.

Out of a job himself, Langdon returned to Amenia to work for his parents or perhaps work for himself. That was the job of the postal inspector to determine.

My father may have had a tough week, but my mother's was no breeze. By Friday, she was at her wit's end trying to keep me from jumping up and down on the floor over Grandma's head. Her bag of tricks, as usual, worked magic. She suggested that my doll Carol, the baby-faced infant with rosy, porcelain cheeks, needed a new outfit to celebrate my father's return. Mother cut it from a torn dimity dress handed down from Aunt May. I basted it with long stitches before sewing it on her old sewing machine. She trimmed the neck with lace and hemmed it in swift, skilled stitches.

That done, I decided Carol needed a bib of my own special design. I chose a scrap of wool plaid left from the jumper that my mother made me for the Sunday school Christmas party. The dress originally came from Grandma's city relatives who gave to the poor. This palm-sized patch was just what I needed to practice fringing, pulling the threads one by one from three sides. Then I sewed a strip of blue bias tape to this tiny bib and tied it behind the doll's white china neck.

When Emma called, "Lunch is ready," I raced down with Carol and set her In a doll's highchair between Grandma and me. I waited for Grandma to release her crisply-ironed, damask napkin from its engraved silver holder. Then I told her how I had sewn the outfit all by myself on the sewing machine.

Looking across the table to Aunt Em, I described at a fast pace how I had stood in front of the sewing machine with one foot on the pedal and used my right hand to pull the shiny steel wheel. Frowns of doubt were quickly followed by words of disapproval, challenging my mother's sanity and judgment. How could she be trusted with my safety? They imagined I would sew through my fingers.

I caught on fast, as I recall, sensing this was no time to claim I had been sewing on her machine since I was tall enough to see the needle. Perhaps their onslaught was an unwitting expression of anxiety over what was going on in Amenia. Without my father here, my mother was more vulnerable to the stream of unabated criticism they heaped on her both verbally and silently.

For my mother, it must have been almost more than she could stand. Did she ever entertain the thought of taking me by the hand and running away? But where could she run? Where could she find a place where only my father could find us? She was helpless, trapped here as she was with no money, no car, and no answer.

My mother may have received a letter from him, which she shielded from me, knowing it would be a burden for me to keep secret. If I were to reveal that word had come from him, the old folks would press my mother for details he did not want her to be forced to answer. Those he would fashion himself in a seamless account when he returned.

But one evening there was great excitement. I was near the top of the narrow back stairs headed to bed, my mother close behind me, when the phone rang: two shorts and a long. She turned on the stairs, as tricky a feat as that was, to go down the narrow steps, her feet slanted for safety. I was so close behind her I even forgot about the bears I envisioned lurking in those dark corners. It must be him. I was just beside myself to know when he would be home.

"Mary?" asked the voice at the other end. My mother replied briefly, her voice clearly not responding to my father. The man's voice, suddenly embarrassed and confused, uttered little more than, "Sorry, wrong number." By then he may have wished he had just hung up.

Had his voice been recognized? He surely hoped not, but this was not the first time our number had rung when the person at the other end was seeking the services of our town's "lady of the evening," whose first name happened to be the same as my mother's. This service might be provided at "two longs and a short." I heard my father wish this lady's business would become prosperous enough for her to afford a line of her own. Excitement for me had to be put on hold until another day, but I was already well trained and used to that.

Although these two shorts and a long had not come from him, my mother was accustomed to silence when he was away. In Washington, working for J. Edgar Hoover, he was sometimes sent out for weeks at a time, unable to be in touch. He always kept a packed satchel at the office and sent a colleague to the apartment with the simple phrase, "Mary wouldn't you like to visit your folks?"

After canceling telltale signs of the morning milk and newspaper deliveries, she would pack her small black bag and walk to Union Station. Arriving by train in Poughkeepsie, she would take the one-car local, known affectionately as the "Dinky." It would take her to her parents' home in Verbank, a tiny farm town where she was safe from possible acts of revenge from anyone my father might be investigating. She could trust in the knowledge that there would be a day when he would contact her to return.

Thus she was geared to his silent absence this time. They both knew she would be in for a curious inquisition, were he to call. She was not spared my rapid-fire questions upstairs, however. Throughout the last day, their pace had escalated. "How do you know Daddy will come tonight, Mom?"

"The postal inspector never works on Saturday," she told me, as if I knew this mysterious figure by more than his impressive title. Who was this man? Was he a nice man? Did my father like him? What was more to the point, did he like my father? Would he ask him to work again? Who was he working for? It was not clear. Aunt May asked my father to come. Was he working for her or for this mystery man? There were so many questions to figure out.

That afternoon I watched my mother change to her best shoes, the ones that matched the afternoon dress she ironed before putting it on. "It's a quarter past five," I announced, so proud I could tell time.

It was too hard for me to see the Big Ben on the tall dresser, so during the morning as I was basting Carol's new dress, my mother let me climb up for it and put it on the floor close beside me.

"Look, Mom," I shouted in astonished discovery. "The bell on the alarm clock is just like those that ring on the telephone!" She nodded and stared into the distance, as if an alarm had gone off in her mind.

It had already been dark for half an hour. We could stand it no longer. Even though Emma had not called us for dinner, we went down to the living room. So uncommon was it for Emma to cook dinner at night, she was getting irritated that my father was not here when it was ready.

Hearing a car drive up, I raced to the front window. My father called, "Thanks again for the ride," and slammed the car door. Knowing how excited I would be, she had released the stubborn lock well in advance to ensure an immediate and loving welcome. I ran to flick on the porch light and fling open the door, which Mother caught before it hit Grandma's antique candle-making tin in the corner.

As I grabbed him, my father reached over me to give her a brief kiss. I'd never seen them do that before, but the hall light was not on and Grandma's face was hidden behind the Tiffany lampshade. Emma was not in view either; she was coming from the kitchen, wiping her hands on her apron.

A quick visit out back, a splash in the sink, a wipe on the old gray towel, and my father was ready to do Emma's bidding. "Dinner's ready." He sat down, facing questions Grandma fired from the opposite end of the table.

Then, as quickly as he could reasonably do so, he turned to admire my doll's new outfit in her highchair beside me. I remember that I no longer sat in a highchair myself, but on the Sears & Roebuck catalog in a chair for adults.

"Daddy, Daddy, did you bring me a present?" I had waited so long for Grandma to be through with her questions that I had nearly burst.

"Yes I did. I'll have it for you as soon as you've finished your supper."

"Ohhh, I can't wait that long. I don't want to eat anyway. Mom, please, can't I be excused to get Daddy's satchel?"

"You'll have to ask your grandmother," she answered in an atonal voice without turning her head.

"Please, please, may I be excused?" I pleaded, drawing on the correct grammar of "May I," a child's game I played recently at a birthday party. I turned to look her straight in the face as I asked again, "Please, Grandma, may I be excused?"

"I suppose you can, but stay out of Emma's way when she clears the table."

That was no problem; I always tried to stay out of Emma's way. Even while sitting in your own place, there was no telling when you might be speared by a falling fork or a hollow-handled knife.

I ran to the front hall where he had dropped his old satchel, its bow handle unraveling at the ends. I lifted it with effort, energized by the long delay and my eagerness to see what he had brought. I set it beside his chair so he could open it immediately. He had bought my present at Al Dubie's store, next to the post office. I recognized the white paper bag with the picture of a sitting bear beside letters representing the store's name. This present could not have been better, dark glasses for my biggest doll, Alice. I was thrilled. My baby doll Carol could have no complaint. After all, she had a new dress and a flashy plaid bib.

From under the living room table all was calm, or so I thought. I sat cross-legged, close to my father. I was happy, adjusting Alice's new dark glasses. Then I looked at the paper bag from Al Dubie's store. It was just the right size for me to use, but I was not prepared for the loud bang it made on the first swat. He jumped like I had never seen before. It was wonderful to watch. I burst out in an unabashed giggle. Then he yelled at me to come to the kitchen for more than a little talk.

As I crept out, I saw my mother's hand cover her mouth, but her eyes were smiling. There she was, caught between the two people she loved most in the entire world.

She understood why he had reacted this way. She also knew how anxious I was to show off this new trick I had learned the day before from Jim Brennan, the tall, handsome guy who delivered our groceries.

Obviously, she had been unable to clue my father in about all the events of the week. I wanted to greet him with a trick worthy of this occasion, as important to me as any Fourth of July. It was worth an unaccustomed paddling to see his response.

My father must have felt that his jaws were clamped tight as a clam. He could not discuss his week in Amenia. He could not respond honestly to Grandma's questions. It was only with my mother that he could share the real truth about his nephew, Langdon, the angry truth, the deceptive truth, and then only in the security of their bedroom.

The post office

The living room in more modern attire. The windows face the road.

While the chandelier, radiator, and mantle are the originals, the wallpaper, curtains and carpet are more modern additions.

While I was living there, this room was painted, and curtains didn't exist for us. There was a threadbare Axminster maroon rug and newspapers for insulation beneath—to keep the coal dust down when shaking the furnace.

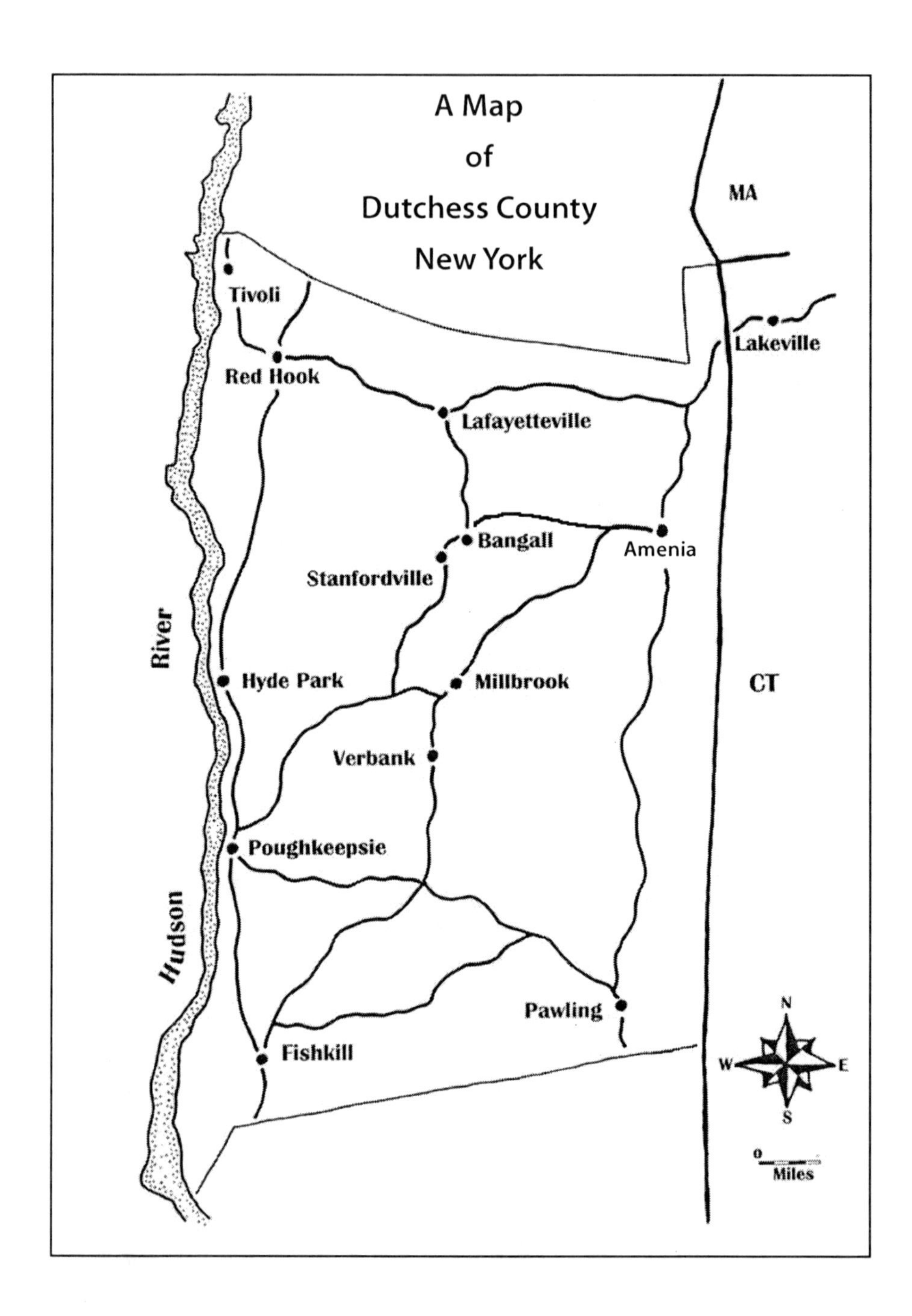
A Map
of
Dutchess County
New York
MA
Tivoli
Lakeville
Red Hook
Lafayetteville
Bangall
Amenia
Stanfordville
River
Hyde Park
Millbrook
CT
Verbank
Poughkeepsie
Hudson
Pawling
N
W
E
S
Fishkill
0
Miles

4

Letter One: Dear Langdon

August, 1971

Dear Langdon,

I never wrote you a letter when you were alive. I only remember seeing you half a dozen times, you being 18 years older than I. But now I'm an adult and you're dead. You have been buried for many years, but your deeds live on. I've been thinking about these as I close the house for sale.

Langdon, I knew you only through my parents' eyes. I claim no objectivity, but lots of curiosity. I'd like to ask you about the time you were helping your parents at the post office. What's more to the point, you'd been helping yourself. I've wondered how you managed, what scheme you used to get away with it. Did you forge your parents' signatures or simply take the deposits from the cash box on your way across the street to the bank?

Langdon, was your father in on this scheme with you? Did he cover for you? After the Crash of '29, there were many bank closings, like the one where you worked. Maybe that helped him to convince your mother that banks weren't as reliable as they used to be, and that they should keep the cash in their safe.

How could you be so stupid as to tamper with government funds? You knew your parents had an impeccable record for honesty and accuracy. At least, Aunt May did. I don't know about Uncle Clayton's record. He scarcely moved to do anything, so how would anybody know if he were honest? In fact, I was in sixth grade before I realized your father was the postmaster. It was never apparent when I was there during summer visits. Your mother did all the work. Your father rarely left his chair.

Only because Mr. Hoose owned the Amenia bank and was such a good friend of your parents was he willing to cover this deficit with personal funds. I can't believe he would back them for nearly $6,000!

That's a lot of money any time, but in Depression days, only a banker had such resources. Your parents must have commanded a good deal of trust for him to do that! Only because of his generosity, were your folks able to keep their jobs. Loss of a job in the Depression meant plummeting to the bottom. What is more amazing, townspeople never learned about this fiasco.

I was confused, Langdon, when your mother phoned that night, but I could see how tense my father was. From what I've heard, Dad knew your history well—first hand, you might say. You know what happened when you brought the old folks to visit us in Washington the year after I was born. As my father told it, when you left, his wallet was significantly thinner. You know full well what I mean! Don't play coy or stupid, or worse yet, innocent.

You may have gotten away with stealing in front of Grandma, but how did you think you could get away with taking government money? Had you forgotten my father specialized in postal fraud for the FBI? Or did you think because of his connections he might get you out of trouble?

He felt you should have been locked up in the Atlanta Penitentiary with other embezzlers. You might have, if they'd found you. Where did you hide? Did you leave the country? But, jail would not have been a corrective experience. You'd have been in training with pros, bigger con men than yourself and come out an even greater menace to society.

Your good looks, your charm, and your lies attracted nice women. Each of your wives was a lovely person. Too bad. You stole their money, hocked their jewelry, and ruined their self-respect. Besides that, you conned Grandma out of those first editions of her favorite classics by Emerson, Longfellow, and Thoreau. And what about my father's prized stamp collection? It might have helped relieve his depression, but the strong possibility that you "lifted" it out of the attic while he lived in Washington contributed further to his mental anguish.

Let me ask you one last thing, Langdon. Remember the French doll I had? She was a beautiful antique, delicately balanced so she could stand alone on her little leather shoes to show off her hand-sewn silk gown. I remember exactly what she looked like. Her hat sloped down over her tinted porcelain face. It was a doll Grandma had had as a child but was never allowed to play with. I played with her under watchful adult eyes and eventually Grandma gave her to me. I named her Frances, after my mother's sister who died of polio.

One day, not long after you'd been to visit, I looked for her, but she was nowhere to be found. Maybe Grandma thought she could give her doll away as many times as she liked. Maybe she had forgotten she'd given it to me when you asked for it. But what on earth did she think a man then in his mid-twenties was going to do with a doll, play with it? You got away with that, too. Did she end up in the hands of an antique dealer to enrich your own coffer? We'll never know.

Langdon, I've been thinking a lot about the relationship between you and my family. Perhaps there were long-standing reasons why, in addition to your sticky fingers, my father was so angry with you. Your mother was Grandma's first and favored child and, as I heard it, she set no limits on you. Dad even called you "Little Lord Fauntleroy." Maybe his resentment arose from your carefree life. That figures.

Your mother, too, assumed only token responsibility for the old folks. Dad had to provide for their support and care. Worse than that, we had to live with them! And it wasn't for a year as your mother had led him to believe. It was 19 years before your mother finally agreed to take Grandma, and then she died a few months later at the age of 96.

There were plenty of reasons for Dad's anger with you for stealing and cheating and lying. But it was, perhaps, your ever fun-loving, untrustworthy behavior that marked you as a target of his frustrations. While shouldering full responsibility for the old folks as well as his own family, he must have envied your life of reckless abandon. No wonder he became so depressed. It's a good thing my mother had her sewing and knitting to help keep her sanity. I had my dolls—or most of them.

One thing I can say on your behalf, Langdon, you weren't lazy. In fact, you were extremely ambitious. You had ability and you could act, too. What a shame you didn't play on Broadway instead of Main Street, USA. You had a commanding presence, posing first as a graduate of Columbia University after a few night courses there, then as a mid-west college professor of an unnamed institution. Later you passed yourself off as a political campaign manager, and finally as a frocked Episcopal priest.

You could have convinced a theatre audience and it would have been better that way, especially for those who paid the price for believing your acts. It's a shame your intellect couldn't have been focused on honest pursuits because you could have been successful in any of these.

Too bad for your family—or families. Were there more marriages we never learned of, families planted here and there under an alias? Bobby, the son we knew, deserved a better father. Your parents and Grandma deserved more from you. Of course, Dad never told Grandma of your shenanigans, but then she wouldn't have believed him if he had!

If ever there is an organization by the name of the Society of Psychopaths of America, you could be a charter member. It's hard to imagine you carried any genes handed down from Johannes van Barghen Knickerbakker. His character was forged in the 1672 Battle of Solebay in the Dutch Navy under the command of de Ruyter and Tromp. With a last name like yours, Langdon CARD, you must have been the joker in the deck.

Maybe there is another side to you I've never heard. Maybe you did give all the money you acquired to the poor urchins of Newark as you claimed. Who will ever know? It doesn't matter. All I know is my own limited experience. Stealing from a child, even if it was for the poor, didn't endear you to me. There's nothing you, nor I, can do about our relationship now, but wherever you are, I hope it is very, very warm.

Your first, your last, your only cousin,
Barbara

5

Letter Two: Dear Langdon

September 24, 1991

Dear Langdon,

I'm writing again because of something very strange that happened today when I was back at the house in Bangall. It was up for sale and the owner wanted me to be interviewed by a local newspaper reporter in hopes that his article would generate historical interest and a sale.

Even though the bizarre incident I refer to lasted only a few moments, I'm certain you'd recall it if you were still alive. I didn't understand it when I was five. I begin to, now.

Remember that Sunday afternoon in the summer, when you brought your mother over in a fancy car, one with a big trunk. Toward the end of the visit, she and my parents were out in our garden. Mom picked some flowers and fresh vegetables for her to take home. We left you in the living room chatting with Grandma.

Suddenly I dashed back to the house for my doll, Alice, upstairs on the landing. At the bottom of our stairs to the third floor, I flung open the door and there you were, coming down, carrying a heavy cardboard box. You looked so startled I thought you might drop it on my head.

"What's in the box, Langdon?"

Sitting down on the steps as fast as you did, I thought surely you were going to open it for me to see. I was so entranced—I remember every word you said. You whispered to me that it was a very special secret, one just for the two of us. You told me, inside this box was a fairy who could wave her magic wand. When I asked to see her, you said you couldn't let me. If you did, all her magic powers would be gone before I could blink my eyes. Besides, if I told anyone about this fairy, or her magic, she could cause dreadful things to happen to me or to my parents.

So terrifying was this prospect, that only now have I recalled the event. I couldn't be certain what was in the box, but I knew it was heavy and it was powerful. I could tell the fairy was inside too, because I heard it jingle all the way along the back hall, through Grandma's room and down her front stairs.

Then I ran up to the third floor, grabbed my doll and headed for our front window. I saw you lift this wonderful box into the trunk of your new car and lock it. The fairy and her magic wand were gone from our house and soon from my memory.

I was so disappointed to realize I couldn't run and tell my folks of this great discovery. It was painful, too, keeping my special secret from friends at Sunday school. I never told. I did forget.

That is, until now, many years after it happened and 20 years after I sold the house.

But on my return this time, 50 years after I'd left for college, an equally bizarre incident occurred. The owner and his wife plus the newspaper reporter and I climbed the stairs to the third floor.

Langdon, I wonder, did you ever notice how pitifully small my parents' stark, boxed bedroom was under that mansard roof of slate? Even empty, it was small. How did they manage to fit in all their bedroom furniture? Tears welled up in my eyes as I stood there, thinking of all the years these four walls were home to them. I would be graduating from college before the house would be theirs and Grandma's front bedroom had them as new occupants.

The owners, sensitive to my pain, walked over to the front dormer window to look out toward the Catholic cemetery on the far hillside. When I had regained my composure, the gentleman turned to me with a question.

"Barbara, was this house ever part of the Underground Railroad," hopeful an historic slant such as this might enhance the opportunity for a sale.

As you can guess, Langdon, I was puzzled, and tried to consider that possibility. I said I was sure it wasn't. Instant recall of Grandma's story of being 12 years old when Lincoln was shot confirmed my calculation that the house wasn't built until after the Civil War.

"Why are you asking me this question?"

"Did you know there was a secret hiding place?" he said, as he fixed his gaze on my face.

"What do you mean? What kind of a hiding place?"

He opened the door to the small dark closet with its slanted ceiling, its every surface covered with dark furring strips. Of course there would be empty space behind the knee-wall of the bedroom, but I had never thought about it. In fact, I'd only seen the closet empty once, when I was preparing the house to be sold.

I crept in on the bare floor, then reached back for his flashlight. There, almost perfectly concealed, was a sliding panel. It would have been big enough to hide a slave from the Underground Railroad. I was shocked. I was curious and surprised, but I also found it scary. I was reminded of the bats and the bears I thought lurked everywhere when I slept on the landing.

The closet had always been so jammed with clothes, suitcases, and my mother's cardboard box of cloth remnants, I seriously doubt my parents ever knew of its existence. "But who could have built such a masterpiece, and why?" This was the question on my lips as I rose from my knees.

The owner's hopes for added historic value were dashed. I was about to discover, however, this elusive nook had played a role in history; although not as altruistic, it was no less colorful.

With a shrug of the shoulders, we turned to leave this empty closet and its puzzling history. I put my hand on the rickety guardrail still in place next to the landing and started down that steep, dark canyon. Langdon, as my foot touched the third or fourth step, the whole scene flashed in my memory. There you were, carrying the heavy cardboard box down those narrow stairs. Remember, how you were so shocked you nearly dropped it when I flung open the door at the bottom. I could almost hear the jingle of that fairy wand you snowed me with.

I started to laugh and I made a quick and risky turn back up the stairs. "Wait," I said to the others, confused by my sudden actions. "Give me the flashlight," I muttered as I dropped to my knees to slide back the secret panel once more. I peered into the corners nearest my knees but no bottles of bathtub gin remained. Suddenly I could see how my parents' return from Washington curtailed this clever marketing and distribution center you managed throughout Prohibition.

Langdon, as abhorrent as I found all your nefarious activities, this one was a hoot! What safer place could you have chosen? Here it was, right over Grandma's head as she slept, she a loyal member of the Women's Christian Temperance Union. If there had been a raid, she'd have died of embarrassment!

And I just doubled up at the thought of how her friend, Mrs. Paine, so righteous, so religious, so right, had been only a floor below this handsome-size cache, sleeping peacefully in Grandma's guest room. As you know, she made annual visits to preach the gospel of the WCTU.

Langdon, how could you keep from laughing, all the way to the grave? Maybe you are laughing still. I am.

Your first, your last, your only cousin,
Barbara

The inside attic space. It was another space like this one where Langdon hid his hootch beside my parents' closet.

6

Sins Incorporated

Mrs. Paine, the female counterpart of Teddy Roosevelt, was three times the size of my petite grandmother. Her face, round and rosy cheeked, could have been jolly. A long black dress hid tubular legs that supported her stately frame. Trimmed with wide white lace, her outfit piqued my curiosity. As an inquisitive first grader, I asked, "Mommy, is she a Pilgrim?"

Mrs. Paine never failed to arrive for her annual stay. Even as an adult, those visits remain among my earliest memories; they were clear memories for my mother as well. This guest never learned to drive, but not because of age. It was beneath her dignity. She was transported by friends and relatives in Poughkeepsie who fell under her thumb.

"Mrs. Paine is a lecturer," my mother explained. From sixth grade on, I met this fact face-to-face on an annual basis as well. To my embarrassment, this dour person had to be the house guest of my grandmother, the only guest she ever had. Pontificating before the school assembly in her high-pitched, stilted voice, she lectured about evils we could not understand. During one presentation, when she referred to me by name, I was ready to crawl under every seat the length of the assembly room. I heard her voice in my sleep. In fact, her voice was all anyone heard around our dining room table. The family never needed to polish its conversational skills. No conversation ever ensued.

As president of the Dutchess County Women's Christian Temperance Union, her annual monologue covered a predictable set of topics. What she said at our table differed little from her lecture at school. Without urging, she expanded on the local and national accolades that had been heaped on her for her dedication in spreading the "word" since Prohibition began in 1919.

Like Teddy Roosevelt, she led the charge with her single-minded viewpoint about the evils of alcohol at schools, churches, and granges. She told of admonishing derelicts lying in the gutters, warning them once again, possibly for the last time before their demise, of all their worldly sins. When she spoke to schoolchildren, her voice was just as condescending.

The news of recent bootleg busts drew rapt attention around our table. For another hour after dessert, she continued telling tragic tales arising from bathtub gin and wood alcohol in her self-righteous, shrill voice.

I remember how curious and confused I was, when she told of copper tubing found in the most unlikely places: a bank vault, a casket at the funeral home, the tool shack at our cemetery and "extra" vats at our milk factory. Without effort, her discourse expanded to include sins in general and extended long after I had willingly trotted off to bed. But in their wildest nightmares, neither my grandmother nor she could have envisioned Langdon's "bottled sin" stored just over their heads.

With the repeal of Prohibition in 1933 this "temperance over tolerance" organization, the WCTU faced possible demise—a threat as great to them as the evils of alcohol to society. Undaunted, these single-minded stalwarts marched forth with even greater vehemence, their message ever more strident. To every child, Mrs. Paine preached the undisputed evils of imbibing even a swallow. In her eyes, a single glass of beer consigned one to certain and immediate doom, to life as an alcoholic.

Having lost a son in World War I, she held the justly respected title of Gold Star Mother and, predictably, was president of that organization, too. This role gave her the unquestioned right to expand on the dreaded horrors of war and its impact on her personally, a rallying point as powerful as her stand against alcohol. Furthermore, as a widow, she was consigned to endure eternal suffering. Mrs. Paine never failed to reap the most from any tragedy, factual or imagined, hers, those of friends, or of society.

At the beginning of each meal, this flood of gloom and doom was held in check by bowed heads. My father's annual silent prayer was unusually long. Although it was a ritual for her benefit, this grateful moment of quiet may have been planned more for our relief. No sooner had my father's "Amen" been uttered, than she inhaled deeply to launch her next monologue. Even as she ate, she could lay claim to the air space for her next thought with an "uum."

"Too much is too much," I complained to my mother between lunch and dinner. "One of my dolls is sick. Can't I eat in the barn with them?"

That failed to work, but I managed to leave the table early, complaining I was feeling ill. An earlier experience dissuaded her from challenging my veracity. For nearly a decade, the three of us had dreaded these visits like the return of the locusts. When Mrs. Paine visited, it was my mother's duty to keep me quiet during meals, even more so than usual.

My parents told me about what happened one year, when I was still young enough to be sitting in my highchair. I summed up my point of view succinctly. With the look of cherubic innocence, they said, I stared straight ahead toward the source of this incessant verbal stream. Our varnished parquet floor suddenly echoed a sound my parents recognized in an instant. My mother gasped. I had not wet my pants for more than a year. "What has gotten into you, my child?" Wasn't it clear?

Compared to Mrs. Paine, ever pompous and prideful, my inflexible grandmother seemed as gracious and beneficent as an early-day Mother Teresa. When Mrs. Paine left, her fearsome lexicon was mothballed for another year: beer, alcohol, and saloons, prohibition and repeal, drunks, winos, and death by delirium tremens. Along with her other official positions, she would be unchallenged as president of Sins Incorporated.

7

The Four-leaf Clover

"One—two—three. One—two—three." Silently I searched and counted, fingering clump after clump of clover on our front lawn. What else was a five-year-old to do on a hot Sunday afternoon still wearing a Sunday school dress? My hand flattened a bed of grass. A lone stem sprung up between my thumb and first finger. I peered closer and counted aloud, my voice intense with discovery.

"ONE—TWO—THREE—FOUR!" With a quick snatch, I recall I scrambled to my feet and yelled, "I found one! I found one!" Dashing up the porch steps, I ran to each of the adults in their rocking chairs, for them to acknowledge my find.

My father lowered *The Sunday New York Times*, his weekly 25-cent indulgence. He rocked forward in his high-backed, dark green chair to look at it with the attention such a specimen deserved. "Four-leaf clovers bring you good luck," he said, adding, "Your Aunt May could find them most anywhere."

"Did it bring her good luck?"

Like other questions, it was cast into silence. Attempts to answer it might have drawn more questions. Except for my mother, the prevailing attitude of adults seemed to be: "Why would a child need answers?" Innocent queries such as this often rekindled my disappointment. "Daddy, did she have good luck?" I persisted, my voice conveying the importance I saw in this matter. "That's a matter of opinion," I heard him say, but this response failed to tell me much, either.

As long as I can remember, news accounts referring to a certain gentleman, spoken of as "he," drew veiled comments from Grandma. Naturally I expected to address this unseen individual as "Mr. He." Looking back, Grandma's tone of voice seemed wistful as she spoke.

I later learned that "Mr. He" started out as a prominent young trial lawyer in Poughkeepsie. I gathered from Grandma's comments that he was smart, ambitious, and destined to go far; he had been at the forefront of Roosevelt's local campaign for governor of New York State and later followed him to Washington when he was Under-Secretary of Navy.

From the first time she met him, Grandma could see he had a great future. She would have been proud to have him as a son-in-law. She daydreamed still of Aunt May going with him to enjoy the political scene in Washington. The subject of this nameless, faceless man never surfaced when Aunt May and Uncle Clayton came for their regular Sunday afternoon calls.

When I was older, my mother told me, "Mr. He" and Aunt May were engaged to be married, but a few months before their wedding, he called it off. Six months later, she married Uncle Clayton on the rebound, as it was called.

The Moreys on one side of Uncle Clayton's family traced their ancestors back to Revolutionary War stock, but little was known about the Card side. With his energy level, Uncle Clayton, whose neck folded in rolls, would never have fought in any war, or cared enough to choose sides. It was said he married up from his social class.

With all the four-leaf clovers Aunt May found, it did not seem to make her so lucky. While Uncle Clayton was nominally the postmaster, it was Aunt May who carried the load.

8

Living in a Paper House

Grandma's heavy oak card table was stored behind the door between the living room and the dark hall. Rarely was it used. I helped my mother dust off the cobwebs so my father could set it up beside the reading table. In Grandma's house, it was unheard of to leave the card table up more than a day, let alone a month. My parents must have asked permission. What an important event!

I remember how they carried straight chairs from the dining room each evening, careful not to chip the paint on the door as it slowly drifted shut. They sat face-to-face to focus on the same task. There was scarcely a chance they might win this contest sponsored by Montgomery Ward, but it gave Grandma's living room a glorious glow of hope.

The contest provided the floor plan of a $3,000, two-bedroom bungalow with a budget of $1,000 for furnishings to be chosen from the store's catalog. The frayed pages of this two-inch tome held promise of the reality I longed for.

Rural families customarily had an allegiance to either Montgomery Ward or Sears & Roebuck. This commitment ranked as seriously as one's loyalty to a political party or religion. Such fealty was rarely broken and, since prices were competitive, they were not a factor. Our family was dedicated to the Sears camp, but at a time like this, my mother could transgress and go into Montgomery Ward's Store on Market Street to ask for a catalog and contest application.

The project drew us like a magnet, taking on a life of its own. We lived in it. We loved in it. It was ours. Thoughts of prize money never upstaged our rich fantasies. We were "family" here, an island in a turbulent, silent sea.

By now this project had been ongoing for weeks and we were down to the very fine points. My mother suggested a garden hoe; he vetoed it, saying, "Only things inside the house should be considered." I championed for a baby carriage, crib, and highchair. My father chose a pipe stand then withdrew it in favor of a floor lamp, an unseen luxury in our house. We were just glad to have electricity, since kerosene lamps had become too dangerous for the old ladies to carry up the dark stairs.

My mother listed the cost of each item and my father, who was justly proud of his mental arithmetic skills, tabulated the final bill in his head. There were the sofa, chairs, dining room table, beds, bedclothes, pots, pans, and dishes, plus kitchen appliances.

"We're over by 20 dollars," my father reported firmly. "Where do you think we should cut?" My mother offered the mop pail and kitchen curtains, but that still was not enough.

He suggested cutting out the change of sheets and towels. Together, that did it, with 35 cents to spare.

My parents viewed this contest with utmost seriousness. They made their decisions as if every penny would be extracted from their own savings account. They selected furnishings with taste and discretion. Crucial to this was the fact that items in the catalog were offered at three prices, reflecting a range in quality. Thus kitchen appliances where durability was paramount would have to be balanced frugally by savings elsewhere. Attractive color schemes were carefully considered.

My father reminded her that the due date was now but a week away. Once more they reviewed the rules and checked every detail of their entry. My mother gave her full attention to the exact listing of each identification number, name, quality, and price before copying them line by line onto a separate page for each room. With her pencil, she tallied these pages once more.

Last-minute changes were negotiated until every penny was accounted for. The balance of 35 cents of unspent funds was refined until they were within pennies of the $1,000 limit. A penny over could mean automatic disqualification. A thousand or a million all seemed the same. Living in this paper house was as wonderful as if it had been a fairy castle. Here we were a family of three or maybe more if only my parents would hear my ardent pleas for a baby brother.

Completed and packaged with the fondness of a Christmas gift, we carried it together to the post office. I glanced up and saw them smile as my mother reached for his hand. The date the contest winners would be announced was never discussed. My parents may have waited anxiously for each arriving mail, but they kept this secret to themselves.

I recognize in retrospect, how my mother was trying to relieve my father's long and deep depression. This treasured project enabled her to engage him emotionally; it also provided untold value for me. I can sense her intuitive actions that I would understand much later, as those of the first occupational therapist I knew. However, the name of this profession, the one I would follow, was unknown to us then.

I never heard the outcome of the contest except to realize that our entry probably had not been selected. I never asked. It would have been too painful. We already had our prize: the joy of doing it, living it, and loving it. Here we had a "home all our own," if only in our dreams.

9

The Ping, Ping, Ping of Buttons and Beads

"But, Mom," I whined, "*I don't want* any old buttons on my Easter dress! I want new pink ones to match the trim on the collar!"

"I wish you could have them," she replied with pained regret, "but you know we don't have any money."

"Yes you do. Just yesterday I saw Mrs. van Benscoten give you 25 cents for eggs."

"Well, it takes more than that for bus fare and buttons, too."

"But Mom, I've looked through the button box and there aren't any pretty ones there." In tears, I added, "I can't find five alike either."

I recall that our tin button box was round and deep. In its previous life, it was big enough to have carried one of Emma's frosted angel food cakes to church suppers. Now, its contents passed through my fingers weekly. I heaped them from one side to the other in search of one of the right size and color for my mother to make needed repairs on pants, housedresses, or school clothes. I recognized every one by its size, shape, and color, and also knew on whose old pajamas, dresses, or coats they had served.

Buttons, snaps, and hooks and eyes were diligently removed from every tattered garment before it landed in the ragbag. Hundreds of matched and unmatched buttons, big ones, little ones, metal or bone, cloth-covered or bare, were all compressed into that yawning, jam-packed, sky blue marshmallow container, so heavy to lift. Long before, our button box had seen many years of service in Grandpa's store where it contained layers of large fluffy marshmallows, powdered to keep them separate and layered on thin cardboard dividers.

Tiny buttons filtered to the bottom. They had not been dust-free for decades. Which of them I wondered, had adorned Grandma's dress when she watched Lincoln's funeral train make its brief stop in Poughkeepsie. She was only 12 then, just twice my age. She kept the black-bordered newspapers that told of his assassination in the tall cherry secretary behind her Boston rocker. Additional clippings were glued in her bulging scrapbooks. To think that Grandma had witnessed such an historical event was captivating. To hear her dramatic recollections of it, one would think she had shaken the hand of God.

Other buttons befitted the styles of Queen Victoria. Still others were the moth-eaten buttons of black flannel that I was told came off Grandpa's morning coat, the kind I had seen in pictures worn by those World War I peacemakers at

Versailles, Lloyd George and Georges Clemenceau. I wondered where Grandpa, this fine gentleman known for his fairness, generosity, and compassion, ever wore his. My mother must have wished he could be here, to bring a peace accord to those silent skirmishes in the powder keg where we lived.

And then there were broken strands of old beads, the half-inch white pearls and some black marcasite of Victorian vintage. The thread, yellowed from dust, sweat, and wear, broke easily. Maybe it was not worthwhile restringing these beads, but nothing was ever thrown out. Odd ones of all varieties rolled and tumbled as I shifted the contents from side to side while sorting a few onto the lid.

That afternoon in the week before Easter, I sat on the bare wooden floor close to my mother's chair. The bedroom floor was painted battleship gray like those in all the rooms, stairs, halls, and kitchen. My bony knees straddled the button box while I pushed the tangled mass in one direction, then the other, one more time.

Suddenly, I came upon a tiny pearl button and held it up for my mother to see.

"Oh, I remember those little buttons," she told me. "That one came off the smocked dress I made for you as a baby," she added, memories of early motherhood still rich in her mind.

Bored and tired, I leaned back against the footboard of their bed and gazed at the low wooden chest. There lay Sad Sadie, my oldest, most worn and torn, baby doll. Her eyelids closed mysteriously, weighted so that, when she was laid down, they closed automatically. This was curiously unlike the dead I had heard Emma talk about, whose eyes had to be held shut with pennies.

"Who in our whole household needed a new Easter dress more than Sad Sadie?" I asked myself. Without a word, I bolted to my feet and ran toward her. Clumsy-footed as I was, I caught the heel of my shoe in the button box. Compressed contents gushed forth. Buttons bounced. Beads rolled. Pandemonium poured across the dusty floor. My mother uttered a grievous "Ohhh" at the dreadful sight and sound.

Her disgust was ill-concealed, but after all, it was an accident. She stopped her handiwork to get down on the floor and help me scoop up the mess. Errant beads hid in distant, tight places beneath the dressers, far under the bed and her drop-leaf table. Hardest to reach, were those beneath the black treadle Singer sewing machine, which was wedged between the plant-stand in the front dormer window and the radiator. The trickiest ones to retrieve had rolled into the gaps of the tongue-and-groove flooring. It took a while to bring order back to this cramped third-floor bedroom.

My Easter dress had attended church services regularly for years on the back of Mrs. Haight, my Sunday school teacher. Mother had ripped the seams and laundered the pieces before re-cutting a dress for me from these narrowly proscribed shapes. Even with the pink trim she added to the collar, this dark blue rayon crepe still looked better on an old lady. I was accustomed to having new clothes made from old. What I really wanted this time were pretty, new, pink buttons that would merit some recognition from my friends at Sunday school, Easter morning.

I forgot about Sad Sadie's needs and began to pout over my dilemma. I pushed this heap of trash and trivia around one more time. Suddenly I made up my mind. If I could not have new buttons for Easter, then I would get some excitement out of these old ones. I was old enough to know better. I knew I could expect consequences, but the impulse that grabbed me in an instant was too compelling to dismiss.

Jumping up without a word, I picked up the heavy button box with my broomstick arms and held it against my body. I stepped across the bedroom doorsill at the top of our stairs. With unaccustomed grace and a hidden giggle, I made a deep bow. Rolling clatter cascaded over the top step like water at Niagara Falls. The sound was fantastic. Every button fled. Even half-strung beads escaped the thread that had imprisoned them. A rhythmic chorus of ping-ping-pings punctuated every step. The sound stopped when the last one hit the closed door at the bottom and bounced back.

My mother's lips were tightly pursed in controlled exasperation at the terrifying sight and sound. She had never thrashed me for any misdeed. The window stick used to prop up the dormer windows was threat enough to correct my behavior. This incident pushed her closer than any other to carrying out that punishment. In a clearly enunciated cadence, she said, "I think you better pick those up."

No move, no word, no regret was forthcoming, mesmerized as I was by this sight. After a few moments she followed with a second admonition: "Barbara, I strongly suggest you pick up all those buttons and beads." Silence froze around me.

"Barbara! Did you hear what I said? Either you pick up those buttons or you'll stand in the dark closet until you can. Is that clear?"

To her shocked amazement, I said, "I'll take the closet." Although I was usually afraid of bears in the dark, I reasoned that my parents' crowded closet did not have enough room for a bear. I went in and turned around to face the door as my mother closed it, backing my slim body against the wall of clothes.

Beneath the padded hangers with my father's suits was the big cardboard box we always called the "piece" box. Its contents were as familiar as the buttons. I could identify the remnants of every garment my mother had made, neatly rolled and tied. In addition, there were the adults' hand-me-down dresses, jackets and coats, each ripped apart, washed and rolled. Like my Easter dress, some day they would be remade for me. Only last week the piece box had been emptied and re-packed. Our orange tiger, Fluff, found this to be a cozy place to deliver her litter, two memorable marmalade kittens we named "Snuff " and "Puff."

My mother opened the closet door in a few minutes and asked if I was ready to be a good girl and pick up the dreadful mess I had made. After a moment's delay, I gave my unequivocal answer: "No." Darkness resumed. When she returned once more to ask if I was ready to come out and behave myself, I changed my answer. Now my plan was complete.

Before she knew what was happening, I stepped over stray buttons and beads until I reached the bottom step. There I opened the door. One final cascading sound sent these beads into the old age zone. From my perspective, the term "aging" meant "sentenced to life without laughter"—or at least none I ever heard.

At this advanced age of six, I recall I was becoming aware of the power I might exercise in this sticky, domestic situation. Never before had I intentionally put my mother in an untoward light with my grandmother. Instead, I tried to protect her position and our interests. This was the exception.

The door to Grandma's bedroom at the front end of the dark, second-floor hallway was closed as usual. I knocked. With some timidity, I turned the white porcelain knob.

"You want to come see where my mother shut me in the dark closet?" Never before had I offered Grandma my hand, but as we neared the button-riddled stairway, I held it firmly to help her up the steep risers to the dungeon of my imprisonment.

My mother was in a state of wordless panic. Greater than her humiliation was her fear for this tiny, brittle-boned, old lady. If she slipped, she could bounce down those treacherous stairs just like the buttons and beads. With the ping-ping-ping sounds still echoing in her ears, my mother had few options. She did not want to insist I pick them up and chance a defiant "no" this time in front of a "weighted jury."

Freedom was brief for those buttons and beads. Step by step, my mother backed down the stairs, scooping them into a shoebox lid while Grandma stood in silence at the top. Every last errant button and bead on the steps, and throughout the back hall, had to be retrieved and returned to its own life of confinement in the round blue button box. When she had finished, I brought Grandma down by the hand. As far as I can remember, it was the only time this tiny woman ever set foot in my parents' third-floor bedroom.

After returning Grandma to her cloistered space, I went to the kitchen and re-issued the invitation. Gritting my teeth, I reached out for Emma's sticky hand with its long ribbed fingernails, yellowed and curved at the end. After all, it was an unusual event. I led this aging "aunt" to the third floor as a corroborating witness to my mother's wrongdoing. I wanted Emma's shocked surprise to document this dreadful deed, knowing full well it would kindle a fiery discussion between the old folks. No one asked the reason for my sojourn in the closet. No explanation was needed.

For weeks, stray beads crept out from the nooks and corners. The kittens were the most excited when months later they were still finding these toys. I was no closer to getting new buttons. It was doubtful whether I would get to Sunday school and Easter services. I do not recall that I did not go. I do know that never again did I touch that old button box without hearing the ping-ping-ping pulsate in my ears.

10

Emma's Church and the Jesus I Met There

Church bells struck in deafening peals from the steeple squat and square. Shimmering bands of heavy summer air hung above the hot asphalt as we approached.

"Mommy, can we leave soon?" I shouted above the clamoring strikes.

Mother squeezed my hand in affection more than to answer the question. The Bangall Methodist Church, bold sentinel of righteousness, faced the road as it had for nearly a hundred years. Greek Revival was its style; badly chipped was its paint. Tall, clear windows were bordered with dark green blinds. Slats were missing here and there.

The tall double doors were opened for funerals but otherwise they were kept closed. As my mother turned the left knob, she felt a determined tug on her right hand.

"What's the matter, Barbara?"

"Don't want to, I'm 'fraid."

"Afraid of what, pray tell?"

"Ghosts.... Ghosts in there! I've heard 'em."

"Stop that foolishness," she chided me.

The idea, once sprung, translated directly to my feet that were firmly planted, toes pointed forward. My knees locked and my hips were braced like a mule. Stooping down to lift me into her arms, I muttered a plea she could not comprehend.

"There aren't any ghosts in there, you'll see," she said, trying to placate me. Inside she put me down, grasped my hand as we walked down the side aisle, and stepped into the pew. Unlike the Methodists, my mother leaned forward to pray, as was the custom in her Dutch Reformed Church. She put her head on her hand and rested it on the pew. I squatted down to peek; her eyes were closed. Her prayers were long. She had a lot to pray for.

Emma followed a few minutes later, huffing from her climb to the village. A sagging, cream-colored Panama hat with a tired blue ribbon shaded her head from the penetrating August heat. Beneath the hat, her sweaty scalp was sparsely covered with very fine, gray hair. Slippery hairpins protruded from an untidy bun.

Emma was not overweight, but her short body collected in the middle like a sack pushed from the top, pushed so hard her knees bulged out as wide as her pillowed hips. She rocked down the center aisle to the front pew, where she sat alone, a few feet below the podium. In this silent sanctuary, her false teeth clacked audibly, and the metal chain of her purse clanged against the back of the sloping oak pew. In addition to her linen handkerchief trimmed with Grandma's tatting, her purse held a thin pledge envelope. This number, printed in red ink in the upper corner gave her status. Her quarter was safe inside for God alone to see.

Emma never missed a Sunday. The pastor may well have wished she would. But Emma, as a self-appointed steward of the Bangall Methodist Church, viewed herself as being sent straight from God to watch over the pastor's sermons, funerals, weddings, and in somewhat regular succession, the pastor's dismissal as well. I was the only child in the congregation; no other children from Sunday school had parents who came to church. Like everyone, we always occupied the same pew, close to a window. Since my mother felt the oppressive heat dreadfully she hoped the aging sexton would try one more time in his fruitless ritual to open the windows.

Wiggling and restless, I lay on the uncushioned seat, unable to keep from sliding back on its slippery, varnished surface. Lying on my back, I could look skyward through those huge clear windowpanes. I watched cotton clouds in silent collision against the maple trees, wondering if I could find a way to fly, as any five year-old might do. Old Mr. Duell's back was frozen in prayerful posture from milking cows and hauling apples. As sexton, he passed the plate, cleaned the church, and if he remembered he put toilet paper in the outhouse.

Throughout the service, especially during the sermon, those in the congregation would lift cardboard fans from the hymnal racks that were stapled to flat wooden handles, to stir the hot summer air. Everyone stood when the organist started the first hymn. My face was nose-high to the open hymnal that my mother had rested on the pew ahead. A moldy scent passed my nose.

"Mom, this book smells just like Grandma's attic," I complained in a voice loud enough for her to hear above the organ. At the same moment, the old organ gasped and quit, leaving my voice to flood this hushed void. "Be quiet!"

It was too late. Emma turned to glower, the organist stared, the minister looked down from his pulpit. Eyes from behind stabbed like an ice pick, but I had already launched into a full-volume rerun.

"Mommy, it does too smell like Grandma's attic."

"Never mind," came her reply, delivered low into my ear. She, above all others, was grateful when the organist reattached the foot pedals that had fallen off. In alternate succession, they breathed life into the old relic. Further remarks from me were safely obscured. Once more, the organ wheezed through the opening bars. Eight mournful voices sang out. There was no choir, or we would have no congregation. Each of the ladies, there being only one man, sang as loud as the next, maybe in another key. From her pew, Emma led in volume, much as she did everything else. "Onward Christian Soldiers" was her mainstay.

My attention was sustained best through the singing and the passing of the plate. I recognized nickels, dimes, and quarters covering the moth-carved felt that used to be red. Once I saw a dollar bill pass by. I turned around to see if there was a visitor. No one in our little village had folding money, at least not for the collection plate.

"Who gets all the money?" I asked, but a pat on my arm indicated, in yet another way, I should be quiet. The sermons were the worst, the longest. Maybe the grown-ups were bored, too. For a while I sat with my legs outstretched in front of me, but soon an endless army of ants seemed to attack my feet. For relief, I lay down again, this time with my legs over my mother's lap. I saw her face tilted up toward the minister. Whether she agreed with him or not was hard to say. Then came a moment of silent reflection as the minister gazed dramatically toward his Maker. It was the moment I had been waiting for.

"All done?" Instantly this brought my mother's white-gloved hand over my mouth. Crimson rose in her cheeks. Then she resumed her listening posture. Over at last, the sermon was followed by the Benediction. In a voice as stately as this ill-nourished young pastor could command, he said, "In the name of the Father, Son, and Holy Ghost." I jumped to my feet, my ears assailed by this long-frightening word.

"Ghosts, Mom, didn't I tell you there were ghosts?" Nothing could keep me quiet then. A rare smile passed over the minister's pale face as he waited for life to be pumped into the organ for the postlude. It was time to go. I ran toward the back and made a sharp turn toward the door. My mother ran in chase lest I dash toward the road. Living in a house where bats were real and bears an unseen presence, just the mention of ghosts could be alarming. There were generations of ghosts in our attic, both dead and alive, and to hear it from the pulpit was indeed unsettling.

Counting the villagers and those in the outlying farms, Bangall boasted a population of 200, that is, it was said if they were all home, and who knew anyone who was not. This town, nestled in the undulating green hills of the Hudson Valley and 20 miles east of Poughkeepsie once supported three churches: Methodist, Catholic and Baptist. By 1925 only the first two had survived, and the first of these barely so. The Methodist Sunday school was held in the parsonage across the street from the church.

For 40 years, the widowed, old Mrs. Haight had taught a handful of wiggling youngsters. Her fearsome admonitions about Jesus registered all too clearly in our young, impressionable minds. The best part of Sunday school for me was to see other girls my age. Above all, we wanted to go out and play. But there we sat, as was expected of us, sharing the living room with boxes of Hoover vacuum cleaners. The pastors, all young, single, and recent seminary graduates, rarely made this their home. Rather, they used the parsonage as a place to sleep while making a living doing whatever they could during the week. Most often, they inherited the territory of the previous one, selling vacuum cleaners or Fuller brushes. Emma determined that one pastor failed to meet the standards of this church because he was a horse jockey on Saturdays.

As I clutched my nickel for the collection, the girl next to me giggled and accidentally jarred my arm. I lost my grip and watched the coin roll out of reach toward the square metal register in the center of the living room and drop to the furnace below.

Mrs. Haight, this virtuous lady with arms that jiggled like Jell-o and a bottom that extended past the piano stool, hammered out the children's song on a tinny upright piano. The original went like this:

Jesus loves me,
this I know,
for the Bible
tells me so.

Outside we devised our own ditty:

All I do,
He sees, I know,
for my teacher
preached it so.

From behind a face, puckered and lined, she delivered her demand: "Now girls, I want each of you to promise by next Sunday, you hear me, you will find someone new to bring to Jesus."

Her powerful voice convinced us all that she was the agent of God whom we dare not disappoint, but her face was too jolting to confirm that Jesus loved us.

The following Sunday, four guilt-laden little girls sat in the same uncomfortable straight-back chairs we had occupied the previous week. Beside me, Evelyn Churton, the grocer's daughter, curled her black patent-leather shoe with a buckle and strap around the side rungs. As Mrs. Haight pointed her finger, we each confessed. None of us could deliver the individual on demand. What were we to feel if it was not that we had failed? Failed ourselves, our teacher, our Christ. Maybe the teacher's getting into heaven depended on our performance, like a quota, the door-to-door magazine salesmen of those days claimed that they needed in order to pay for college.

This Sunday she presented an even more arduous assignment. She insisted we bring our parents to God so they could confess their sins, join the church, and attend thereafter. If that had really happened, counting two parents each for the four of us, church membership would have increased by 100 percent, but we did not know math then. Of course, my mother attended church already, so that would disrupt this computation.

Having failed miserably the previous week, I made a more determined effort this time. I pleaded with my father to meet the mandate with which I was charged. Nudging the Rock of Gibraltar would have been easier. My father's mind was set in stone. Emma had exerted such relentless control over him as a child regarding religion, her religion, her God, that he still bore scars. He would not be budged. With pressure from each side, I felt like a piece of balsa wood squeezed in a vice.

I was very quiet as we walked down the long hill in stifling heat. My father, our resident weatherman, quoted the latest reading, "temperature 90, humidity 80."

A low rumble groaned from the distant dark cloudbank. "We'll get a corker this time," he predicted. "It should cool off then."

As usual, we climbed the stairs to their sizzling-hot third-floor bedroom. My mother changed into more comfortable shoes than the Sunday best she had worn to church. "Barbara, what *are* you doing?" my mother's voice cried out. "Ouch," I cried, as my shoulder hit the edge of her dresser. The linen runner was pulled askew and with it, hairbrush and comb fell, but worst of all, her gold-trimmed, Dresden tray followed, smashing into bits as it hit the floor. The floral border scattered everywhere. I looked back in horror to see the handle of her engraved silver-handled mirror perched perilously close to the edge.

How could I stop to answer, I had to keep twirling. It was urgent. I had to see Him! My head made rapid jerks first to one side, then to the other. Pigtails flew straight out, then curled against my lips. "Missed again." Have to try harder I thought, determined to succeed. My mother met my continued gyrations with a stronger admonition:

"Stop that nonsense right now. Look at that tray! I've had it for years, and now it's in a hundred pieces." She muttered, "You know how much it meant to me." She shook her head. Tears welled up in her eyes. "That was a shower gift from the Titus girls when I got married."

The name "Titus girls" was a child-puzzling oxymoron. It challenged my imagination to envision these bent and sagging old maids as ever having been young girls. Feeling closer to success, I forced several more twirls, even though it meant stepping on the broken china. These patent-leather shoes were a size too big for me, but they had become a size too small for Ruth van Wyck, a distant cousin on my mother's side. She could have fancy new shoes since her father had a job. I envied her for that, but I was sad to be told she had no mother. I heard them say she had died in childbirth, whatever that meant. Looking back now, I remember wondering if she had done something to make her mother die? That was scary.

"What on earth are you trying to do?" my mother screamed as never before. But my goal was so important not even her screaming deterred me.

Emma called up the back stairs, "Dinner's ready."

Exasperated, my mother spoke even louder, so loud Grandma could have heard her in her bedroom below if she had not gone down to dinner. "Barbara, I said stop that, and I mean it. Stop before you fall down and cut yourself," she said from her knees, as she tried to scoop up the fragments of Dresden.

"Can't. Gotta see."

"See what? You're just making yourself dizzy."

"I gotta see what He looks like."

"What who looks like?" my mother queried. A puzzled look crept over her face. She feared that my fantasies about bears, or church ghosts, were behind my bizarre behavior.

"JESUS," was the reply I delivered in a firm voice, confident that anyone would understand. "He's right behind me. I've got to see what He looks like."

"Who told you that," she asked, anxious to get to the root of these actions.

"Dinner's READY!" Emma yelled again, dropping her voice in self pity at our delay.

Without acknowledging this command, my mother persisted. "Tell me, Barbara, who said so?"

"She did. In Sunday school," knowing there was only one important "she" there.

Like most children, my mind was easily impressionable. Fertile fantasies flew. I was imbued with a monstrous sense of guilt for any sins of omission or deeds of commission. It was what they taught in Sunday school. I thought that was what you were supposed to live by. These last two Sundays were classic examples of heavy-duty sins: not bringing another child to Sunday school or worse yet, failing to drag my father to church. How much of a load like this could a child's shoulders bear?

On a weekly basis, Mrs. Haight pronounced with such authority that "Jesus sees everything we do," I believed every word. In my literal translation, it naturally followed that He had to be right behind me or sitting on my shoulder if He is to see everything I do. Thus, it seemed only fair that I should be able to see first-hand what He looked like. I never caught Him. My only conclusion was that He moved awfully fast, faster than I, for I really tried. By the time we reached the dining room, Emma had already put dinner on the table. We released our napkins from their silver holders and at the same instant, a sharp bolt of lightning shot out of the sky behind my chair.

Solid walls of water dropped from the heavens. An artillery of hailstones sprayed the tin roof over the summer kitchen, now used for storage. Fierce lightning was followed in close intervals by sounds as deafening as a locomotive. Then God himself reached down from the heavens and split the locust tree in two at the White's farmhouse down the road. If His power could do that, imagine what He might do to a serious sinner like me. And knowing He was perched on my shoulder, it seemed my true punishment would be just as swift.

By the time we finished dessert, the rain had stopped; the air had cleared. No matter how much the storm lowered the temperature and cleared the air outside, it would take far more to normalize the climate within.

Courtesy of Stanley Benham

The Bangall Methodist Church, built in a Greek Revival Style, where Emma attended regularly.

11

Our Priest of the Potato Patch

Father Norris was the most beloved priest that Bangall had ever had. This talented, humble gentleman was sent to our town as penance instead of being assigned to a large New York parish. His "sin" was to have joined the Army as a chaplain in World War I against his Cardinal's orders. So blemished was his career by this defiance, his rise in the ranks of the priesthood never attained what his mentors had originally predicted.

His early background had been very different from most in his calling. Orphaned at an early age, he was raised by a Quaker family. Later, he adopted his new faith and attended Catholic seminary. He was comfortable among Protestants, befriended their clergy, attended their benefits, and outlasted a succession of them in their short-lived pastorates at our church.

Father Norris never complained. He never considered being sent to our town was like "Napoleon's banishment to Elba," as he might have. Nor did he confine his ministry to his own parishioners. For a number of years, he offered my father space beside his own vegetable garden to grow potatoes. This gave us room for more vegetables in the limited plot behind Grandma's house.

His smiling round face and good humor appealed to a youngster like me. I remember him vividly because he often sat down on the grass to talk to me when I went up to the potato patch with my father. As I petted Shep, his collie, Father Norris told me stories.

Shep feared thunder and lightning as much as I. He could hear the gentle rolls of thunder from distant hills long before humans were aware of it. Father Norris told me that Shep had dashed up the hill from the rectory to the Catholic church one Sunday morning. He took the flight of steep outdoor steps three at a time, crept through the door, and up the aisle.

I remember that Father Norris told about turning around from blessing the Sacraments, to see frightened Shep at his feet. I wished I might have been there to see this sight, but I would have been just as scared as Shep.

The yellow tiger kitten we named Snuff "got religion" and went to Father Norris's house to live. The table scraps his housekeeper offered were tastier than ours. Every Thursday afternoon the priest's housekeeper had time off, and Snuff could be seen dashing across the road to appear at our back steps for dinner with his own family. He would stay for a brief visit, lick his paws, and saunter back across the lawn to return the following week.

From the front windows of the third floor, I delighted in watching Father Norris hold burial services. There, in the cemetery on the hillside past the potato patch, Snuff could be seen winding his tail around Father Norris's robes as Shep lay close by.

For three or four summers, my father and the priest grew potatoes together, planting, weeding, and harvesting their own plots and helping each other. My father gave our fine neighbor the highest accolade he could offer: "He's more than a priest. He's a prince!"

Father Norris always addressed my father as "Mr. Knickerbocker." The priest was probably the only man around that my father could talk with. Perhaps it was the priest's understanding of my father's intolerable situation that led him to offer the potato patch. My father's return to Bangall was no more related to any shortcomings of his, than was the priest's sin of wanting to serve men in combat.

Working, talking, and sweating side by side, they shared a fellowship that bonded them man to man. This bond was as close to religion as my father ever got, but it provided him the warm human contact he so richly deserved. Perhaps this friendship also offered the priest an opportunity to relax and step away from his customary role. In this unspoken bond, it seemed as if they were serving out their time together.

One hot summer afternoon I was playing with Snuff while my father worked in the potato patch. Father Norris stopped to chat before walking up the hill to his church. He carried a wide, flat basket with church candles, incense, and other items under the freshly laundered altar cloth. I ran over to see what he had in the basket and ask what they were for.

As he obligingly lifted the starched linen cloth, I saw a colorful doll in blue robes and outstretched china hands. I asked who would get to play with her.

"No one. She's not a doll. This is the Virgin Mary," he replied patiently. "She's the Mother of Jesus." Now I was on familiar territory; I knew the name "Jesus" first hand. But it was this new word that puzzled me.

"What's a virgin?" There was a long silence and glances between them to see who would offer an answer. Finally my father said, "It's a young lady," in hopes that this would satisfy my query.

I was always being reminded to sit still and be a lady, so the natural question to follow was, "Am I a virgin?" I noticed the priest turned to wave a hand toward my father, saying he had to move on or he would be late to hear confessions. Pressing for an answer, my father replied slowly, "Yes."

When the afternoon's work was finished we walked out to the road, past a stone wall that held back a weed-infested lawn and a decrepit looking cottage beyond. It was in sharp contrast to the priest's lawn at the rectory of the Church of the Immaculate Conception.

Before we crossed the road to our house, we saw several young girls approaching. They wore lace head covers, so it was very possible they were going to confession. Proud to display my new-found word, I asked him if they were virgins. Since his answer was not immediately forthcoming, I feared that this window of opportunity was fast coming to a close. I had to find out for myself, so I shouted, "I'm a virgin. Are you?" I could not understand what made them giggle and turn so red. I never heard their answer.

12

Great Escape, if only Temporary

Finally we had a car and I could be like the others when I started school. But there was one drawback I had yet to learn. It was not my father's car. Together with the money my mother had earned from sewing, plus a sizable contribution from her parents, she bought our $600 car, which long ago had been new. Naturally, her name appeared on the title. I was so embarrassed by the fact my father had no work and could not afford to buy the family car that I carefully monitored any reference to it as my parents' possession.

Our town had a band-aid doctor but no emergency medical equipment. This was typical in 1930. Other towns much larger than ours had none either. When the hearse from the next town was not in use, it doubled as an ambulance. Woe, be it, if you were to come to on the way to the hospital and think you were en route to the morgue. One reason my mother felt we should have a car was that the old folks were becoming more vulnerable with each passing year.

My mother and her parents discussed the situation. Perhaps Grandpa and Grandma Ham recognized the benefit to her emotional well-being could be even more important. In particular, she wanted to earn money as a sales representative for a paper products company from Ann Arbor, Michigan. This company carried items unobtainable locally, such as colorful paper tablecloths and matching napkins, paper doilies, party decorations, and fancy pastel paper frills to wrap around drumsticks for a party. These caught my eye. I had never seen anything like them.

We did not know anybody who gave parties, so my mother was at a handicap from the start. Talented as she was, she was no salesperson. She seemed to back up to the doorbell and apologize fervently for any interruption. This was especially true at the house of someone referred by another customer or friend.

I was taken along. Never would my mother acknowledge that we needed charity but having me along gave the unspoken message of increased expenses of a growing child. I sat quietly and watched her slowly unpack her display case, using just the right pitch in her voice, I had heard her practice under my father's guidance.

Sales work did not make my mother happy and her commission barely covered the gas. What it did achieve was to get each of us out of the third floor and give her an opportunity to see other people and other things. Her renewed spirit helped ease my father's depression too.

What I got out of it was the cardboard packing boxes. I could make playhouses or set a narrow one into the bed of an antique wooden wagon handed down by Grandma Ham. I played covered wagon in imitation of the ones I had seen on Emma's box of Twenty Mule Team Borax. One by one I would put the cats into the covered wagon. Some stayed until the wagon moved, shooting out before they could enjoy the ride. The dolls were my most tolerant passengers.

For a number of months, my mother made her weekly tours in hopes of earning more than her expenses. A $10 order was a rarity and really made her week. Most people bought the bare minimum for the salesman's free favor or to avoid the embarrassment of turning my mother away after she had displayed it all so conscientiously. A minimal order meant returning the following month with scant hopes of another sale. By then, the cost of the gas had eaten up the profits.

My father helped her prepare orders and willingly unpacked boxes left by the trucker. Sorting orders for delivery had to be done upstairs in the old barn. That was not hard in the warm weather when the big door could be open for light, but she dreaded to think how she would manage in winter. Although she had no inkling of it at the time, she would not have to worry.

By the time it was cold, we would be driving our car to Florida. Giving up her sales job was no hardship.

13

School on the Horizon: History on the Hudson

I pulled a heavy dining room chair along the parquet floor and gently bumped it over the doorsill to the living room. Kneeling on the seat, I could write at the old card table, predecessor of the featherweight variety.

My father sat in another straight-back chair, smoothing out a piece of butcher paper. "Before you start school next week," he said, "you should know how to write your name." Soon I did. I wrote all 13 letters of my last name in the right order.

A few evenings later, he gave me a greater challenge: "Schaghticoke."

With my crayon, I traced each capital letter he had written across the wide paper before copying them on the line below. He turned the paper over for me to repeat from memory, but that proved to be too difficult.

"Remember the first seven letters sound like 'scat.'"

That appealed to me. He spelled it out for me in rhythm. "SCH...AGH...TI... COKE," just as he had learned from his father: same age, same rhythm, same table.

Schaghticoke! What was it? Where was it? Why did I need to know?

Actually, this weird name had been part of the lexicon I had heard in Grandma's house all my life. I soon learned that family history at home was considered to be as crucial to my education as was American history at school.

When I was old enough to invite a school friend to stay overnight, she could easily be overwhelmed by our mealtime servings of history and politics. Some never wanted to come back, but I had no escape. My grandmother handed down family history, legend, and lore with breakfast, dinner, and supper. Her account focused solely on the Knickerbockers.

Addressing my father exclusively as he sat at the opposite end of the table, she would say, "Remember, it was only 65 years after Henry Hudson discovered his river that your ancestor followed the same route," as if he needed reminding.

It was not because Grandma was senile that she repeated these stories. Far from it, she was physically and mentally adroit until the day she died at the age of 96. However, there may have been other reasons for her litany.

Perhaps she was force feeding my father the dose of history he escaped when he left home before finishing his senior year of high school. Perhaps she resented her son who had returned, a son whom, at birth, she did not want and could not love. Perhaps she resented him for being so much like his father: kind, gentle, and generous. More importantly, perhaps this allowed her to reinforce her territorial rights from what she envisioned as our encroachment.

The Knickerbocker Homestead was built on the site of the Witenagemot Oak. It was here, Washington Irving came to visit his friend and owner, the great grandson of the original family member to come to America. During Washington Irving's visit, he became inspired by the fanciful costume of Dietrich Knickerbocker, a fifteen-year-old nephew, and it was this name he used as his 'nom de plume' for ***The Knickerbocker History of New York*** published by Putnam Co., New York in 1830.

Thus, recital of family history became Grandma's lifeline to security and a strong weapon in her arsenal. It gave her ownership over the air space when we sat down together for a meal. For the most part, communication flowed south to north. On occasion, I could sense my mother's back stiffen as if to distance herself from this verbal sluiceway.

On rare occasions, my father might introduce an alternative topic to remind Grandma that the taxes were coming due or that the attic roof had sprung another leak. Before the Crash of '29, her meager stock dividends could cover these expenses. After that, routine maintenance suffered. Emma, too, often chimed in with her well-crafted comments to influence family decisions. Little table conversation, if any, was relevant to my mother or me. Neither the ambiance nor the food was appealing. No wonder they would comment that my body was "fat as a slat." Eating was intrinsically linked to keeping quiet and enduring the boredom around the table three times a day.

Grandma's heavy oak sideboard was far too large for this modest dining room. Sturdy oak table and chairs filled the remainder of this emotionally weighted space. The furniture was not antique then; it was vintage Grandma, and it was in vivid contrast to her diminutive size. Grandpa was tall. Could he have made the final selection of such bulky furniture?

For years before I started school, I could repeat much of our family history verbatim even though there were no exams and I was never asked.

In 1609, Henry Hudson's Dutch ship, the *Halve Maane*, dropped anchor at the upper end of this long river, near what would become Fort Orange. Hudson sent his oarsmen upriver in a skiff to check its depth. The Dutch seamen came ashore to learn who lived there and what they could grow. So entranced with this fertile tract of land above the Mohawk, they named it Halve Maane. It was not for their ship, but the crested hills beyond. Having visited there, little of this seems evident. The name was changed to Half Moon by the English; the name it carries today is Mechanicville, New York.

It was too much for me when Grandma went on and on, telling how this land remained in the possession of the Mohegan tribe until 1664; according to Grandma, Pieter Schuyler and Goosen Garretsen had purchased this land from these Indians.

Now my ears perked up. "Goosen" was such a funny name. "Was that because he had a long neck?" I asked. It seemed reasonable, but answers were not forthcoming.

I wanted to hear about the Indians and what kind of headdresses the Mohegan wore, but Grandma rarely focused on details of interest to me.

"Did they smoke pipes?" My mother tapped me on the arm to be quiet.

Never wanting to be interrupted, Grandma continued, "The reason Pieter Schuyler purchased it was to prevent the English in Connecticut from doing so." It was part of this land at Half Moon that Grandma said my earliest ancestor had purchased from Pieter Schuyler.

On hearing the word "Connecticut," my ears were alert. I knew the word Connecticut. It was near Amenia, where Aunt May and Uncle Clayton lived. But, how could I even guess that this name, Pieter Schuyler, would surface hundreds of years later, in my own young life?

The story Grandma recited most often was how Harmon Jansen Knickerbakker survived the 1672 Battle of Solebay. I remember her telling that he was aboard a ship captained by his father, Johannes van Barghen Knickerbakker.

Even though I had no understanding of the word "England," let alone its coast where the battle took place, I knew the Dutch "fought like lions" under their hero, Admiral Michiel de Ruyter, and the second-in-command, Cornelis Tromp.[1] Grandma loved to say those names. The latter rhymed with "stomp," and when she was upset, stomp she did in her child-sized, black shoes.

The strategy this naval commander laid out was to wait for clear weather under full moon to send one ship east to locate the French, another west to sight the English. His scouting ships reported their respective locations.

According to Grandma, the Dutch fleet of only 70 ships surprised this much larger combined force, at sunrise on May 28, 1672. Grandma's version maintained that the English fleet of 115 ships was at anchor off the English coast at Solebay. She told how the French, rather than stay and fight, headed out to the English Channel. Her story, indicating that five Dutch ships and an English vessel were sunk, may have been askew. It is a fact, however, that both the English and the Dutch fleets were knocked out of action for more than a month.

1 Admiral de Ruyter, admiral of the fleet, became successor to the famed Admiral Maarten Tromp, who died at the Battle of Schevingen. His son, Cornelis, had been the likely successor, but was named second-in-command to de Ruyter, who had become famous for his strategy in naval engagements over the years in the Caribbean.

I preferred to hear about the battle from my father. I remember often climbing up in his chair to sit on the broad oak arm, in hopes he would be in a mood to tell me a story. Sometimes he never budged from his cast-like posture, head low, eyes closed, hand supporting his forehead. I would sneak a look at his eyes to see if they opened. If they did not, I would creep down to leave him alone as I had been told.

But if I could get him to respond, he would straighten up in his chair, light his pipe, and begin a story. Over and over, I would ask him to tell me about the Battle of Solebay, just so I could provide the sound effects of war under these valiant Dutchmen.

"Who won?" I always asked, even though I knew. In the annals of Dutch naval history, the Battle of Solebay was a draw and the wars of supremacy would resume another day. I had memorized most of the details, but as a preschooler, the dates presented a problem.

If Grandma were up from her afternoon nap, I was allowed to mimic the surprise attack by sending out the boom of cannons in all directions. Mainly, they were directed up the front staircase.

Of course, I knew Grandma was not the enemy; she just made us feel that we were. Maybe like de Ruyter and Tromp, our continued presence had surprised her, not at the "sunrise," but at the "sunset," of her life.

Had she believed, as my parents had, that we were coming to live in her house for only a year? Maybe she had good reason to stomp. When my parents moved in with a year-old baby, it surely had disrupted life as Grandma knew it. As unrealistic as it was for these elderly women to live here alone after Grandpa's death, no help, no hope ever appeared on the horizon, the horizon, that is, between our house and the hills in Amenia. Thus, our care-giving role slid silently from a 12-month tour of duty into a lifetime endeavor.

Could it be that Aunt May had fantasized that after a year, relieving us could spell relief for her? Maybe she came to realize, however, she was shackled with a care-taking role of her own, one she could never get out of, taking care of her volitionally inert husband and managing the Amenia post office. Long before the Depression and certainly after the Crash of '29, this protected her financial well-being. Had she left, her security surely would have been lost.

But in this house, nothing was ever discussed. The motto "Keep your powder dry," was translated here to mean, "Keep your questions at bay." Questions from a curious child like me were considered disruptive. Questions of my parents about the future, questions of how to support a five-member family without any income, could have been explosive. Communications, at best, were kept quiet and tranquil.

It was up to me to discern what it all meant. I figured Grandma did not really dislike me, but she never said she loved me either. That was not so unusual, neither did anyone else. In this house, neither questions, nor affection were ever put into words, but, without a doubt, I knew I had the warmth and devotion of both my parents.

As to Grandma, perhaps reciting history was the only way she could relate to me as a child. It seemed, at the time, I was not so much a grandchild in her eyes, as I was a product of history.

I was always delighted when I could get my father to tell about the Battle of Solebay. According to family legend, the warship commanded by Harmon's father took a direct hit, and Harmon himself received a serious leg wound. However, before returning to safe harbor with the injured, and dead, on deck, his father was able to put several more British vessels out of action. Harmon recovered enough from these injuries to fight a year later in the Battle of the Dunes which, according to Grandma, was not far from The Hague.

Sometimes he told me the whole story of the action of the Battle of Solebay. This gave rise to my immediate re-enactment. Besides the booms of cannons, the best part of his story depicted Harmon's leg being injured on shipboard. I would fall on the floor, and grab my leg in mock pain. Usually my father and my doll Alice were my only audience but that never deterred me from launching an acting career, one which reached its zenith right there.

Other times, it might take more effort than my father could exert, so details I eagerly awaited were abbreviated. Pleading, I would say, "Do it ag'in!"

Our historical re-enactments served in lieu of play with children my own age.

"I can't do it again. You go find something else to do. I'm very tired."

"Just the part where the cannons go BOOM. Please, Daddy, just one more boom."

"You go boom by yourself. I can't tell it again."

"Well, then tell me about the Indians at Schaghticoke. Ple...ea...se."

"Another time, not now, I really need to rest."

"Barbara, come out here with me," my mother called from the front porch. "I have something to tell you."

"What?" I ran out, with a degree of expectation. She had to think fast. Maybe her resources were exhausted, too, but she had given my father the relief he needed. "Go get your dolls. They need your attention."

"I don't want to," I whined. "They are old, and sick, and I'm tired of taking care of them. I want somebody 'real' to play with."

With a sigh of frustration, she said, "Ohhh, go play with the woodchucks."

"But I can't catch any, not even the little ones. They won't play with me like kittens." Resigned that nothing better was going to happen, I sauntered down the front steps. Then, stomping across the neighbor's freshly-cut hay field, I watched the grasshoppers jump in every direction, and heard the locusts predicting that tomorrow would be another steamy, hot day.

At the far side of the field, I worked my lean body in spider-like movements between the stretched and sagging strands of rusted barbwire. Above the soggy swamp, three or four deeply-shadowed holes were gouged into the steep bank. They linked a colony of woodchucks through a labyrinth of tunnels. I would gaze at these woodchuck homes, and daydream that each of these families had a private apartment all to itself. My mother's garden was their dining room. No matter how my father placed traps, or poison, in these holes, the woodchucks always found a way to escape.

Days later, I climbed onto my father's lap, with hopes he would tell me Harmon's story again. I needed to vent more booms. If he declined to tell that story, I would ask to hear about the Indians. They were my colorful, imaginary playmates.

This early Indian story that would evolve was the one I liked best. It started like this. Several years after Harmon had arrived, Governor Andros, the new, English governor who had renamed Fort Orange, Albany, feared the Indians from the north would try to retake the land purchased from the Mohegan tribe 12 years earlier.

In 1676, Governor Andros delegated Harmon to recruit 12 families to join him at Half Moon and create a settlement on the west side of the narrowed Hudson River. This was to prevent the Indians and the French who had provided them with their firearms, from advancing south down the shores of the Hudson.

Such a move could have created a divisive split between the still-fragile and emerging colonies. To hear Grandma tell the story, from her point of view, Harmon could, without doubt, have accomplished the deed single-handed, if he had been asked.

In Grandma's version of the story, it was Harmon also who was responsible for convening a thousand Indians for the Onandaga Council.[2] Although it didn't happen just the way Grandma described, this momentous event did take place. The location was east of the Hudson on a wedge of land between the Tomhannock Creek and the Hoosack River. The Indians aptly named this fertile spot Schaghticoke, for "mingling waters." The thousand Indians from the Mohawks of the Caughnawaga Village in Canada and the Hoosacks of Schaghticoke assembled and, together with these new white settlers, they forged a lasting peace.

I recall my father telling me how, surrounding the evening campfire, they sat pensively, and slowly passed the peace pipe from one chief to another, each signifying his agreement with a few, slow puffs.

"Did they have marshmallows?" I already knew from previous recounting, that I would be disappointed in his answer, but I could always hope.

Then he described how, at daybreak, they planted an oak sapling beside the white man's campsite. The Onandoga Council's name, "Assembly of the Wise," called this fledgling tree by its Indian name, the "Witenagemote Oak." This "Tree of Peace" became a towering giant and remained standing for 275 years. According to available research, the Witenagemote Oak was the first monument to peace in this country.

"And then," he continued, "the Indian tribes broke their bows and buried their hatchets of hand-hewn flint deep in the rich soil beside the tree."

The Witenagemote Oak shaded the site of the Knickerbakker Mansion for nearly three centuries, it having been constructed several generations later. According to Grandma it was Harmon Jansen Knickerbakker who was present when the tree was planted, but we shall see whether this is true. This beautiful brick mansion still stands and is under restoration as an historic landmark.[3]

"So Daddy, how'd Harmon Knickerbakker get here?"

---

2 The name was later spelled Onondaga, which is still in use today.

3 The variation in the spelling of the name Knickerbacker/ Knickerbakker reflects the change represented over the intervening decades.

"Well, that's a very good question, for he nearly missed the boat."

"You mean he slipped, and fell in?"

"No, but unknown at that time, there would be a very narrow window of opportunity for him to come to America. If he had missed the boat then, he wouldn't be our ancestor, and we wouldn't be here." This concept was much too difficult to understand.

I heard Grandma's quiet footsteps descend the carpeted front stairs. Perhaps she had been alerted to my "history in action" as the cannons boomed. She immediately took up the stance of the staunch, all-knowing school teacher that she had once been. However, her explanation was clearly made in terms more suited to an adult's understanding than mine, as she told how the English had captured Nieuw Amsterdam in 1664. The Dutch were so angered that half of the population returned to their homeland.

"No one from The Netherlands would have considered coming here while the English held the colony," she said, glaring down her nose as she spoke. "The English even renamed it New York, which greatly offended the Dutch," she continued with haughty pride.

Eight years later, the Dutch regained control for a brief period in 1673, and the greater part of 1674. My father added that by then, Harmon had fought enough for his "patria," or homeland, and was anxious to exchange the hazards of war in Europe for the promise of peace across the Atlantic. With the Dutch in control, Harmon and other Dutch adventurers sailed for the New World.

As a preschooler, I found much of this over my head, but you can bet that the afternoon discussion set the stage for our supper-time monologue.

The history I was brought up on came principally from an article in *Harper & Brothers Magazine* in 1878, written by General Egbert Viele, a direct descendant, entitled "The Knickerbockers of Schaghticoke." Some of this is verifiable, some was later refuted, but in our house, it was gospel. Even if Grandma had been told that not all the material in General Viele's article was accurate, she would not have accepted it. She rarely listened to any ideas that were not already entrenched in the fabric of her belief system.

Grandma drummed this into my head that: "Harmon Jansen Knickerbakker," (as the name was spelled until it was simplified by Washington Irving generations later,) "was the only person of that surname ever to arrive from Holland."

So, for me, the question and the mystery evolved as to why this name so universally claimed as Dutch in our country, is unheard in The Netherlands. Over the generations, descendants, including me, searched there for this family name, but never found it. Only recently have I begun to solve this mystery.

Although my father's family name is legendary around New York State, ancestors on my mother's side were among the earliest settlers here, pre-dating the Dutch for more than a decade. There is little common knowledge of the fact that the first people to arrive in Manna-hattin, as the Indians called it, were Walloons. A brief overview follows of the little-known history that figures prominently in Part II and Part III.

The name Walloon is virtually unheard of in this country. Walloons were French-speaking people who were not French. Neither, were they Huguenots. These Walloon Reformists were followers of John Calvin who, prior to the 1530s and '40s, had been devout Roman Catholics. About fifty-percent of them continued to follow Catholicism at the emergence of the Protestant Reformation.

The ancient Walloon tribes, so named because they lived below the River Waal, had occupied the Belgic Lands before the time of Caesar. The Lowlands were known as the "pays bas" under French rule, and later became the Seventeen Provinces of The Netherlands. It was all under the oppressive rule of Spain, as part of the Holy Roman Empire. After the 1579 Union of Utrecht, the southern Walloon provinces chose to remain Catholic and under Spanish rule; they were designated then as the "Spanish Netherlands."

The northern provinces were Protestant. When they were granted their independence, they became the Seven United Provinces of The Netherlands. Nearly three centuries later, in 1830, the southern provinces became the kingdom of Belgium. This occurred after an intermittent, often stormy, alliance with The Netherlands over the previous century.

By the 1530's, many early reform-minded Walloons began to flee religious oppression in the Spanish-controlled Netherlands. The flood of 100,000 refugees fled during the Two Year War (1567–1569) in protest against the Duke of Alva and the little-known Second Spanish Inquisition that spanned 12 years. More Walloons fled to Holland after 1579 when it became independent of Spain.

It was not the Dutch but the Walloons who first came to the New World on behalf of the Dutch West India Company. This was done to promote Dutch trading and to keep Spain, their lethal enemy, from claiming these territories.

The Dutch had trapped for furs and bought them from the Indians over the period between Henry Hudson's discovery in 1609 and the arrival of the Walloons in 1623, but none of these traders created settlements. They simply bought fur pelts and tobacco, and then returned to reside with their Dutch families.

Lost to history is the fact that it was the Walloons who were the first to bring families, flax, and farming tools to settle this Dutch territory. Before this shipload of 100 settlers sailed from Amsterdam, the directors of the Dutch West India Company designated which men and families among them would be "planted," as the term was then used, in each of four locations. Eight of the 30 families on their ship the *Nieuw Nederlandt* would go to Manna-hattin, so-named by the Indians they met there.

> Legends of my childhood indicated that those eight Walloon families named their tiny settlement Nova Belgica, for their lost homeland. Novi Belgii, meaning new lowland in formal Latin, is found on maps that signify this to be the name of the whole territory of Nieuw Nederlandt.
>
> There was good reason that the Dutch did not come here to settle. With comfortable, prosperous lives in Holland, they had no reason to risk the dangers of the New World. The Walloons, on the other hand, as refugees in a crowded land, had nothing to lose and needed a new place to settle. Only after 1640 did a number of Dutch begin to join the Walloons, building their settlements along the Hudson River banks.
>
> Adrian Vincent, the earliest Walloon ancestor on my mother's side, was said to have been from a family of flax farmers outside the city of Tournai, near the French border. Tournai was a hotbed of the Walloon Reformist movement on the east bank of the River Scheldt. As a young child, he and his family may have resided temporarily in Leyden, Holland, where many Walloons had taken refuge, before moving on, to settle in England. If so, it seems possible that this youngster would become the grandfather, of the young man by the same name who sailed from London on the *Mary and John*, to arrive in the New World in 1634.

The fact that ancestors on my mother's side arrived 40 years earlier than the first Knickerbocker would not have pleased Grandma. No one considered presenting her with such effrontery, but it was one of the few sources of chuckles my parents had.

My mother respected the fact that I faced a daily plethora of family history, so she did not burden me with hers. What she did, was to establish in me a strong ancestral identity that made me curious about its origin when I grew up. I can vividly recall from the time I was four years old, hearing her words: "Don't ever forget, you're a Walloon."

Besides mastering the spelling of "Knickerbocker," and "Schaghticoke," I also learned to write this new word. My mother, an elementary school teacher before her marriage, helped me spell "balloon," first. After that, "Walloon" was a breeze.

Momma says I'm a Walloon. Daddy says I'm Dutch. How can I be both? This was a mystery to me, especially in a fractious household such as ours.

"Don't ever forget you're a Walloon," were the words that rang in my ears that day as I stepped into the first grade classroom. I did not forget it, or that equally pressing issue of "escape," which was often on my mind.

But, first things first. At recess I asked everyone, "Are you a Walloon?" This created distance like the ocean that separated my ancestors from their homeland.

In a loud, rejecting tone, a frowning playmate asked, "What's that?" I could not remember any details, but if I could have, it might have caused me to endure an even greater gulf.

My mother was anxious to hear about my momentous first day at school. I ran to her waiting arms at the edge of the schoolyard. Before I could tell her that I had tried unsuccessfully to find other Walloons, I filled her in on my immediate goal by shouting something she was not prepared to hear.

"Mommy, Mommy, can I marry Adelbert Campbell? He's not a Walloon. He's not even Dutch, but I want to marry him anyway. Is that alright?"

"It's alright," she said, "but you might want to wait a while."

Right away was what I had in mind.

Many times I had heard the adults speak of someone, particularly Aunt May, who married and moved away. From this I gathered that marriage could guarantee my escape, too. I lost no time implementing my problem-solving strategy for relief of our stressful living situation.

On my high school aptitude tests, I always scored highest in American history, prompting my counselor to suggest a career in teaching or historical research. Not surprisingly, I fled at the thought. History was an anathema for me. I had other ideas, ideas I had developed in early childhood.

I dreamed of becoming an inventor. This seemed like the natural outcome, drawing on the problem-solving skills I had honed all my life. Of necessity, I had developed a highly imaginative adaptation to our living circumstances. In addition to creating my own clothing styles, I designed and constructed my own toys. As I was completing high school, I envisioned a career in which I possibly would invent kitchen devices or other items of utility. Realistically, my poor math grades made engineering studies impossible, but aside from that, I was informed by my guidance counselor that girls were not accepted at engineering schools. As usual, I was on my own to find a career that would utilize my innate instincts.

Midway through college, I accidentally stumbled upon the occupational therapy profession. The daily demands of this work were a perfect match for my hidden talents, and my lifelong hopes materialized.

Problem-solving remained at the forefront of my work throughout a 46-year professional career. I loved the challenge of creating adaptive equipment that enabled orthopedic and neurologically-handicapped patients in army hospitals to resume an independent way of life.

In my private practice as a civilian, I treated learning-disordered children and adults. Once more, creative problem-solving techniques were needed to motivate these individuals, and reinforce their sensory-motor pathways for learning. I designed inflated therapeutic equipment for children to develop better balance, and obtained a generic patent for a number of them.

Now, much later, I am coming full circle. At long last I can revisit that dreadful overdose of history that I could not escape in childhood. I can also acknowledge that in part, I share my grandmother's intense interest.

In retrospect I can appreciate the roles of those early settlers and the actions of my ancestors on both sides, to preserve their own families, their colonies, and our country.

14

Kitchens of My Childhood

"Hitting the ceiling" in Emma's kitchen was just a figure of speech, but she could unleash stormy squalls with the fury of a hailstorm. The glare, the gloss, the gray all reflected the character of this square box.

Known in our family as the "kitchen of the six doors," none matched. According to family legend, the carpenter who had built this house for himself acquired a door at each of the other houses he built. They all leaked cold air in winter. Outside doors opened east and west onto cold, covered stoops as the Dutch called them.

The coldest spot was the adjacent pantry. A flimsy door was built of thin furring strips; its thumb-latch clattered like loose false teeth. Referred to as "Greenland," its large, four-paned window was coated in winter with layers of diamond-studded frost. On the rare occasion when I went in, it was too cold to scratch my name on the windowpane, even when I knew how to write.

Opposite the pantry, in the corner beside the west door, the hand pump stood like a sentry above the black soap-stone sink. This archaic device was as reluctant to yield water as Emma was to give up her fresh molasses cookies.

Among the six doors, the two that matched best opened on each side of the clock shelf where Grandma's tall, walnut clock struck a harsh and rapid reminder of advancing time. The door to the left, always kept open, led to the sunny dining room.

In bold contrast, the door to the right was always kept closed and led into a dark hallway. Darkness intensified toward the far end where another closed door deterred traffic into Grandma's living room. Other doors in the hallway were also kept closed: one to the back stairs, one to the cold, damp cellar stairs, and opposite it, one to the parlor where ghosts might live.

The route to our cramped quarters took us through Emma's kitchen, into this darkness and up the steep back stairs. Sharp turns at the top beside Grandma's closed door, and again at the other end of the second-floor hall brought us to the stairs for our floor. The landing at the top I could call my own.

Our kitchen had a center worktable like most country homes at the time. What appalled my mother most when she came here to live was to see how the old housekeeper disregarded the value of this antique, drop-leaf table. Warped from sloshing dishwater for nearly half a century, the table now had a jagged crack down the center.

The cherry table was not all Emma abused. She often broke tumblers as she jammed pots and kettles on top of them in the dishpan. My father claimed he had to buy a dozen replacements a year at Woolworth's. Sitting in the living room after the evening meal, it was not uncommon to hear still another crash coming from the kitchen.

Emma had developed the habit of talking to herself. She could conduct both sides of a heated argument as if she were preparing for an audition. My parents implored Emma to conserve grocery money, but their pleas were in vain. Since she had always had access to Grandpa's store, she was accustomed to generous use of butter for cooking and baking and refused to substitute margarine. She viewed as punitive having to economize in her buying habits. Hearing Emma's mock audition from the kitchen this evening, came as no surprise.

"Just ridiculous, that's what. I'm not going to do it!"

Barely changing the pitch of her voice, she mimicked my father, emphatically saying, "Well, if you don't start cooking with margarine, Mary and I will take over the grocery shopping. Butter costs too much."

She countered, "How can I cook if I can't shop?"

Thrusting the heavy iron skillet into the dishpan she heatedly challenged my father's mandate.

"Can't cook without butter. Never did before and won't do it now. Just won't do it. Oleo looks like lard! Who ever cooked with margarine in a dairy state? My reputation at church suppers would be ruined!"

To me, Emma seemed plain clumsy. She accidentally hit things, knocked them over, and literally ran into people at home, at church, and in the grocery store. On wash days, my parents were fearful as she wrestled the big copper boiler of hot water on top of the stove. Refusing help, she sloshed it everywhere, over the stove, on the floor, and on herself. Occasionally she got burned, but she seemed oblivious to pain. Beyond that, Emma was gullible enough to believe that the promises on the Rinso box would yield snow-white laundry from her ripple-glass scrub board and that the sturdy image on the Twenty Mule Team Borax box would guarantee spotless saucepans.

On the shelf next to these soapboxes were numerous cookbooks, but seldom did she read more than the listed ingredients. Surprisingly, Emma had taught in a one-room school for two years before coming to work for my grandparents, but she could read and write at only an elementary level.

Emma's expertise lay in knowing how to wield power. No one defied her nor encroached on her space. Her kitchen was the "no trespass zone."

Now that we had a car, Emma's great-niece invited us for an overnight visit at the old family residence in Schuylerville, north of Albany.

Arching elms shaded the streets. A low picket fence and trellis ushered us from the sidewalk to the front steps where colorful hollyhocks and delphinium embraced the low white clapboard cottage. Here, in this storybook setting, some of Emma's ancestors had lived. This unexpected glimpse of her background puzzled me, a child of six.

More puzzling, and a bigger surprise, was the kitchen. Even as an adult memories of the countervailing emotions I associate with kitchens are vivid. On this occasion my emotions escalated for the first time.

Before we went in, I could tell there would be no sticky doorknobs.

What I never expected in a house as old as this was a new kitchen.

Emma must have been out of her mind with envy. When I saw it, I was so excited, I ran for Alice, the doll I had dropped on the sofa. I took off her red-rimmed, dark glasses and held her up to see the refrigerator while I spelled out the letters on the door: K E L V I N A T O R. On the top was a stack of glossy, white coils nearly as large as Emma's washtub.

"Even Grandma Ham doesn't have anything like this," I said. Like most farmers, they cut blocks of ice at the pond in Verbank. Nearby in the old icehouse, these 40-pound blocks were insulated by layers of sawdust to last through the summer and cool grandma's Hoosier icebox.

At our house, without even an icebox, food was kept in the cool cellar between meals in what was called the safe. This was a simple cabinet with open screened sides that kept food safe only from flies, cats, and rodents. Milk never soured; my father walked to the White's farm each evening to exchange an empty milk pail for a full one. This outing might have been his only glimpse of the outside world on those dark days when his head was bowed low and braced in his hands.

But here was an electric refrigerator. I would have a lot to tell Grandma Ham the next time we visited.

Although our hostess and her husband had no children, I could tell Miss Marjorie, as I was to call her, loved them. She had borrowed a child's table and chairs, and a set of doll's dishes for me. I sat Alice in one of the little chairs, with her flesh-colored, papier-mâché legs sticking straight out. Before I could join her, something at the end of the kitchen drew my attention. Marjorie's sink had two faucets, one for cold water, the other hot. I pulled over a kitchen chair to stand at the sink so I could wash the doll's dishes over, and over, and over.

More than toys, her kitchen was the fascination for me: a kitchen stove that was heated without wood and a refrigerator that made blocks of ice the right size for dolls. Surrounding her sink was a shiny counter with cabinets overhead and drawers beneath. I wanted to stay. I knew we could never have anything like this.

Marjorie loved to cook, and her husband, Alfred Fecht, who was employed at the Albany post office, had recently had her kitchen renovated. What a joy. No sticky handles or doorknobs here. I had never known such heaven.

Marjorie set a fine dinner table. From my place at the table, I could see the glistening silver service on her sideboard. My mother pointed out her beautiful Spode china, the Tiffany silverware, and Waterford crystal. In the soft candlelight, colors danced from the cut-glass goblet in front of me.

"Just like your diamond, Mommy," I told her. I could see how nervous she was for fear I might upset this delicate piece of stemware that Miss Marjorie had set before me with such trust, but I knew Emma was a bigger risk. As the adults talked, I watched the baby blocks of ice move like magic. Never before had I seen water glasses perched on tall stems, nor any filled with ice.

After dinner we gathered in the living room. The antique walnut furniture and heavy brocade drapes reflected the tastes of earlier inhabitants. I remember that Marjorie told us that the brass candle holders and snuffers belonged to the original owners and were nearly 200 years old. As the adults hovered over the family Bible, speaking in reverent tones about this ancestor of Emma's, I started copying his name from the first page letter by letter: P H I L I P S C H U Y L E R.

I heard them say he was the grandson of Pieter Schuyler the white man who originally bought the land at Half Moon from the Mohegans. My ears perked up. I remembered my father had told me how Harmon Jansen Knickerbakker bought land his land from this man.

How, I wondered, could our reckless, messy housekeeper, Emma Earle, possibly be related to someone who had owned and preserved such delicate things? How could she ever have been a descendant of the influential landowner and patriot in early American history for whom Schuylerville was named? Could it be that Emma inherited her power from these early ancestors?

Our overnight vacation, the only vacation of my childhood, ended too quickly. As we said our good-byes, I knew how awed my family was by the antiques and living history of this house. However, it was the kitchen that made the greatest impression on Alice and me.

At last, I was old enough to go to school. For children who had siblings or playmates, waiting until age seven might not have been so bad, but for me, it was an eternity. School seemed like a magic carpet, transporting me to a new life. That, too, was about to change.

I had overheard tales of Old Doc Richardson, fat in the stomach from too much liquor, and a philanderer, as well, but this term made no sense to me. I understood that he was not much of a doctor if you were sick, but for us, he ranked among the greatest. My mother had not felt well the fall I started school. The day after Thanksgiving, she went to his office.

That night, outside their locked bedroom door, I listened carefully at the keyhole as she told my father that Dr. Richardson, red-faced and bleary-eyed as he was, could see how desperately she needed relief. Our painful living arrangement was bad enough anytime, but he told her it would be especially difficult as she faced this "change of life." I heard her say that it was the doctor's orders that he was to close the house and take us to Florida for the winter.

I did not know what the word Florida meant, but I knew it must be good news.

This would be a change of life for everybody.

My father prevailed on his sister to take their mother for the winter, which was in itself a miracle. Rarely did she invite Grandma for overnight. Emma spent the winter cooking for a minister across the Hudson River. No doubt he welcomed spring.

While many in our community had lost respect for Dr. Richardson, he shone like a bright light in my life. I looked up to him as God—my God, at least. His orders made life more normal. He created this miracle of menopause. For many, many reasons, this became the happiest, the most memorable winter of my childhood.

What was this whispered adult word my ear caught on occasion? I was not expected to ask. There would be little explanation if I did. I was on my own to figure it out. As a child, I remember thinking it had to do with men. Men will pause, was the best I could make out.

One thing was certain: by the end of our winter in Florida, my parents often laughed and they drew together as one. This funny word must mean magic, some magic condition; that was what I concluded. It certainly was magic for me. Would she have this condition every winter? I surely hoped so. In Bangall, magic was our only hope.

Before we could reach the promise of what Florida might hold for us, we would travel for days. Excited as I was to be taken out of school for the trip, I was getting tired and very restless after passing through miles of boring pine trees in the Carolinas.

Then we came to Georgia, where the weather was much warmer, even hot.

Suddenly we began to see strange and disturbing sights. They generated many queries from me. My parents, too, raised concerned questions. Clearly, this was a study in black and white.

By the side of the road, we saw a row of men with picks and sledge hammers in hand, wearing uniforms with two-inch black and white stripes.

Above each collar, the skin was charcoal black. Around one ankle a sturdy metal cuff chained each one to all the others in this crew of 10 to 20 men.

Chain gangs were lawful then, and provided free labor for road building in the South. This hard labor was part of the punishment for their misdeeds. Prisoners with more serious crimes against society spent their dismal lives in the dark cells of a nearby prison for blacks. Even this bit of fresh air and sunshine, harsh as it was, might have seemed like relief to them.

But for these hard-working men little relief was possible as they crushed rocks by hand. They endured long, sun-baked hours with little food. They drank from a dented aluminum dipper, hung on the rusty water bucket that was passed down the line.

In strident contrast, two white prison guards wore starched gray uniforms and broad-brimmed hats to protect their faces and sometimes their sunburned necks. Each drank cool, clear water brought in a shiny Thermos bottle from a well at home and carried a loaded shotgun over one arm. Neither of these white men worked the sun-up to sun-down shift of those whose every movement they guarded, and menacingly commanded.

Only one family of dark-skinned people lived in my town. Two little girls from school occasionally came with their grandfather when he plowed our garden each spring. At school, they wore freshly starched print dresses, had bright eyes, and crisp braids.

These girls were strikingly different from children I saw in the South, whose clothes were tattered and none had shoes. Even by winter's end, I had never seen any of these children attend my school, or my Sunday school, nor come to our grocery store. I do remember hearing about bathrooms at the gas station for "Whites only." Negroes, as they were called then, were told to go around the corner.

Crunched beside suitcases, blankets, and boxes for so long, my legs could hardly wait to be free. My parents were exhausted by frequent outbursts of "How much longer before we get to Florida?" My mother invented new car games on the spot, one after another. I read and reread *The Gingerbread Man*; that is, I had memorized the story and knew when to turn the pages.

For further amusement I dressed and redressed Alice in the new outfit my mother had made for the trip. I wiggled in my cocoon-like seat and asked "How will we know it's Florida when we see it?"

It was noon on Christmas Eve when my father pulled back the handle of the squeaky emergency brake that stood upright between them. Peering over the mound of baggage, I saw it: a perfect doll house. Before my mother could get out, I squeezed past the hinged back of the passenger seat and bounced up the steps to swing open the screen door.

Our little house numbered among many in what was called a tourist camp, or communal setting that provided relief in winter to northerners at a modest rate. It had a front porch not much larger than Grandma's card table, a bedroom slightly larger than a double bed, and living space with a couch for me to sleep on. It also had a lavatory. Showers, which I saw for the first time, were housed in a central area, as were community washing machines with hand-cranked rollers on top.

The most exciting feature of our doll house was the kitchen. "Mommy, come quick!" I shouted from the other end of the tiny living room. "Look at this! Water faucets just like Miss Marjorie's, even hot and cold!" Here we were with

Our tiny 10' x 20' treasure where we lived briefly, after arriving Christmas Eve 1931 in St. Petersburg, Florida.

a kitchen all our own and running water too. I pondered for a minute. If only we had running water in the kitchen at Bangall, it might be the end of jellied spoon-handles and dough-covered doorknobs. I hoped my parents could see the answer to this sticky problem as easily as I.

My mother had purchased a branch of holly, rich with red berries, as we came through North Carolina. When tied to the back of a kitchen chair, this spray of color functioned as our Christmas tree, the designated spot for Santa to put our presents. This was the greatest Christmas ever for here we were, just the three of us, like a normal family, in a home of our own.

This treasure, a true doll house, would serve us well for a few days until we found another place to rent for the winter.

At last, we had a home. Larger than the house where we spent Christmas, this was one of a dozen cottages, set in two rows. Each had a screened porch front and back and two small bedrooms. For the first time, I could stretch out and roll over on a bed in a bedroom room all my own. I was in heaven. Besides, we had a bathroom with hot water and a tub with legs just like the one Grandpa and Grandma Ham had.

This house was sparsely furnished, but we could afford it at $12 a month. The living room was too small for a sofa, but we would not miss that; Grandma K.'s living room had none either. Her horsehair sofa in the parlor was for company, but I never saw anyone sit on it. They would never want to sit for long; those prickly tears and breaks pierced right through clothing.

Promises my mother had made as we packed for Florida were about to come true.

Before lunch I would see for the very first time those treasures that were packed long ago and stored upstairs in Grandma K.'s barn. This was the way we both addressed my grandmother in the softest tones we could.

In response to my frequent questions, my mother had often described her precious dishes. Now I could finally see this wedding china, her shining flat silver, and the pots and pans I had always heard about. I did not even stop to unpack my dolls. When compared with our Christmas a few days before, this was more eventful by far. I had longed for this moment as long as I could remember.

There it was: her blue-banded, white china with pink rosebuds around the edge. She unwrapped each piece as if it were a newborn baby. I watched her eyes tear up as she and my father held them again. My father, never demonstrative, shared my mother's loving glance. I know my parents did not embrace, for I surely would have remembered it if they had. Restrained for so long, their outward responses could not change that fast. Their unspoken love was always dependable; no one could sever those lines of communication.

Wrapped in compressed folds of newspaper, each piece of china carried news of Washington that was six years old. How my father chuckled, as he read the headlines about politics and government from this now-distant perspective.

The next morning I saw him wash the old Plymouth that had gotten us here and would get us back. It was as if he was giving his horse a well-deserved rubdown after a long, hard trek.

"Why is Daddy whistling?" I asked as I watched him through the kitchen window.

"It's a sign he's happy."

"I never heard him whistle before."

"Oh yes, he was always whistling when we lived in Washington. It's so good to hear it again," she said, turning her head away.

When she resumed her dish washing, I asked, "Will he whistle when we go back?"

That time she drew her lips inward and after a long pause she looked toward me and said, "I wish I could tell you, but I can't answer that question. We'll have to wait and see."

Later, I went outside. Two little boys from the cottage next door came out to play. One was a bit older than I, and his brother was younger. They introduced me to their wrestling game which consisted of rolling over and over together, wrapped in each other's arms. Suddenly, my father called from the back porch.

"Barbara, stop that and come right in."

I never understood his reasoning then; he did not elaborate. I claimed I was not getting my clothes dirty, but he seemed to have some other reason. Well, so much for boys, but I still liked them. Whenever my parents were visiting with neighbors out in the front, we resumed our games in the back.

For the first time in my life, I saw my mother in a kitchen. I could tell she felt right at home. My father picked lemons for her from the tree in the back yard.

Our next-door neighbors, Ora and Flora Porter, had come to Florida to escape the cold winter of Oswego, New York. We became lifelong friends. In the evenings we often sat around our kitchen table and my mother would serve one of her delicious lemon meringue pies.

These neighbors were childless, but they loved children, so they gave me lots of attention.

Mr. Porter said I could call them Ora and Flora just as my parents did. I was thrilled he thought I was so grown-up. Ora was such a whiz, often entertaining me with sounds that accompanied the shadow figures as they danced across the warm, yellow kitchen wall in the evening.

Never had I had so much attention. Ora would do almost anything for me. Thus, my birthday was most memorable. First, he took me fishing at the St. Petersburg pier where I caught an eel. When I came home, I rushed through the front door to announce that I had caught a whale. Eels or whales, they were all the same, I was having so much fun.

All I wanted for my birthday was a cake of my own design, not the traditional angel food of Aunt Em's kitchen. Nothing would do but a three-tier cake with white frosting, like the one I had seen recently at my Uncle Eugene's wedding. Naturally, Ora asked the bakery to oblige.

Here, in our little home, the kitchen was the magnetizing force. My father and I sat together around the small table as we watched my mother make dinner.

Our kitchen was definitely the place to have fun when the neighbors came over. The Porters, who lived in a less protected, end cottage, came to ride out tropical storms in our kitchen. In Bangall, the kitchen itself was the storm center.

The economic depression for most of the country came with the stock market Crash of '29, but in our family, with my father having had no job after we moved from Washington, the depression both financially and emotionally had started four years earlier.

While the crash was catastrophic for the whole country, it was the big boom and bust of the real estate developers in Florida that plunged middle class and poor alike into a state of deep despair. Men walked along the St. Petersburg pier carrying bamboo fishing poles, their heads sagging, shoulders bent and their future less certain by far than any bite on their line.

Their posture was familiar to me, but in contrast, my father's depression had lifted. Here in Florida he could enjoy his family. We had everything: a place we could call home and close friends. I even had playmates. This was the most exciting place I had ever known.

I had been in my new school for three months. That spring the first grade teacher suggested that I be moved up to second and my parents approved.

My father sat at the kitchen table and gave my mother a big smile as he finished his second piece of lemon meringue pie. As she looked back from the sink, I could see all the joys of their winter captured in her face. However, when he began to discuss plans for the trip back, her smile dimmed.

She was deep in thought, as she plunged my tin lunchbox into the dishpan.

Lifting a soggy piece of notepaper, she exclaimed, "Barbara, what's this?"

"Oh, Mommy, it's a note from the teacher that says we're all going to see *Old Ironsides*, docked at the pier this week. I told her we had a car and you could drive."

Our old car with wooden spokes and black rubber steering wheel had undergone a most unique transformation. In Bangall, I felt that our car must be the oldest in New York State. In Florida, my classmates had less than I, no car, no shoes, no hope. Instead of having the oldest car, my family had the only car.

Friday morning, the teacher's car and ours stood in front of the schoolhouse as the entire class piled in. Ten barefoot little chatterboxes squirmed and squeezed around my mother as she drove. I felt so proud.

Although my mother had been trained as a teacher at Columbia University, neither that nor anything else could have prepared her for what would happen to one of her charges. She later described her cargo as a bunch of wild little Indians whose first names she had barely heard.

Along with hundreds of school children from Pinellas County, we stood in line on the long pier for hours under scorching sun. Teachers and parents were thinly spaced in this sea of white faces. Several boys started punching and shoving. At the same instant, we heard the screams, then the splash. Hundreds of pairs of eyes looked down, none more anguished than my mother's. The little seven-year-old blond bobbing up and down in greasy black water 20 feet below was one of her nameless charges.

Moments weighed like concrete while we gazed at this floundering little boy. His head bobbed up twice, he splashed, he screamed with fright and went under once more.

On the other side of the long pier, two muscular Coast Guardsmen in crisp, white uniforms heard the screams, and plowed a path through hundreds of terrified youngsters. One dove from the pier, while the other searched for a hemp ladder to loop around a low iron chock. In the deep, dark water, the sailor swam blindly toward the terrified bundle.

Then his broad hand reached toward a threadbare shirt, faded and already torn. The sailor's quick grasp ripped the shirt further before his hand could cup the chin of our drowning classmate.

The seaman groped for the dangling hemp, then slowly worked his way up the shaky rope ladder. All eyes were riveted on the limp load hanging over the shoulder of the sailor whose grease-streaked uniform had, moments before, been crisp and white.

The sailor was helped onto the pier by his friend. These men promptly applied their coal-black hands to pump water from the child's lungs and air into his body. Gradually this child's pale face and purple lips resumed their natural color. A grateful smile crept across his face and ours, too. My mother extended her hand in grateful thanks to these courageous seamen.

It is hard to say who was more shaken, the child, the teacher, or my mother. No one could have been more thankful than she, that a tragedy had been averted. Her face was near tears for reasons that reached beyond the moment.

This frightful incident had been a stark reminder of an earlier experience that had not ended so happily. While making breakfast the next morning, she told my father in a whisper I could hardly hear, that the nightmares had returned. I could not understand the significance of her remarks, but years later she told me about the drowning in Grandma Ham's fishpond.

Grandma had hired a lady to watch over the two youngest of her five children during haying season when she always fed the hungry farmhands their noon meal. Two year-old Lewis escaped the sitter's vigilance, only to be discovered moments too late by his terrified mother. The oldest child, age ten, was my mother, who suffered nightmares about it for years.

Because I had seen my young classmate nearly drown and sensed my mother's responsibility for his safety, this event has had a lasting impact on me. After more than 75 years, seeing *Old Ironsides* still pales by comparison.

That winter sped by so fast. In just another week, our respite was to end and we would turn back for our week-long journey. Migrating birds heading north bore hopes of spring, but we were returning to a house cloaked in the chill of winter year-round.

Each of us dreaded it in our own way. Most of all, I would miss being a family of three. There was love and lightness in our life here. How fortunate that I did not know then that this would be the only time when we would ever live under our own roof as a family of three.

For my mother, it meant more than repacking the pots, pans, and dishes. I heard her wonder aloud when she might ever see them again. My father must have worried that the sunlight in his life might again dim into the darkness of depression, a frightening prospect.

Our dear friends and neighbors, the Porters, and my parents realized how painful it would be for me to leave, so they started preparing for this, months in advance. The event itself took place a few days before our departure.

Throughout the winter, whenever we had gone to our corner store, I had stood in awe of the beautiful doll with flesh-colored arms and legs sitting on the shelf behind the cash register. She could be mine for 25 coupons. One was packed inside each 29-cent box of gingersnaps.

All winter long, we ate gingersnaps. Between the Porters and my parents, they bought five more boxes the week before we headed north. We added these coupons to those held safely in a kitchen drawer.

The five of us walked down the sandy road to the grocery for the last time. In front of the shiny cash register, I saw Ora and Flora exchange smiles as my father counted out the coupons for my treasure. Then the grocer lifted her from the shelf and put her in my waiting arms.

She was more than I could ever have dreamed. When I squeezed her soft rubber legs, she would cry. In her pink organdy dress and white booties, she was almost the flesh and blood baby sister I had begged for. I cuddled her all the way home, giggling whenever I squeezed her legs to make her cry. The adults, too, had smiles, and possibly some tears. Of course, I named her Flora.

It would be painful for all of us to leave our little home. After having a bed in a bedroom all my own, I would find it hard to return to the quilt-covered chest on the landing. I wished for magic, some magical way—just any way—to avoid going back to Bangall, back to the life I dreaded, back to our lives with Grandma and Emma.

To my parents' dismay, I was to get my wish, if only temporarily. We had stopped at a tourist cabin in Atlanta overnight, and the next morning, they found me peppered with measles. Whatever advantage this delay gave me, it put unexpected stress on the family budget. My father was embarrassed to have to wire Grandpa Ham for the loan of $100 to cover our additional expenses.

After leaving Atlanta, we stopped to visit grandpa's sister, Helen Ham Merritt, and her family in Ashville, North Carolina. This aunt of my mother's was elderly, but she was kind, and she could still smile. There, under the same roof, were three generations of Helens. Her daughter, Helen, and husband, Charles, had met at a tuberculosis sanitarium outside of town, sent there for rest and mountain air, the only cure for the disease at that time. Their children, "Little" Helen and a younger brother, Stephen, were a few years older than I. As I was to discover, they had been educated as staunch Southerners at home and at school.

Here in Asheville, Stephen and his sister were in grades four and five, while I was a proud second grader. They were far more mature, lived in a city, and had tremendous advantages. Stephen complained about losing his savings when the banks failed in the Crash of '29, and professed keeping his money in his sock thereafter. In my limited experience with money, I imagined that the Indian head pennies and buffalo nickels I took to Sunday school would be hard to walk on.

The original Merritt family had left the Hudson Valley in the early 1800s to buy farmland near Appomattox, Virginia. When the Civil War began, the husband returned to fight with the Union, leaving his wife and 14 year-old son, Stephen, to safeguard the farm. It was Stephen Merritt whom my great-aunt Helen would subsequently marry.

Throughout the four years of fighting, Confederate soldiers often came to their farmhouse demanding that Stephen's mother cook them a meal.

They once brought her a Union soldier's hat filled with bullet holes, and claimed it was her husband's. Stephen Merritt survived the war and their heirloom silver at the bottom of the well was preserved, too, while the hat with the bullet holes became a significant family possession.

When I was an adolescent my mother took me to visit Eugene Merritt the oldest son of great aunt Helen, who still lived on the family farm outside Appomattox. I saw these objects of family history I had heard about: the old well and the bullet-ridden Union hat.

What intrigued me most was his impressive collection of Indian arrowheads and the buttons from Confederate uniforms that filtered to the surface with each spring plowing. It was a stark reminder of the troops who trod this ground and defended their fluctuating lines.

Hostilities came to an end at the nearby Appomattox Courthouse on April 9, 1865. Five days later, on the other side of the Potomac, Lincoln was shot. Grandma K. never let me forget that she was 12 years old when this happened.

The Civil War had been over for many decades, or so one would think. Not so, as I was to experience first hand. Before we arrived in Asheville, my mother had tried to explain that this family had a Mammy, but I was unprepared for the concept. Smiling, her snow white teeth gleamed as she asked me about my dolls. With no other name to use, I, too, addressed her as Mammy. My biggest surprise was yet to come.

Sunday morning, we three children were left with her while our parents piled into their family car to tour the city. Outdoors, a game of hide-n-seek ensued, but it was short-lived. With a toy pistol in hand, Stephen, his grandfather's namesake, bounded around the corner of the house shouting, "*I'll shoot* your head right off, you *damnyankee*," using the customary, one-word form favored by Southerners after the Civil War, and may still be heard on occasion.

I didn't know I was a "Yankee," but I did know I was terrified. I screamed and dissolved in tears. Before I knew what was happening, Mammy appeared and bundled me into her big round arms to protect me from the in-house bully.

Unbelievably, she took me into her kitchen. The aroma of ham and yams filled the air. She cut a slice of fresh-baked bread for me and spread it with butter and jam. Her kitchen was both haven and heaven, the polar opposite of Emma's fortress.

My parents got their surprise at the Sunday dinner table. The giant-sized ham was placed in front of Charles. As he stood up to slice it, the kitchen door flew open and in rushed his three hound dogs to sit in rapt attention beside his chair while Mammy held their dishes to be served first. Indeed, Charles was a Southern gentleman, brought up in a hunting tradition where hound dogs came before family and visitors.

The next morning, as we were saying our good-byes, I dashed back to the kitchen to throw my arms around Mammy's neck. How I wished she could cook at our house.

The trip back held none of the excitement we had experienced on our way to Florida. In fact, for my parents, it must have been akin to birds being returned to their cage, to their own ten-foot by fifteen-foot patch of privacy on the third floor. Sadly, this would remain the status quo until I finished college.

My parents decided that the time had come for basic changes. Emma's eyesight was failing, so she could no longer cook safely. Occasionally, she put unintended ingredients into the food. We never got sick, but we were not always sure what we were eating.

Contemplating how to break the news that from now on my mother would be in charge of the kitchen must have sent tremors through their bodies as, day by day, we drew closer to Bangall. Perhaps they were silently preparing themselves for the explosion they knew would erupt.

They were right. Emma could hardly speak a civil word to us for weeks. Not that Emma stopped talking, she spoke with everyone: at church, at the post office, at the general store, and with neighbors down the road. Her angry message was loud and clear. She felt she had been totally displaced.

In absorbing the shock waves emanating from the kitchen, it seemed as if the mansard roof on the third floor moved perceptibly up and down, as the house virtually approached combustion level. Emotionally starved all her life, this maiden lady was extremely jealous of my mother, but the reason behind Emma's attitude was not her fault alone.

Emma had been hired by my grandfather shortly before my father was born. Not wanting another child, my grandmother willingly gave him over to be raised by Emma. To compound this complex situation, he was born on her 25th birthday. Having been invited to lay claim on him from birth, it is not surprising that she, a domestic servant, complained bitterly when my father brought my mother home from Washington as his wife.

Apparently my father's reluctance to marry earlier had been colored by the reality of what she might be subjected to. Thus, these high school sweethearts did not marry until my mother was 37 and my father a year older. They had made their home in Washington, where my father worked for the Department of Justice for a number of years, before going to the FBI in 1919.

In further violation of Emma's fantasies and her turf, my parents had brought me, a toddler who could be troublesome when the smell of baked goods escaped her cloistered domain. But now, insult of insults, her very own kitchen, her territory for over 50 years, had been invaded, and by my mother, at that.

Emma proclaimed that she felt like a nobody and was no longer needed. Feeling she had no reason to live, she uttered profound threats of suicide at every meal. It came as a surprise to me to find her sitting there at the next one. With great regularity she renewed her pledge, death by nightfall. Relief never came, for her, or for us.

Upstairs in Grandma's bedroom, she and Emma spent hours commiserating over an untold variety of complaints, real or imagined, often resulting in the writing of a new codicil to Grandma's will.

The intent was clear; Grandma's door, usually kept closed, was now kept open. Emma spoke loud enough for my mother to hear her in the kitchen even if the door had been shut. Convinced that her standard of living had been compromised, Emma complained that there had been no molasses cookies for breakfast for an entire week. She proudly pointed out that she had upheld this Dutch tradition, one perhaps of her own invention, without fail for those many years. And, despite a variety of fruits and healthy desserts, she whined that there had been no pie or cake for more than a week.

Change was coming too fast for Emma. She was shocked that my mother never baked bread.

"Why should I, when I can buy Ward's Wonderbread at the store for nine cents a loaf and they slice it, too."

For a lifetime, Emma's bread slices were wedges an inch thick on one edge and, as my father used to say, so thin he could read *The New York Times* through the other. Emma could bake, but she could not cut. For as many years as she had practiced, slices always ended up the same way. A double wedge sandwich was more than my jaws could handle.

The winter in Florida had done wonders for us all. Now my mother had enough self-confidence to withstand Emma's ceaseless battering. As when Britain ruled the waves, so it was here. Whoever controlled the kitchen had the upper hand and determined the grocery list, the menus, and the schedules. All these household responsibilities were difficult for Emma to relinquish. It was hell upstairs and down.

What fortitude it must have required for my mother to keep from screaming to my father: "Take her, she's yours, I'm leaving!" The most vehement remark I ever heard her say was "My dear man!" This usually preceded a plea for him to intercede. It was always my clue that her emotional fabric was becoming tattered and frayed.

Over the following weeks the kitchen-dining room routine gradually settled down. My mother delegated appropriate responsibilities to me, such as setting the table and pouring the glasses of water.

After one particularly turbulent afternoon in this daily war of nerves, I considered what I might do to mitigate my mother's distress.

It was a bone-chilling evening in that long damp spring when I took matters into my own hands; to this day, I remember the dramatic effect. Now that my mother was in charge, she changed the main meal from noon to evening, which did not please the old ladies. Not only was I in school all day, my father had a full-time bookkeeper's job, so now it was dinner at night, not supper as it had always been. Rules chiseled in stone were suddenly being demolished.

A few moments before I was to call the old folks to dinner, my mother noticed that I had failed to serve either of them a glass of water.

"Okay," I said in childish disdain, acquiescing to her stern mandate to behave.

Opportunity jumped in front of me. A few minutes later we were seated around the table. All were accounted for, five people, five glasses of water. Grandma reached for her glass of water as always before starting her meal. The last two glasses served were filled to the rim. No one could drink from them without spilling, least of all someone with aging hands.

As she tilted her glass for a drink, water poured into her lap, just as I had hoped. Pushing her chair back in fury, she spilled still more and jumped up faster than I had ever seen, screaming: "Oh...That's cold." I knew she was still wearing her heavy winter underwear and would have to change down to her skin.

Grandma climbed the front stairs faster than ever, without a word or a glance back. Good thing, for I was unable to hide my joy, joy that is, until I caught the full sentiment of my mother's response.

"Go pour two glasses of water the way we usually do!"

The implication was clear not to try that trick again. I never did, but I found others. I had no siblings with whom to spar, and I needed to vent childhood revenge for the injustices I witnessed. Ice cold water was my most effective weapon.

15

A New Bedroom: Mine!

It had been six weeks since my mother had taken over the kitchen. The level of turbulence was gradually subsiding. The storm clouds rumbling from the second floor were now reduced to silent skirmishes without smiles. It was time to launch the next salvo into whatever tranquility remained. Would Grandma let me move from the landing to a bedroom of my own? What would she say when we asked? Such a request promised to be tricky even in this large house.

The quilt-covered chest was too short now for my long legs.

The bedroom we had in mind was the square room above the kitchen; this room was off limits to me, as the kitchen had been, and the parlor still was. Frozen in time, its furnishings were unaltered since the day Aunt May married. Nevertheless, it was referred to as May's room and always would be. The risk we faced was that the old folks would interpret our request as further encroachment upon their world.

Now I was eight and skilled in the art of selecting the optimal opportunity to broach a painful subject. Over several days, Mother and I discussed how and when we might best approach Grandma K. for this timely favor. My mother always addressed her as "Grandma K." Since she regarded her own mother with such warmth and affection, it was unthinkable for her to address Grandma Knickerbocker as "Mother."

It was a warm spring afternoon. Emma had left for a Ladies' Aid Meeting at church. Outside the east stoop, Grandma leaned over her long, narrow flower garden where she would weed for hours. This would be the best time to approach her for several reasons.

Emma would not be there to reinforce Grandma's position. Secondly, we could speak to her, or rather my mother could, from the garden's edge. Then Grandma could give her reply without having to look at us. This way, we hoped she might be more comfortable discussing the issue and grant us a favorable decision.

My mother and I mobilized ourselves in the kitchen. We reviewed our tactics. We were ready. We crept quietly out the east door so as not to disrupt the setting and ruin our hopes. My mother leaned over the garden as if pulling an unwanted weed and cautiously opened the conversation.

"I guess you've noticed how much Barbara has grown while we were away," she ventured in soft, neutral tones.

"That she has," was the most my grandmother could offer as she brushed dead leaves from the crocus bulbs struggling to burst through the rigid soil.

Silence settled over the crocuses and along the entire garden. My mother waited a respectful length of time, so as not to appear as eager as she surely was. Again she broached the subject.

"Barbara is so tall now that her feet hang off the wooden chest on the landing."

Another long silence ensued. My mother wondered if she should mention that I was accustomed to a bed now so it was hard for me to roll over without falling off. Grandma weeded instead, and kept us waiting.

"Is that right?" she said at last, her response lacking any invitation for discussion.

My mother hoped my presence might tap Grandma's compassion. There was none. She was not to be stopped now, but she carefully maintained her delicate tone of voice.

"I was wondering if it would be possible for Barbara to have a room downstairs on the second floor."

This reply came immediately and was firm.

"Well, not the guest room. Mrs. Paine sleeps there when she comes to visit. If you're thinking about May's room, you'd have to ask her about that."

We knew May and her husband were away for two weeks celebrating their wedding anniversary, and we wouldn't see her until the Sunday after their return. There was nothing more to be said. Mother tried to make as graceful an exit as possible, moving to the far end of the flower bed as if to pull up one last weed. Her free hand flew up to wipe her face. I knew it was a tear.

We retreated to the kitchen, relieved that the opening foray was over but disappointed about the long wait. We reassured ourselves we had done our best. We had provided Grandma the opportunity to come forth in offering May's room in a spontaneous, warm, and generous manner if she could. She could not.

That evening I sat cross-legged under the table as usual while the family read the evening paper. Suddenly my father leaned forward in his chair, turned his head to the left, and pressed the newspaper flat against his knee.

His voice was firm in a way I had seldom heard unless he was scolding me.

"Mother, I have to speak with you." He laid down his pipe. "We need a bedroom for Barbara. I'm asking you for May's room."

The battle line was drawn.

Grandma, too, lowered her newspaper to acknowledge that my father had thrown down the gauntlet. She turned her cold gaze in his direction. Even from my spot under the reading table, I knew exactly how her face looked. Her skin was like transparent silk. Her snow-white hair was pulled back as always and secured in comb-drawn lines into a tight bun. Beneath the softness of her china-white skin, her jaw and cheekbones were as unyielding as stone. In uncompromising tones, she released a reluctant response.

"Well, I already told Mary this afternoon, we'd have to see what May says. After all, it is her room."

My father shifted a bit in his chair as if to realign a phalanx of troops. "Look! May married and moved away 25 years ago. Unless she's thinking of dumping that lout, she won't be back."

He picked up his pipe, having safely made the first advance. A blue smoke screen preceded his next words. "And we're not waiting weeks to ask her. We're settling this tonight!"

Under the table, my heart pounded. My head swiveled left and right toward the source of each voice. I was so proud of my father's stand. Never before had he said such things. My grandmother used silence, her strongest weapon. It took so long I wondered if she would ever speak.

"Well, I don't know what May will say," my grandmother offered stiffly, trying to safeguard her ammunition and make the most honorable retreat possible. It was a battle she sensed she had lost despite her position.

"You forget, don't you, your only granddaughter carries her name." countered Dad.

It was my middle name, which later I would disavow when asked how my name should appear on my high school diploma. This was an act of defiance not condoned in the politics of this family where my grandmother was owner of the house and matriarch of our lives.

My father's voice grew in confidence with each sentence.

"In a house with five bedrooms, you could give one of them to a growing girl. She needs a bed and a room of her own."

From below, I smelled another screen of smoke, heavier than the last. It was the only way my father could vent the feelings he usually kept silent.

Like those Dutch stalwarts Admirals de Ruyter and Tromp, my grandmother was unaccustomed to experiencing defeat, but finally she was resigned. She acknowledged that I could have May's room but insisted that I could not use her good, pink porcelain and gold-trimmed washbowl and pitcher. I could see how desperately she needed to preserve part of the family myth that May might someday return to live at home.

Was there more to this than I ever knew? Had May really intended to return here to live? Was she thinking of leaving Uncle Clayton? Was that the answer to the mystery I never understood, when we moved here expecting to stay only a year?

Whatever the family politics might be was of no interest to me. This evening was mine and I was ecstatic. I sprang out from under the table. I swung open the door to the scary back hall to lunge for the stairs. Before I could put my foot on the bottom step, I was stopped in my tracks.

"Barbara!" my mother called. When I reached her chair, she told me in a soft, quiet voice, "You must go around and thank your grandmother." It hardly seemed that she should be thanked it was my father who had saved the day.

As I glanced at my grandmother's face, I could see that her expression was unchanged. I said, "Thank you," as briefly as possible and then I dashed upstairs two steps at a time to push open the bedroom door with a crash. I took the one step down from the hallway and walked across the room to reach for the overhead light cord. With pride of possession, I shouted to myself, "This room will be Barbara May's now."

I was so happy that I could hardly contain myself. I bounced on the lumpy mattress that covered the weary coil-springs. Then I rolled from one high end of the bed to the other and back again until I was dizzy. Suddenly I thought of the fun I had had in Florida rolling on the grass with the two boys next door. How I missed my playmates.

This was my room. It no longer mattered that Grandma continued to refer to it as May's. It was the best room in the house. The open register over the woodstove made a warm place to dress, whereas hugging the radiator had warmed my body in ridges. More than that, the see-through register offered a unique listening post.

Now that my mother was in charge of the kitchen, I often heard her discuss serious matters of the day when my father came home. Listening intently, I sensed the strains of the moment, stresses to come, and sometimes their solutions. When my parents were together in the kitchen, I was only a few feet away. We were almost a family of three.

My first bedroom on the landing. The railing was put up to prevent me from falling down the canyon of stairs to the lower left. There is a window behind the wall on the right. There was little room to squeeze between the wall and the railing to get to my "bed."

16

The Wall of Freedom

The gray walls of the back stairs grew darker as I climbed. Grandma's door at the top was again closed and locked, now that Emma's tirade over the loss of her domain was subsiding. The second-floor hall, gray on a sunny day, again became a dark tunnel.

Whenever I was sent me to the third floor on an errand after dark, I darted quickly, often returning without the object requested.

"Bears up there," was the common excuse. I grew braver when I could make these scary creatures vanish with the flip of a light switch but still this was at the farthest end of the hallway.

Grandma never used the back stairs as they were steep and risky, but she made many trips a day on the carpeted front stairs. Her brisk pace never faltered. Alerted by the four clocks that struck each hour in unison, this keen and sprightly woman came promptly for meals and kept an unalterable schedule of daytime radio programs and soap operas, such as "The Goldbergs." Her all time favorite, "Divorce Court," unfortunately for me aired on Saturday mornings. The theme music was Mendelssohn's "Wedding March," the customary recessional, creating a needless travesty against its composer and lifelong distaste in my mind.

Grandma's evening radio schedule matched the dedication with which she read the newspaper. Without fail, she listened to Lowell Thomas at six o'clock. To her, he was a favorite son. He lived in Pawling, some 30 miles away, and often broadcast his program from home. His recorded broadcasts from Tibet, where he met the Dalai Lama, were my favorites.

It was Grandma's radio, so she owned the airwaves and the schedule, tuning in for a full diet of Sunday evening commentators, beginning with the alarmist Walter Winchell, followed by Gabriel Heater and H.V. Kaltenborn.

These gloom and doom boys always sounded as though the world was about to come to an end, and, in many ways, they were right. As predicted, people in Europe did lose their freedom and many lost their lives.

At my father's urging, we heard entertaining programs to help offset this dark mood. We really enjoyed Amos and Andy, Jack Benny, and Edgar Bergen, the ventriloquist with his famous sidekick, Charlie McCarthy.

Alone among these personalities, Charlie McCarthy was my idol. I listened to him with a passion and would hear none of it when my parents told me he was not real. I knew better. I needed Charlie to talk back to Edgar, and make him look ridiculous. I also needed Charlie to be real as a companion, which he was, except for the few months in Florida when I had live playmates.

While storm clouds gathered over Europe in the 1930s, we, in our tiny microcosm, were gaining our freedom in increments that the three of us could both see and feel.

My father finally had a job as bookkeeper at the local lumberyard, where he earned $35 for a six-day week. We were definitely stepping up in life. But it was more than finances that enabled him to ask his mother's permission to paint the second-floor hall. Now, as an eight-year-old, I could see the change. He no longer held his head in his hands when he sat in the chair by the living room window.

While I was too young to understand the word "depression" when we were in Florida, I remember seeing him enjoying his family. His self-esteem continued to flourish when we returned, since he was earning some money now. Asking Grandma if we could paint the back hall came easier for him.

Perhaps he could even envision the potential this benchmark event might offer me. Without even turning to ask Grandma, he told me that until it was painted, I could scribble all I wanted using a pencil. Crayons were forbidden. This ten-foot-long wall became a monument to free expression. It provided a license to freedom never before granted in this house. This surely, was my "Freedom Wall."

I could hardly believe what he said. With a pencil in each hand, I scribbled down to the baseboard and as high as my spindly arms could reach.

One Saturday morning, I lay on the floor and in letters too small to read standing up I wrote two lines in careful block letters. I HATE GRANDMA. I HATE AUNT EM.

I had a scribble wall for friends and myself, something no one else in town could boast. Perhaps no one else needed this simple pleasure as desperately as I. Inviting an occasional classmate home from school, I proudly shared this special opportunity. It no longer mattered that we had an ancient car and no indoor plumbing; I had the magnetic attraction of the moment. I was one happy child.

Holding our pencils, we ran along the wall and watched the trail left behind, some straight, some wavy, others with sharp peaks and valleys. Then with two or three pencils held together, we giggled as we created parallel lines like those in our songbooks. This wall was ours. It was my pride of possession. This Freedom Wall met a desperate need in me. No space larger than a thumbnail was left unmarked.

Painting the upper hall was our first luxury, even if it was only calcimine. This was a cheap water-based paint, one grade up from the whitewash farmers used in the cow barns, but calcimine was already colored.

Here, we were to have something new, clean, and cheerful, and we were free to choose the color as well. It was as close as we had ever come to feeling that this house was our home.

Immediately, we agreed on sunshine yellow like our kitchen in Florida. This project was a source of instant pride. I could feel it ripple through me.

After several weeks of our wonderful play, I had to face the fact it must come to an end. With some regret I saw that my treasure was soon to vanish. Watching my father stir the big pail of yellow liquid, I heard him start to whistle.

"What are you whistling," I inquired.

"Humoresque," he replied. The title meant nothing to me. I was just glad for humor of any kind, especially from him.

When the paint was fully mixed, he showed me how to pull the paint brush along the baseboard. He drew me in through the excitement of painting, to override any disappointment at seeing our cherished experience disappear. We closed the chapter on our Wall of Freedom, but I could live with it. We had had our fun. More than that, Grandma's preference for battleship gray had been overruled. The bears left at about the same time.

My father was empowered as never before. Now, he still chuckled on occasion. We saw him break into a smile the first time he pulled a paycheck from his pocket. Seven years was a long wait.

Having a bedroom all my own, painting the back hall, and even choosing our own color comprised unheard-of changes in our house. While yellow symbolized our unity as a family of three, it was my father's challenging my grandmother that elevated him to become the head of the household.

17

The Mystery Package

I pulled open the door at the bottom of our stairs and called to my mother that I was home. My faded book bag landed on their bed with its third-grade spelling and times tables inside.

Her face had an impish smile as she said, "I have a surprise for you. We're going to town on Saturday." In her hand was a penny postcard, and I recognized the handwriting. This was exciting, because it promised work, and then she would have a little money.

I reached for the postcard to read it for myself. Like those that had come before, it asked my mother to stop when she came to town. This was easier for her now. She no longer had to walk from the bus terminal. A translation of this postcard meant that the Wilkinson sisters, like others of their social class, who never admitted that the Depression touched them, were running low on money. Once more, they had gone to the attic to pull out a family heirloom. Often these pieces needed repairs. Then, they could be consigned to their trusted antique dealer.

That afternoon, as my mother looked at the cream-colored postcard again, she pondered whether this would be a small item she could repair upstairs, or whether she would need to work on the dining room table. That would be fraught with problems and required careful planning to use the window of time between meals.

More crucial was the fact that Emma had been in this household for more than 50 years and was territorial to say the least. As housekeeper, she had cooked the same meals and dusted the same furniture all that time, and when she had a mind to clean, things flew. Even though she no longer was expected to clean the house, Emma could not pass anything without moving it in an automatic, compulsive response. Thus, my mother was distressed if she had to leave her work unattended downstairs. Frequently, she left me to safeguard her project, inspiring this ditty:

Project in progress
we'll all give a cheer
if on our return
we find it's still here.

We seldom went to the city, so our trip was exciting for me in many ways. Even though we would be doing only serious window shopping, that was fine. It meant that we would study the latest trends. We would scout for new ideas to impart life into those clothes that my mother could make for me from the piece-box remnants. On our next trip, when she had a little money, we might buy buttons or school supplies.

Uppermost in my mind as we drove to town was a secret, singular hope. I studied every house we passed. It would take magic to find a place for us to live, but I was ready to try anything.

"There Mom, there's a house nobody lives in! Why can't we move there?" I endowed every bungalow we passed with bliss, and babies, and birthday balloons.

My mother did not answer; she merely gripped the steering wheel tighter.

There would be no answer to this dilemma, an answer I longed for, prayed for, and dreamed about.

The impressive, brownstone home we were to visit on Clinton Street in Poughkeepsie was so different from ours, it intrigued me. Here, the elderly, aristocratic Wilkinson sisters lived in their family residence and still dressed in the long, black skirts worn at the turn-of-the-century. Perhaps they had not been out of the house since then either. They puzzled me, for not even my grandmothers dressed like that.

I was curious about the throat-piece of layered, white netting that my mother had fashioned for one of the sisters, to artfully conceal her sizable goiter. She explained that this medical condition was rare, now that table salt, by law, was iodized to prevent this thyroid deficiency.

Whereas their house was unique to me, it was not different from those of their contemporaries who shared the same social status. After climbing the outdoor stone steps, we came to a set of double doors, distinguished by decorative frosted windows and always left unlocked. It was here where the mailman delivered his letters, umbrellas were left in the glossy brass umbrella stand, and one could ring the doorbell.

Bridget, the maid, would open one of the inside double doors and, if you were coming to call, she would hold a silver tray for the guest to place their engraved calling card. Nothing of the sort occurred when we arrived, as we were there on business.

Readily recognizing my mother, Bridget ushered us in. This wisp of a young girl, barely a head taller than I, said only a few words, but they sounded so foreign to my ears, I could not understand them. Her bright red hair was in sharp contrast to the long-sleeved, black uniform with starched white collar and cuffs, she wore. Her very existence seemed to be at variance with the outside world.

A dainty, white cap bounced on her head and the ties of her white organdy apron flew, as she hurried up the long staircase to announce our arrival. We stood quietly on the snow-white, marble floor and, in due time, the Wilkinson sisters would descend the winding staircase, as if they were arriving from some distant era.

I noticed one of them was more erect. She followed, clutching a package wrapped in brittle, brown wrapping paper and tied with dusty twine.

I hoped she would open it for me to see. Instead, she handed the package to my mother in obvious reverence. As if to shield themselves from embarrassment if the maid might heard this, she whispered a few words of instruction that I could not grasp. One of those ladies had to be younger, or older than the other, but how could anyone tell? To me, old ladies were all one age, old.

The Depression had touched everyone, but some people could hide its devastating effects better than others. Since the Civil War, the Wilkinson family had been on the cutting edge of industry, but no longer. There was not much call for swords these days. The family endowment was now reduced to pieces of parchment in the safe deposit box. At such advanced ages as these maiden sisters were, they might never see another dividend check.

On our way home, my mother's thoughts on this particular occasion evidenced concern over how she could possibly manage the repair of such a large project. Using the dining room table would be an absolute must, she mused aloud.

My problem-solving instincts surged. I was always trying to find more space for us in Grandma's house and thought of the dark back hall, and the door opposite the one to the musty cellar that had always been a curiosity. I had forced open the door of this unused room and found the blinds were closed and shades pulled throughout this room. Sheets covered the furniture, creating ghost-like images everywhere. It was too scary to stay long.

"Why don't we use the dark room downstairs? Nobody's living there."

"You mean Grandma's parlor?"

"Yes, yes, the one with sheets hiding the furniture."

"That's Grandma's best furniture. Old people always keep the parlor this way. Then, in case someone dies, they'll be ready for the funeral."

"Will it be soon?" I asked with an acknowledgment of hope.

Grandma and Emma were quite old, but nothing happened. Throughout the next 12 years, this dreary, dismal space saw no life, nor was it the scene of my grandmother's funeral either. By the time she died in 1945, ways had changed; there were funeral parlors available to the public. However as a child, from then on, I always referred to that room as our funeral parlor.

One afternoon early the following week, my mother cleared the dining room table and gingerly unwrapped the stiff paper, darkened with age. I was close by, eager to glimpse its still-mysterious contents. A whiff of mildew from long years in an attic trunk startled me. I backed away fast and watched from a distance as my mother carefully lifted a heavy lace tablecloth, yellowed with age, out of its wrappings. As she spread it out over the table, she could see there were small breaks near a stain in the center, and a few tears along the edge, but these did not present a serious challenge.

She estimated it would take a couple of hours to return their cherished possession to its original dignity. The precision and skill with which my mother revived textile relics would have ranked at the master's level, but whenever she was restoring these delicate antiques, she was very anxious.

Suddenly, she realized that she had left her spool of extra-fine number 80 ONT cotton thread behind. This meant climbing two flights of steep stairs, so by the time she reached the third floor she needed to sit for a moment to catch her breath. Next to the thread on a small table was a letter from her mother that had arrived in the morning mail. Since her aging parents had become stone-deaf, she could no longer speak with them on the phone. Letters were ever so cherished.

I waited downstairs to stay near the project. From the living room window I watched the eighth grade roughnecks' snowball fight. Emma watched, too, her false teeth clattering each time a snowball struck its mark.

When the snowball fight was over, Emma headed toward the dining room on her way to fire up the kitchen stove. Her side-to-side gait forced her pillowed hips to graze the edge of the table, dragging the antique tablecloth along with her. As she turned to snatch this slippery piece, her right foot ground a pile of lace into the hardwood floor. In an effort to catch the falling fabric, she used both hands, yanking the tablecloth upward like a conductor of the *1812 Overture*.

My mother was coming down the back stairs. She held tightly to the railing, carefully lowering her foot at a 30-degree angle on each step. At the exact moment her shoe touched the hallway floor, her ears caught the wrenching, ripping sound of fragile threads. Rushing into the dining room, she met Emma face-to-face. My mother stared in disbelief at the dark and jagged gap, three inches wide and 18 inches long. Intact only moments before, it was severed and rent.

"What have you done?" my mother screamed as Emma began her retreat to the kitchen.

Never had I seen her so angry!

"I...I...I don't know what happened. It just started to slide off and...and I caught it, before it all hit the floor," she stammered in rhythm with the clicking of her teeth.

From the expression on my mother's face, I could see there was no way to discuss the disaster. It would take hours of unpaid work to restore this treasure. And when she returned the valued antique to the Wilkinsons she would, of course, have to acknowledge what had happened. She had no estimate of how much its original value had been compromised. More crucial was the fact that now, her best clients might consider her unreliable.

Word of this might spread. No matter how skillful she was in repairing textiles, she felt that maintaining their trust, which assured her some small livelihood, was in jeopardy.

She dropped into a dining room chair, dazed and totally spent. Her head drooped. Grimacing to hold back the tears, she gathered the long tablecloth into her sagging arms. Slowly she stooped to pick up her workbasket before plodding upstairs. There, she slumped into her chair beside a pile of family mending and wept in silence.

I sat beside her on the rolled arm of her drab wicker chair and rested my hand timidly along its back. Even as a child, I recognized that in our family, it was not customary to touch, especially at a time of deep emotion.

I hesitated. Whatever remained of my mother's composure I feared could be demolished with my fingertip.

I felt so helpless, not knowing how to console her. I, too, had angry feelings about this clumsy cook, some of which I would carry well into adolescence. Ill-equipped to do more, I launched a phrase I had heard Jim, my older cousin, use disparagingly about his big sister, when we were visiting Grandpa and Grandma Ham. Drawing on his handy epithet, I said, "How dumb can she be?"

My mother shook her head slowly. Finally she was able to speak, and with more grace than one could expect, she said, "Emma can't help the way she is."

Her lifeline and solace lay in the letter from her mother. As she clutched the envelope in her lap, I saw a tear blur the familiar handwriting of Grandma Ham's tender, shaky hand.

18

Anonymous Gift

My mother was mending socks on the front porch. She watched as I meandered up the road alone. The old, blue book bag that swung against my knee carried the fourth grade arithmetic homework that I dreaded doing that weekend. Suddenly, I heard her voice. "Barbara, hurry, I have a great surprise for you!" She could hardly wait to give me the news.

I ran along the gravel shoulder and up the marble walk. Usually these mysterious white slabs captured my curiosity. I wondered if they were tombstones faced-down. This time I ignored them. I ran up the front steps and dropped my tin lunch box, anxious to hear her news.

"Miss Jordan was here this afternoon," she told me in excited tones.

It was always welcome news when our compassionate health nurse stopped by. She was one of mother's few friends, and the only one with a "listening" ear.

My mother continued breathlessly: "She said you had been given an anonymous scholarship to go to Camp Sloane for two weeks this summer. Isn't that fantastic?"

My response was predictable. Questions tumbled out in rapid succession. How could anyone give me a scholarship? I had never been to camp and Miss Jordan knew my grades at school had never been good.

Throughout the entire Depression, I never realized we were poor, we just had no money. After seven years of unemployment, my father had a job now, but on his paltry salary they could ill-afford a luxury such as summer camp.

However, my family could accept a scholarship without embarrassment. Some unseen, unknown individual had recognized how stunted my childhood was in this constricted household without siblings or playmates.

"Camp Sloane," my mother continued, "is a marvelous place with lots of things to do. It's only an hour away, in Lakeville, Connecticut. I know you'll love it there." My long pig-tails swished from side to side, wrapping against my mouth as I pressed her for more details.

"That's where boys and girls from New York, whose fathers have good jobs, come in the summer," my mother explained. Sadly, as I learned later, most of them came for the whole summer.

My next question was a practical one. "But Mom, who will braid my hair?"

"Maybe you'd like to have it cut."

"Yippee," I shouted. Without running water, washing my heavy blonde hair in a shallow washbowl produced anguish for both of us. My hair had never been cut and my braids were long enough to sit on. I jumped up so fast the heavy, green rocker slammed against the clapboards, drawing my mother's automatic caution to be careful of Grandma's property.

I never heard her, as I was already through the front door and headed for the back stairs. As I took both flights at a fast clip, the image of a new hairstyle emerged at the same speed. I returned with the largest scissors I could find. Sunday school was a distant two days away, and I could hardly wait to show off my new haircut and tell about camp, too. Never had I been so lucky.

Quickly undoing my heavy, blonde braids, I was ready for this momentous occasion, ignoring the saw-toothed edges that were inevitable. I was thrilled by my new shoulder-length haircut that would shock my father when he came home from work.

It would guarantee disapproval from the old folks around the dinner table. This was a bonus as well.

My mother promised I could have a real haircut in a few weeks, another tremendous first. I was beside myself with excitement. As we drove to the hairdresser's, she handed me a crisp, two-dollar bill and smiled, implying that I could go in by myself. I felt like a very grown-up ten-year-old. I was certain of the look I had in mind: a short boyish bob, but it was one I had to arrive at in stages, as the hairdresser wanted to avoid displeasing her customer.

My ears were freed as never before. I was elated as much by growing up as by my hairstyle. When my mother saw me, she gasped, but she did not scold. This was her early preview of my impending teenage years.

At Camp Sloane, eight girls shared a tent with upper and lower canvas bunks. Many of these girls had known each other from previous summers. They were even more grownup; they could tap dance and play the piano or the flute. Unbelievable to me, one of my tent-mates even had to continue her piano lessons all summer.

These city girls knew everything. I was so envious. I learned a lot, too, everything anyone needed to know about boys. Amid giggles, they would talk about kissing as they lay under the mosquito netting at night.

"What?" I thought to myself, "Kissing boys?" Was that anything like being kissed by the old ladies who came to visit Grandma and who insisted that they kiss me, too? I hated those spitty kisses and often hid in the musty closet beneath the front stairs to avoid them. And here these girls were talking about kissing a boy. Ugh! I thought that would be worse, but they saw it differently; some had even tried it.

One night, an older girl slept in our tent. She had far more puzzling stories. I heard one of the girls whisper, "Did you go all the way?" It was a question I did not understand. I lay still as a tombstone in my lower bunk, hoping I would not have to slap the mosquito buzzing near my ear. For the life of me, I could not figure out what they were talking about. So much was new to me. In my sheltered life, it would be years before this question made any sense.

These city girls laughed about the primitive outhouse. It was no laughing matter for me, since this was not limited to a camp experience, but I never let on. How I dreaded the late-night trek alone, along the winding path, defined by the shaky beam of my flashlight. Bears returned to lurk by every bush.

I was scared, too, when it was my turn to set tables as there were so many of them in this screened dining hall, long as a barn. Ravenous appetites were spawned by swimming, canoeing, and nature hikes. Our days were filled with theatre productions or craft classes and our evenings, with campfires, songs, and toasted marshmallows.

Other than the campfires, I enjoyed craft classes most. I made a brown calfskin wallet for my mother, blistering my fingers as I tooled her monogram.

The two weeks passed all too quickly. When the last day arrived, I was delighted to see my parents, and to surprise my mother with this priceless gift, but I was overwhelmed by emotion about leaving my new friends. I cried and cried. I was so angry that I pounded the packed suitcase lying on my bunk then dumped the contents on the floor to delay our departure. Sobbing, I stomped all over my clothes before kicking them down the steps.

Without playmates, I had only the fields to run in and the woodchucks to chase. I wished my parents had not come and I told them so. "I don't want to go back." I shouted across the sun-bleached grass, for the counselors and all my new friends and their parents to hear. "I hate it there!" My parents were terribly embarrassed, but they understood.

A photo of me in front of the tent says it all: a skinny girl with bony knees and high-topped ears, so angry, so lonely, so sad to leave her friends that she could not even force a smile.

I envied my tent-mates who could be friends all summer, as they had been years before, and would be in the future. On the way back, I recounted how lucky those girls were. My mother tried to soothe my pain as she pointed out that many of them were rich children whose families sent them away to camp while they traveled abroad.

"They probably don't want to spend all summer there, but they have to." She looked toward my father as he drove, in hopes that he could offer some relief, then added, "Some have parents who are divorced and they don't have the kind of love you have."

She tried her best to put some advantageous slant on my dismal situation, but it did little to assuage my tears. For the first time, I was aware that money could buy things. It did not necessarily buy happiness, but this time it would have helped.

"Maybe you'll feel better when you get home," she said, but her hopeful remark increased my despair. How could she say that when she knew being back there would be worse? As we drew near, the pain returned to my cheeks as I tried desperately to hold back a flood of tears.

I dragged myself out of the car and sauntered up the path toward the kitchen. Puff, our five-year-old yellow tiger, was so glad to see me she rubbed against my legs but that did little to comfort me.

My father walked ahead and held the screen door. I stood, stooped and silent on the top step, reluctant to re-enter this drab world. Then, looking up, I was stunned, unable to believe what I saw. Something big had happened, a surprise they had kept until now. My mother was close behind me, all smiles.

There was the kitchen cabinet from their apartment in Washington. All those years I had dreamed of what it looked like. My mother had always told me her upright Hoosier was like her sister Irene's, but I had to see it for myself.

I rushed across the kitchen and opened every drawer and door. It had slatted, sliding covers in the front and a container inside to hold 20 pounds of flour for automatic sifting into a bowl below; a similar container held 10 pounds of sugar for baking and jelly making.

"And look, the enamel-top table, too."

I was wild with joy. "Mom," I said, trying to keep my voice as subdued as I could. "I didn't know you were going to ask Grandma's permission to bring this out of the barn."

She smiled. I saw a twinkle in her eye. "I didn't." We both laughed. She knew how hard it would be for me to leave camp. This was her way to ease my dreaded return. Here I had more than the anonymous gift that put me through camp. I had the joy of her kitchen furniture from the crates in the barn. This was a gift, too, not anonymous, but longer lasting and fully as treasured.

The summer seemed longer now without those wonderful new friends. I ran across the hayfield and down the bank to check on the family of woodchucks. That was why I never saw Miss Jordan's car.

It would be difficult to say who was more eager, my mother to relate the story, or Miss Jordan to hear it. My mother must have been all smiles as she described how much camp had meant to me and how hard it had been for me to leave. More than anyone else, our dear friend recognized how desperate I was for childhood fun and friends. She assured my mother she would relay her gratitude to my benefactor, smiling as she walked to her car.

I kept in contact with this kindly woman throughout her long life, but it was only after her death that this secret was revealed. My mother had learned that it was Miss Jordan who had quietly withdrawn $50 from her savings account to become my anonymous benefactor.

19

Growing Up in the Roosevelt Era

The Roosevelt era of my childhood seemed so important at the time it remains vivid in my memory. Perhaps this was accentuated because so little happened at our house, what occurred on the outside took on a greater significance. My parents took every opportunity to broaden my education about world events and people in the news when they were happening in our midst. Often this was more educational than what I might learn at school.

Four adults pulled up their chairs around Grandma's reading table, bringing them closer physically and emotionally than at any other time of the day.

Each was frozen in place around this table throughout my entire childhood.

From under the table I whispered, "Momma." I was not supposed to disturb the family, when they were reading.

"Momma, did you vote for Roosevelt?"

She continued to knit until a section of the paper was passed her way. Without dropping a stitch, she looked down in my direction. A curious smile crossed her face. Her eyes smiled as well. My father re-folded his newspaper, rustling it so my mother could answer in some privacy.

"Didn't everybody vote for him?" I persisted in a slightly louder voice.

This was important information for any nine year-old to know, especially in a household where politics were standard fare.

She lifted her eyebrows and stared at me, a familiar signal that meant we would talk about it upstairs. I looked up at my father and saw his briar pipe hang from the side of his mouth as the muscles of his cheek rippled in a quiet grin. Cold silence returned to Grandma's living room.

Before the days of Franklin Delano Roosevelt, I never knew we had a president, but he would have been a Republican. The words "Roosevelt" and "president" were synonymous. I thought FDR was the only one we would ever have. Many Republicans felt the same way. I would be out of college before another name appeared on the Democratic ticket.

The first election I remember was Alf Landon's miserable defeat, challenging Roosevelt. Judging from all the sunflower buttons worn by my seventh-grade classmates and across Dutchess County, this Republican should have won hands down.

Some locals held FDR in high regard. My father, for one, liked the man, if not all his New Deal schemes. When Mr. Roosevelt was Under Secretary of the Navy, they exchanged a few letters regarding some local postal matters over which my father was seeking a political favor. My father proudly saved those replies carrying FDR's famous signature.

In our house, Roosevelt was more than president. He seemed like a member of the family. My father and Mr. Roosevelt were only sons, born 10 months apart and less than 20 miles away from each other. As a child, I thought they shared many facial resemblances. Maybe they did. If so, it could be a throwback to the generations before them who had arrived from Holland. They did resemble each other in their kindly, blue-gray eyes, high cheekbones, and the distinct shape of their noses and lips. More than that, it was the pince-nez glasses they both wore. My father, however, was not nearly as tall, and he had a slight build. He also lacked the heavy jowls and sculptured crevices of the president's face.

Both men were avid stamp collectors. My father told me he had once sent one of his choicest stamps to Mr. Roosevelt. I believe, he said this was a one-cent blue Benjamin Franklin stamp in an oval frame, embossed on the envelop. The exact date of this stamp that was hand-franked with the postmaster's swirling scribble is unknown, but it would have had to be after 1848, the date stamps were first issued.

While these two men had obvious contrasts of wealth, education, and position, their upbringings shared some unfortunate similarities. FDR's mother was exceedingly protective. Wealthy and emotionally hungry, Sara Delano Roosevelt was the second wife of a husband 25 years her senior. She was consumed with the details of her child's upbringing, and it is reported he was almost nine years old before she allowed him to bathe himself.

Under such tight reins, he was ill-prepared for the hurdles facing him in his social and emotional maturation and was dimly viewed by his sports-minded, prep-school classmates at the Groton School and later at Harvard. In his post-polio days, she hovered over him, nearly derailing his career in national politics. She continued her dominating role once he was in the White House.

My father's mother was just as domineering as was FDR's, but it was Emma who curtailed his maturation. Emma's own emotional development, stalled in her youth, left her unable to form normal, mature attachments.

This dismal situation was compounded for my father; his own mother virtually gave him to Emma, to raise. Being born on Emma's 25th birthday compounded Emma's emotional attachment. Her overbearing control of his upbringing must have been daunting. What my father and FDR shared in common was their struggle for independence from psychological prison.

Without question, my father was a deeply devoted family man who never breached his marriage vows. Not so for the president. He and Eleanor both emerged from adolescence with considerable social ineptitude. Perhaps it was here that they found their common bond. Perhaps it was because neither had been attracted to anyone else before their marriage that FDR felt the need to roam. Perhaps it was that they were distant cousins. Perhaps there were issues inherent with Eleanor. But then again, if FDR had any early stirrings toward a political career, he might have felt drawn to Eleanor by the added attraction of her Uncle Teddy, who occupied the White House at the time.

The self-confidence that this shy bride might have developed was soon overridden by the matriarch, Sara, who made all the family decisions.

On the other hand, Eleanor's handsome, young husband emerged from his years of being socially inept to develop a most engaging personality that thrived in public. He honed this trait skillfully to advance his career in law, in politics, and in government, but such a flamboyant style made him dangerously attractive in social circles when he went to Washington as Under Secretary of the Navy.

Because Roosevelt's first inauguration on March 12, 1933, was such an important event, many local Democrats made a great effort to attend.

Now that my father could count on a paycheck, my parents made plans too. They welcomed the opportunity to see their friends and my father's former colleagues. My mother promised that this would be a late celebration of my ninth birthday, allowing me to watch history in the making, whatever she meant by that.

I was more excited about going to the Woodward and Lothrop department store where I was to get a new raincoat.

More than any thrill Washington might hold for me was the promise that I would see an apartment. This enchanted word evoked in me a dreamlike, idealized image of heaven on earth. Even though it would not be the one where we had lived when I was a baby, I would see for myself a real apartment at last.

The car was packed before supper and I was put to bed early. We planned to leave soon after daybreak, but dawn brought an unpleasant surprise. Sounds of whooping cough from my room broke their sleep before the alarm chimed. They quickly arranged for someone to stay with me, someone I could enjoy all by myself, isolated from the old folks.

When they returned, my parents described the cheering crowds and those impressive black tails and high silk hats worn by members of the Cabinet and of the Supreme Court. Out of view of the photographers and the public, Franklin Delano Roosevelt was brought to his feet. Heavy wrought-iron bars defined the margins of his lifeless legs.

Based on my own subsequent connections with the Georgia Warm Springs Foundation, this is what the efforts behind the scene may well have looked like. With his sons pulling the leather cushion of his wooden wheelchair, FDR could edge his heavy body forward. They locked his lifeless legs in line by pressing on his kneecaps until the half-inch iron bands could be slipped over each knee hinge.

The most arduous chore was ahead. His tall, enormous body, nearly dead weight, had to be pivoted from this straight-legged sitting position to a standing one. Beads of perspiration sprung from his forehead and theirs. Locking his arms around their broad shoulders, they could not help but feel the enormous effort embodied in his will, as they struggled to help him stand.

Then with a vice-like grip on Elliott's arm with his left hand and a sturdy cane riveted to the floor with the other, he inched forward in an upright posture.

This physical accomplishment had been honed as fully, and required the same dedicated attention, as the first inaugural address he was poised to deliver.

From all I heard, the world watched this muscle-weak giant step onto the world stage to meet the public and the rigors of the office he was about to fill. He skillfully deflected any hint of physical weakness before a world that looked to him as a symbol of strength. He could never let them down, nor did he.

My father told how as he stood at the podium his deep resonant voice boomed from the loudspeakers, radiating vitality and self-confidence across the sea of people standing shoulder to shoulder as far away as the Supreme Court. He addressed the down-trodden men in soup lines, the millions whose stock certificates were worthless pieces of paper, and men who came into office with him to breathe life into a dead economy. As a natural leader, he inspired his countrymen to trust him to fix what had gone wrong.

His voice was carried by radio across the nation and around the world. Grandma listened to every word this man had to say. It was as if this was a man with legs of jelly and spine of steel who had the voice of a Pied Piper. His message restored hope where hope had been lost.

Together with others from Dutchess County and the larger New York delegation, my parents stood close to the Capitol steps. Beneath his long black cape, his devastating affliction was shielded from public view. My folks described to Grandma how he had taken the oath of office, placing his hand on the Roosevelt family Bible.

As promised, my folks brought me a birthday present, an emerald green, suede raincoat with large brass buttons. It was big enough to grow into, and I did in several years; by then it was nearly worn out.

An unspoken truce cloaked our household with regard to partisan politics. The fact that my mother was a Republican only furthered the distance between her and her mother-in-law. Grandma could look down from her five-foot elevation with a haughtiness that did not invite an alternative point of view. My mother knew better than to offer one. Their chairs around the square table in the living room were back-to-back at the corner, further deterring informal exchange.

On Election Day all the adults went to vote. In presidential elections, the Democrats could depend on Grandma's vote; this was one of the rare occasions she left the house. Although it was common knowledge for which party each person presumably voted, it was considered the height of impropriety, even for a child to ask such an intrusive question. Emma never caught on to this breach of etiquette.

Twenty miles away and a political planet apart, my maternal grandparents, the Hams, lived on their 250-acre dairy farm in Verbank, south of Millbrook. My mother followed in the political footsteps they had set forth, as quiet but confirmed Republicans. For a farmer like Grandpa Ham, to oppose the New Deal farm subsidies, seemed ironic, but in his wisdom, he saw government intervention as foolhardy. It would provide only short-term benefits, I heard him

Grandpa and Grandma Ham, wearing original wedding clothes at their 50th Wedding Anniversary. By the time they had grandchildren, they were too deaf to hear their voices.

emphasize to his son-in-law. This time it was my father who was the political outsider.

I remember Grandpa said something like this, "You wait and see. It may not happen before I die, but farm subsidies will erode the pride and independence American farmers value." I had to ask my father later what all those words meant. Was Grandpa going to die? That was the only word I recognized.

Looking back, there were many discussions I could not understand, but one thing I knew for certain. I loved these grandparents and their farm. There were lambs in spring and kittens in the haymow year-round. The farm could be a dangerous place for kittens, always around at milking time. Occasionally a clumsy Holstein would step on one.

Old Bozo, the faithful collie, let generations of playful seven-toed, black kittens bite his ears and chase his tail until he was called to bring the herd in for milking. He earned his keep, rounding up nearly 100 black and white, lumbering beasts with bulging udders. Cows were not very smart, but they could follow the tail of the one ahead up the long dusty lane, across the road, and into their places. Their lives were pretty dull. Morning and night, snapped into their stanchions, attached to the milking machines, they were rewarded with fresh hay and grain.

Each of the grandchildren, and there were four of us then, could count on Grandma to save the Sunday funny papers. The colorful sketches of our favorite characters with their simple accounts, dashed across the pages of cheap newsprint. "The Katz'n Jammer Kids" were my favorite. Each of us would make a beeline for these treasures, chuckling over the characters' antics and then returning them for another grandchild to enjoy.

I had just gotten into the car after saying my good-byes. Against my father's command, I dashed back to give the black, paddle-pawed kittens and old Bozo one more hug to delay our departure. Our good-byes continued as the car rolled away. Neither grandparent could hear them, but outstretched arms waved from each direction. They had been deaf for so long they had never heard the natural voice of a grandchild and Grandma's bulky, boxed black hearing aid was a poor substitute.

Before we reached the top of the long hill, I tapped my father on the shoulder. "Daddy, why can't we get the Sunday paper with funnies, like Grandpa's?"

"Well, your grandfather prefers *The Herald Tribune*," he said in a slow pace as he waited for an oncoming car to pass before pulling onto the highway. "That's a Republican paper."

"But," I protested, "there's never anything funny in *The New York Times*." There was no response, so after this pensive pause I asked, "Is our paper just for Democrats?"

"Not necessarily, but it has more of the Democrats' point of view, the way they think," he told me, genuinely trying to put a complex answer into terms I could grasp.

After a few moments of thought, I came up with the right solution. "Daddy, why don't you write *The New York Times* and ask them for Sunday funnies too," I whined to emphasize my misery.

He gave a slight chuckle, "I don't think they would take a letter from me very seriously."

"Well then, I'll write them myself." I felt confident they could grasp how serious I was.

Funny papers seemed tied to politics. Since I was old enough to read the funnies, I knew I must be old enough to choose a political party.

I could not look to my parents' choices, one being a Republican, the other a Democrat. I simply had to make my own decision, and I did. I relied solely on the funny papers as my political guidepost.

Seated around the square table, the adults were virtually frozen in place as always, silently reading the evening newspaper. I stood against the warm ridges of the living room radiator to make my announcement.

"Ahem."

No one looked up.

"Ahem."

I cleared my throat for emphasis, setting the stage as any one might do if connected with a political party. Failing to draw any attention, I stepped forward. No one seemed to notice except my mother who wondered, perhaps, what embarrassment she might be in for.

With a clear sense of purpose I patterned my posture after my "local" grandmother when she exerted her authority. I took a deep breath, held my head high and my spider-thin body erect. Without hesitation I spoke in a loud, clear voice like an aspiring candidate: "I am ready to join the Republican Party!"

This brought broad smiles from both parents, but when I peeked over the top of the newspaper that my grandmother held, she was aloof as usual and continued her reading, neither interested nor amused. That was unfortunate for us both. She could not explore, nor enjoy, the rationale for my decision. Nor did the atmosphere inspire its voluntary disclosure. She would never know how her devotion to politics and her historical curiosity might eventually impact me.

I came to recognize our president from various perspectives. I could see him through my father's eyes as an intelligent, polished, and skilled politician. I could see him through my grandmother's rose-colored spectacles.

My mother's interest in the first family had a very different focus. She greatly admired Eleanor. If Eleanor Roosevelt had run for president, my mother might have transgressed to vote for a Democrat.

Although Eleanor's height and posture conveyed a noble presence, she was reserved and uncomfortable in the public eye. How difficult it must have been for her to assume the demeanor expected of her as First Lady. Perhaps this vacuum due to shyness set the stage for Sara to usurp many functions normally assumed by the First Lady. After all, this small but imperious lady commanded the ear of her son and occupied a front seat both literally and figuratively in his life.

Eleanor's situation evoked great empathy from my mother. Even I could see the parallels between my mother's humble setting and Eleanor's unenviable situation. In the privacy of my parents' third-floor bedroom, she and I referred to the president's mother as "Old Sari." We nicknamed my grandmother the same, along with other epithets such as "Mrs. Astorbilt" drawn from the prestigious mansions of the Astors and the Vanderbilts near the president's on the bank of the Hudson River.

The president's mother and my grandmother were characteristically very much alike. Each was diminutive in size, but domineering in personality.

Each lived under the same roof with her only son and his wife.

Each was distant and condescending to her daughter-in-law. Here the similarities ended.

The nation often saw how protective and emotionally close the president's mother was with her son. By contrast, my grandmother led an emotionally sterile life, that is, until this "native" son came upon the scene.

In my grandmother's eyes, Sara Delano Roosevelt barely existed, and it was she who was sitting beside the president, as FDR became her favorite son.

When Grandpa Knickerbocker was a prosperous merchant, he had given substantial financial support to a friend running as the Democratic candidate for a county office. The man lost the election and Grandpa lost much of his modest wealth. What he did not lose at that time, he lost in banking investments before he died.

Grandma shared his keen interest in politics. She was, once and for all, a Democrat. When a native son won the presidential election she was as thrilled as any Democrat in Dutchess County. She became a most impassioned supporter of our new president and as rabid a New Dealer as you could find. His halo never rusted, never slipped, never got too big for her steadfast loyalty. It was inconceivable to her that others, even some Democrats, were less enchanted.

My grandmother was an avid reader. She remembered details of every classic or poem she ever read, memorizing many. However, her daily resources about politics at home or in Washington were limited to the local newspaper, then the *Poughkeepsie New Yorker*. It's not surprising she had a running tiff with the editorial view of this Republican paper, but *The Sunday New York Times* provided her with fervent political ammunition.

Grandma's nephew, Bob, a Democrat from Poughkeepsie, occasionally came to call on Sunday afternoons. He loved to rile up the old lady with unflattering remarks about Franklin's New Deal, his political ascendancy, and vagaries rumored about his personal life in the White House.

"Now Aunt J., you know the Democrats fill pork barrels just as much as the Republicans."

"Well," she retorted, stiffening her short spine to convey the authority she felt was hers. "Democrats may have done it in the days of Al Smith, but I know Franklin Roosevelt is above all those shenanigans. After all, he didn't grow up on the streets of New York. He's an educated and cultured man.

"Just you listen to him speak! Bob, I'm astonished at you, a Democrat, to say such things, as if they were true!"

Bob waited patiently for her to finish her monologue which stopped only when she ran out of breath or started coughing, brought on from the rigorous defense she mustered at his slightest provocation.

Then he would start another tack, just to watch her sputter. "I've heard rumors about his liaisons at the White House when Eleanor is out of town," he said as he looked at my parents with a wink.

"Bob, what's a *lazon*?" I wanted to know. I had sat there on the floor as patient as any third grader might do, trying to make sense of this adult discussion.

Bob looked from me to my mother, then to my father before he said anything. "Harrie, I'll let you field this one. You're more experienced than I."

"Well, Dad what is it?" I had been patient long enough.

I watched my father shift in his chair and draw deep breaths on his briar pipe. Seeing that I would not be put off, he finally said, "Well, it's a kind of pleasure, I guess you could say."

"Pleasure. Umm.... Fun. Maybe like ice cream cones?" I said.

I saw a sly grin curl around his pipe stem at the side of his mouth.

Finally he said, "I guess you could say that it's a form of pleasure, like ice cream cones, as you put it."

Pleased that he had satisfied my curiosity, he looked directly toward Bob and in a lowered voice added, "probably one in each hand."

"Whoopee, one in each hand! I've never heard of that before!"

Bob offered that little pitchers have big ears, a phrase I had heard often, but one that had never made any sense.

Immediately my mother called me over and gave me a strict order: "Barbara, go run in the fields. Chase the woodchucks. And take your doll along."

She was anxious to discharge her primary duty to keep me quiet so that the adults, namely, my grandmother, could talk.

"Oh, no, Alice might get bitten by a woodchuck," I commented as I headed for the kitchen.

My mother chose to ignore my fantasy, and turned back toward Bob as if she, too, had been included in this conversation.

Bob smiled and turned to Grandma to ask what she thought of those White House rumors. She had ignored the family conversation, preferring to focus her thoughts on ammunition for her next assault.

"I don't believe a word of it, you're just dead wrong," she said, her white face turning red, her thin hairline bursting with beads of sweat. Wiping her brow with a white linen handkerchief, she continued. "That's all Republican clap-trap! You certainly can't take that kind of political rubbish seriously.

"They're out to make trouble, the whole lot of them, the Republicans here in town, in Albany, and in Washington, too. They don't want Roosevelt to succeed. I know! They've got their investments. They don't care about soup lines."

"Neither did Grandma before the Democrats took up the cause," my mother mused to herself.

Barely stopping for breath, Grandma continued, full steam ahead: "Even financiers from Wall Street are selling pencils on the street corners! I read about it every Sunday in *The New York Times*."

Finally she stopped for another breath. Her face was flushed with anger. Grandma never backed down from her exalted opinions. I never remember her responding to humor.

For Bob to challenge her keen mind was one thing. He could get up and go home. But for us, these visits spelled holy hell. She often continued her tirade for days about those disgusting comments of her nephew, and he, a Democrat at that. There was no fear she might aggravate any high blood pressure. Grandma's good health, spirit, and determination were relentless. She never went to see a doctor and only twice did he need to come to see her: once for whooping cough that she caught from me and later for pneumonia.

"Here he comes." Those words could only refer to the president. As school children, we got excited whenever we saw him. It was easy to know when he was in the neighborhood. First there was a big, black car ahead and one like it behind, each with men in dark suits, looking out from behind dark glasses.

Lodged between these cars was the president's own. He loved to drive that old tan Ford roadster equipped with hand controls he had asked Henry Ford to install. The canvas top was always folded down behind the back seat. We never saw Eleanor with him. Rumor had it she would never get in the car because she thought he was a reckless driver. But when he was off his own property, the Secret Service tamed his driving habits.

Accustomed to seeing the president go by, we would wave and shout. Once I wrote him a letter telling him I was the one who waved just as he turned onto Hunn's Lake Road, headed for Lithgo. I cherished the typed letter he signed in return.

He loved to look up old family cemeteries in the countryside. While these trips were good outings for him, they could make for memorable moments for his Secret Service agents.

On one such occasion, the president instructed an agent to make a charcoal rubbing of a certain tombstone in a tiny family cemetery that was iron-fenced and overgrown with weeds. Completing his assignment, the agent was heading back, his dark trousers covered with burrs, when he heard the rhythmic sound of approaching hoofs. Envisioning the farmer's bull, he raced toward the dirt road and quickly vaulted the barbed wire fence without a backward glance.

The paper did not mention the length of the tear in his pants, only that he sat in the car for the remainder of the outing. Of course, the Republican paper made a big deal of the incident, chiding this city man who had been scared off by a harmless herd of cows. It seemed to us that Roosevelt had put Hyde Park and Dutchess County on the map almost as much as Washington. Regardless of one's political bent, he was our president, our neighbor who loved to stop his car along the country roads of Dutchess County to talk to the farmers.

Often, they would jump off their John Deere tractors and rush over to the fence, excited to tell him how things were going under the New Deal.

While meeting the "common man" was his hallmark, it was one not all Democrats applauded and a trait some Republicans took every opportunity to condemn.

It was in the fall of his first year in office, when my classmate, Kathryn, and I were trudging home from school, that we heard cars slowing down behind us.

"Hi, girls. How's school going?" came the president's booming voice. Secret Service cars had stopped ahead and behind his vehicle. We were overcome by instant shyness. I twisted the shabby book bag against my left knee. His broad grin came alive and put us at ease more than we ever dreamed. With his left hand still on the steering wheel, he reached across his stout body to grasp my hand. I was startled at its enormous size. Strong from having to substitute for weak legs, his handshake was crushing. I struggled to keep a smile on my face until he let go. Perhaps he wanted us to remember long enough to vote for him when we were older.

Seeing what happened to me, Kathryn moved toward the back as the president's dog, Fala, bounced across the seat. "Can I pet Fala?" she asked. Fala had already settled the matter.

Grins on the faces behind the windshield of the open car following the president told Kathryn that the Secret Service agents were human, too.

President Roosevelt introduced us to a man sitting beside him with bushy white hair. I could not remember his name to tell my father, but the papers told us it was Cordell Hull, relaxing from his duties as Secretary of State.

"How do you like school?" The question was addressed to both of us, but since I was in his direct gaze, it fell to me to answer.

"We both failed math, but today I got my first 100 percent in spelling."

Turning to Cordell, he added, "That averages out, don't you think?"

"I hear you have lots of ice cream at the White House. Is that true?" This was a burning question for me, since we never had any at our house. Having no refrigerator, ice cream was very special.

Obviously he had been unaccustomed to the quirks of childhood reasoning for quite a while.

"I'd say we have it fairly often," he replied slowly, turning to Cordell with a puzzled look across his face.

"My father says you have lots of ice cream in the White House, an ice cream cone in each hand."

"I don't recall that, I'll have to think about it. Cordell, what do you make of that?"

"It's getting too deep for me. I'll pass."

These were the president's personal outings and he reveled in them.

No press corps bothered them. No cars followed. No fanfare marred these casual jaunts.

My hand still hurt, when I threw open the door with a bang and shouted into the empty kitchen that I had just shaken hands with the president.

Grandma heard me from her second-floor bedroom and hurried down the steep back stairs to hear every detail of this awesome news.

That evening at the dinner table was, for me, like no other. Grandma, who always sat at the head of the table, facing my father who served, actually turned to face me as she asked for more details. I had fully described the whole event several times that afternoon, but she hung on every word. I elaborated on details, such as his grin, his painful grip, his slouched felt hat, and the gold cigarette holder.

Although it still puzzled me, my parents were appalled when I recounted the conversation about the ice cream cones. But I caught on fast; this part could well be censored when Grandma asked for any retelling of my fabulous encounter. It was safer and more advantageous to talk about the president's dog.

I told her how Fala stood on his hind legs in the empty back seat with his ears erect. "His bright, brown eyes and floppy, red tongue," I said, "were just like his pictures and almost like Skippy."

She never liked my dog, but that night as she asked more about this world-famous pet, I glorified the status of Fala, hoping there might be some political fallout for my dog. There was none, but that never offended Skippy.

Like Fala, Skippy was a Scottish terrier, but not a purebred. His mother had skipped over the breeder's fence for a rendezvous with a cocker spaniel. Hence they gave us this "cocker scandal." Unlike Fala, Skippy's ears were long and curly like the hair that wound around his short tail. Between nose and tail, he and Fala had more in common. Still, Grandma was unimpressed.

In all the years Skippy had lived with us, Grandma had never allowed him in the house. She was never seen petting the dog outdoors either. Skippy had buried too many bones in her peony bed for that.

The following winter, Grandma was sick with pneumonia. Opportunity loomed.

"Mommy, can't I bring Skippy into the kitchen for the evening?" My mother stopped stirring the mixing bowl momentarily.

"Please, just this once. Grandma can't get out of bed. She'll never know."

My mother agreed reluctantly, but the twinkle in her eye revealed how much she shared my delight.

This was not only her first excursion in the house it quickly turned out to be her last. As we sat down to our evening meal, a blood-curdling shriek shot out from Grandma's room. My father took the front staircase two at a time while we raced up the back stairs. We came upon what I thought was a most hilarious sight. There was Skippy straddling my grandmother's frail body, licking her face and ears, wagging her tail with the glee of a conquering hero.

Skippy was so excited that she left a big puddle before my father could lift her off. Wet and warm, the puddle took only an instant to soak through the bedspread, a quilt, a wool blanket, sheets, Grandma's flannel nightgown, a mattress protector, and the mattress below. The damage was even more devastating to Grandma's authority.

If fury could cure fever, my grandmother would have been well before midnight. Instead, wrath that never stopped sputtering kept her awake until dawn. Skippy and I were both in the doghouse after that.

The radio blared the news at six. The world stood still. It was Dec. 11, 1936 when King Edward VIII announced to the British House of Commons his intent to abdicate the Crown, for love.

Grandma K. was incensed to think he would abdicate for a commoner, and a divorcée at that. He had let the monarchy down, had allowed the strength of the empire to be rent. Around the square reading table, it seemed he had let her down as well, and all because he loved a woman. Love—love of a man for a woman—became a gap in Grandma's remarkably astute memory through which little else was ever lost.

Like many others in this country, Grandma had finally forgiven the British their dreadful deeds of the Revolutionary War and had adopted a loyalty toward the royal family as symbols of dignity. This respect was drawn from the tastes and styles championed by Queen Victoria whose presence was well preserved in the house where we lived. As significant as this date in 1936 was for the world, it had personal importance for me. It was indeed a memorable day to reach menarche.

In addition to all of her other duties, Miss Jordan was also charged with performing annual school physicals each fall. Our square, one-story school building was located high on a hill between the towns of Bangall and Stanfordville, away from traffic where an occasional truck or car rolled along at the speed of second gear. Now that the one-room schools of the surrounding farmland, had been closed, our school numbered about 100 students between first and tenth grades. Four rooms had two grades each; the freshmen and sophomores had separate rooms. Each teacher taught all the grade subjects; sophomores were taught by the principal.

After we graduated, we could go by bus nine miles to the north, to Pine Plains, noted for its sports program, or 12 miles south to Millbrook without gym or playing fields, where academics were all important. There was no question where I would go.

At annual physicals, and occasional visits during the school year, Miss Jordan may have been paying special attention to the health and welfare of the pupils in the fifth and sixth grade room, but we never saw any results. The teacher was a self-pitying widow with four children my age and younger. She had the sympathy of the townspeople, but they did not have to sit in her classroom for two years, a childhood eternity.

"Becky," as we irreverently called her out of earshot, was overweight, stooped, and she wore the same navy blue, long-sleeved, crepe dress all year.

When she walked down the aisle in her dusty black oxfords, a scent of home heating oil, and the lack of indoor plumbing combined to form an almost visible wake.

The four rows of desks were divided into the two grades. She would lecture alternately in front of each grade while the other grade did deskwork. A well-worn, long manila folder contained her penciled syllabus of New York State geography for the entire year; her droning voice conveyed its unaltered content. Sometimes, we felt sorry for her children who had to endure her at home, and sit through two grades, plus having to bear the brunt of her perennial leadership of the Girl Scout troop, too. At school, one of her daughters became the all-time, all-seeing tattletale, which doomed her on the playground.

Every child knew what would guarantee a response from Becky. Henry Karnes, who was a year ahead of his sister, Kathryn, and me, sat in the adjacent sixth grade row. He could irritate her most by intentionally misusing verbs. One day, he launched the word "brung," which sent her into a tailspin. She turned around and threw a pair of scissors she had in her hand, and they landed just below his left eye.

Everyone went home with that story, in hopes this would bring about her immediate dismissal. Nothing happened, but Henry had his own justified response. A few days later, he brought two mice to school. When she was writing on the blackboard, he lifted the hinged, wooden desktop, and let them escape. We hated mice, but the resulting pandemonium was wonderful. We escaped to early morning recess, while the janitor chased the mice toward the cellar stairs with a broom.

When Miss Jordan suggested to my mother that she serve on the school board, I was in sixth grade. I was delighted and immediately became the self-appointed spokesperson for our room. In hopes I could get Becky fired, I went about failing classes as fast as I could. With the same dedication as one seeking academic excellence, I managed a 49% on my final test in art, the teacher's favorite subject and a "D" in both history and geography, but this self-sacrifice yielded our classroom no relief. I did not fail the grade, as I might have done, because we were usually moved along to make room for the poor souls who would take our seats. Becky, however, was fully convinced I had no future.

A few weeks before school closed that year, I did reap some measure of relief. The circumstances were most unexpected. Several years before, Miss Jordan has asked my mother to become the Chairman of the Health Association in our town. She had done so much for our family that my mother would gladly do anything for her and served in this capacity for a number of years.

Eleanor Roosevelt had a strong interest in improving rural health conditions. She invited the officers of the Dutchess County Health Association to Hyde Park as her guests. When the invitation came, my mother immediately envisioned taking me along. She willingly opposed the teacher and took me out of school, knowing this would contribute far more to my knowledge of world events than anything I would be learning in sixth grade. She was right. Not only was I eager to get relief from our dreadful classroom, this experience was a benchmark in my early education.

It created for me a clear impression of the president's home, the hub of events of national interest that were transpiring here in our historic valley.

About 20 of us sat there in the still, humid, June temperature that rose into the nineties. Broad-limbed maples shaded the long driveway, but their branches gave no relief on the porch. The American flag and the deep blue one with the presidential seal hung limply from the semi-circular portico above the classic white columns. The freshly painted balustrade was as white as the fragrant clematis that climbed to the second floor above the porch at Hyde Park.

The ladies were all "in place" half an hour ahead of the event, so they had plenty of time to reflect on the importance of the health care provided the poor in our rural communities. Their role and their dedication as volunteers gave Miss Jordan, our district health nurse, the assistance she needed. These circumstances need to be put in the proper context of the time. It was long before the advent of the medical services and treatment facilities of today.

Rarely did one go to the hospital, short of a farming accident such as being kicked by a cow or gored by a bull. Occasionally a tractor tipped over as the farmer mowed a hillside; auto accidents were rare, as few people could afford a car.

Miss Jordan's district covered five townships and, in each one, she organized a team to assist her. They did so in three ways: (1) by setting up a central point where basic medical equipment could be stored for loan to local residents, and (2) by preparing kits for her to do minor surgical stitching of lacerations, and (3) preparing deliver packs. These 18-inch delivery packs were wrapped in brown paper for autoclaving at the hospital then stored in the trunk of Miss Jordan's car until there was a midnight call to come!

Few people in our town could afford to have their baby delivered at the hospital, 20 miles away in Poughkeepsie, even if they had a car to get there. Therefore, most of the pre-natal and post-natal care, as well as the delivery, were performed by the state-funded, district health nurse.

Volunteers met regularly at the home of the local chairman to fold the muslin surgical towels, cut yards and yards of gauze to be folded into four-inch dressings, and pack them according to Miss Jordan's specifications. Pains of a mother during delivery were matched by the pain my mother endured as she approached grandma each month for permission to use the dining room table. There, seven or eight volunteers met to fulfill their responsibilities. The topic of the afternoon speaker on the porch at Hyde Park would be dedicated to the work of these women whom she wanted to honor.

Since our house was on the main road, it may automatically have been assumed, when my mother became chairman, that the cache of simple medical equipment would be stored there. Crutches, canes, commodes, hot water bottles, and ice packs were available for anyone in need. Whether Grandma's permission to store them in the barn was requested or just assumed to be granted was never clear to me.

What was clear was that some excitement was now possible at our house. When the doorbell rang suddenly, it meant someone had an urgent need, voiced from the dark shadows of the front porch. Viewed from the eyes of childhood, my mother and our house had taken on unprecedented importance. Even Grandma could not negate this.

It was apparent, even as I was growing up, that Miss Jordan's role not only in our household, but in the whole community, far exceeded what the state might have defined. Her concern for one's physical and psychological well-being extended from nursing, to social work, and beyond. Her devout care exceeded the ministerial duties of the young, timid, new seminary graduates, ill-equipped to recognize, let alone address the needs of a tiny rural community in the Depression.

My mother's gracious endeavors helped those in need, as she expected to do. More than that, it gave her a new identity, one that provided me an important example, a role model for serving the community. In a household where largesse and positive reinforcement were non-existent, Miss Jordan clearly saw the unspoken need for approval and recognition.

There we sat in the sweltering heat and humidity in neat rows of folding chairs on the front porch. Some of the ladies brought out fans from their pocketbooks. I noticed a few who felt the heat so badly they even removed their white gloves. I knew I would be expected, under these circumstances, to keep mine on.

My mother and I sat next to Miss Jordan. I heard her say she was proud of her record of the number of babies she had delivered. What she lamented most was her inability to convey the concept of planned parenthood to families mired in illiteracy who could least afford a ninth or tenth child. I understood the word illiteracy right off, but planned parenthood had always baffled me. Did not everyone plan to be a parent? I thought so.

Miss Jordan's face was riveted on the wide front door. It was cracked open a few minutes in advance of the moment the three ladies would pass through it. We stood in unison and sat at the first lady's motion to do so.

The graciousness and humility of the first lady were readily apparent to me, a 12-year-old. Before the program began, I watched as "Old Sari" positioned herself beside the speaker, upstaging the first lady. She proceeded to introduce the lady, with little consideration to the reality that the speaker and guests were here at Eleanor's invitation.

My mother and I thoroughly enjoyed watching "Old Sari," and were glad she did not live at our house. At least our Sari allowed my parents the privacy of their own bedroom. By contrast, when the Roosevelts were first married, Eleanor's Sari had arranged on her own initiative to cut an upstairs door between her New York City brownstone on East 65th Street and the one next door she had bought for her son.

I had little interest in the speaker, so my eyes were drawn to the first lady. It was only when everyone's attention was focused on the podium that I saw her cheeks relax; her eyes were downcast. She looked solemn and isolated.

When the formalities were over, Eleanor invited her guests out to the west terrace overlooking the majestic Hudson. As we drove home, my mother and I discussed our eventful afternoon.

"It would have been more fun," I said with a laugh, "if we had told the first lady, 'We have a Sari at our house, too.'"

My mother smiled but kept her eyes on the road, perhaps deep in thought of what Eleanor's life must be like.

It was in 1939, that the world's eyes were focused on the New York World's Fair. In June, Britain's royal family visited the British Pavilion there, followed by a weekend with the Roosevelts at Hyde Park. Everyone's attention was riveted on these famous people: King George VI, Queen Elizabeth, and their two daughters, 13-year-old Princess Elizabeth, and 8-year-old Princess Margaret Rose.

Crowds lined Main Street of this small but dignified town. We all waited and watched as the royal family and the Roosevelts returned from Sunday services at St. James Episcopal Church, which the president customarily attended. My grandmother, whose frail appearance belied her determined stamina, would have mobilized every ounce of energy to see the president and his guests, but then, nearly 90, she decided not to attend. That was smart, for we stood on the steaming hot sidewalk for several hours until their arrival.

We heard the distant cheers go up minutes ahead as this historic cavalcade approached. My little cousin, who was the same age as Princess Margaret Rose, stood up from the curb and shouted that she could hardly wait to see the crowns that the king and queen would wear.

"They wouldn't wear crowns to church, would they, Mom?" I asked.

"I think they only wear them to coronations and royal events in London," she affirmed. "They're extremely valuable. I've read they're kept at the Tower of London under careful guard."

"Here come the motorcycles," we shouted in unison. Excitement was dulled by the noisy, smelly motors that led this slow, short procession of people, so eminent in the world, but so humble in person.

Waves and cheers went up all around us. The Roosevelts and the royal family passed within ten feet of us. The gentlemen waved their hats and smiled. Our president looked huge, beside the short-statured king, in the back seat of the first open car. In the second black limousine, "Old Sari" presided over the seat of honor beside the queen.

My view of the queen was breathtaking. She wore a soft, blue chiffon dress and matching, off-the-face hat. What Eleanor wore was insignificant. There she was, relegated to a jump seat, waving to the crowd beside the well-mannered little girls.

After they passed, my cousin remarked, "I'd never want to be a princess. Those little girls can't take off their white gloves even on a hot day like this." However, the way she talked all afternoon about what kind of a doll house they might have in their castle, signaled her envy of their fairytale lives.

My mother's cousins, the Titus girls, lived a block off Main Street. These two elderly sisters who never married had, over the years, developed the prune-like faces of the very elderly. Knowing that we were coming to Hyde Park to see the motorcade, they had invited the relatives to come to their house for a picnic on the lawn when the festivities were over.

Florence, the older sister, could not walk well nor stand very long, but neither of them would have gone a city block to see the Roosevelts, even if their guests were royalty. To be sure, in this Republican stronghold, my father's support of the president was not a topic of conversation.

In the late afternoon, Eleanor entertained the royal family with the famous hot dog roast at Val-Kill, her nearby country home and refuge. My mother and I were thrilled that Eleanor put her imprint on this historic occasion.

When my grandmother read about it in her newspaper the next day, she gave her usual "hrrumph" of disapproval. The fact was, neither our Sari, nor Eleanor's, thought serving hot dogs was a proper way to entertain royalty.

No thunderclouds marred this informal event, but within three short months, on September 1, 1939, storm clouds would sweep across Europe, and roll into Poland as World War II began.

20

Unlikely Alliance

In the summer of 1936, I saw my father give his rapt attention to every column of the Reuters news service describing the fantastic achievements of Jesse Owens. I did not understand what was happening, but I remember hearing about a mean man, a bully named Hitler, who would not let our remarkable athlete stand at the podium to receive his four gold medals.

"Why not?" was my mystified response.

What was more remarkable was the composure maintained by Owens at this insult of Olympic proportions. History would soon reveal the difference, in human terms, between these two men whose lives had crossed momentarily.

As a 12-year-old with rural upbringing, events such as the 400-meter dash, hurdles, and races had no meaning for me. I had neither seen, nor heard about track and field events. I had a different understanding of the word "field." While adolescence can be difficult, for me it was an almost insurmountable hurdle.

Our new physician, Dr. Reginald Berry, a kindly, genteel man and Yale graduate was just out of his residency. He arrived with his wife, Lucia, a Yale graduate in physical education, bold, brash, and bumbling. She thought she might practice as a physical therapist in a sleepy town such as ours.

"Barbara's drooping head and poor posture need fixing," she told my mother and convinced her to bring me to weekly corrective exercises. I didn't need her. I hated her attitude, her banal exercise, and just about everything about her.

My grandmother spoke to me at the table now, which was a new twist. Sitting to my left at the head of the table as always, she commented, "You eat like a bird." I never gave an answer, but she did not expect any.

My mother, sitting to my right, said nothing, but she knew how I felt. She was content for me to eat what I could and leave the rest. Nothing on my plate added an ounce to my spider-like frame. In jest, it was said that I had to stand twice in the same place to make a shadow. There were plenty of reasons why my head drooped, why my appetite hit rock bottom.

As much as anyone, I understood how my father must have felt when he sat mute with his head in his hands.

With our school population totaling 100 students from the adjacent small towns of Bangall and Stanfordville, there was a very limited pool of peers and friends. Few lived near enough to share time beyond our school hours.

Having one friend for a sleepover was the biggest event our house could manage. Parties were impossible. In fact, they were ruled out after my fifth birthday, when my mother invited a handful of age-mates I had never seen. I did not even know how to play with them. Grandma let us move her reading table aside for the event. The Tiffany lamp survived, but something else of Grandma's got broken and that was enough to close the door. The price was too high ever to have another party.

Then something dreadful happened that made me too embarrassed to bring a classmate home in the afternoon. Emma, whose eyesight continued to fail, was now beset by a strange, inflammatory condition called erysipelas, which caused her skin to be red, swollen and unsightly. Its remedy could not have been worse.

Ointment intended for her skin eruptions spread rapidly over everything she touched. It made me shiver. As repulsive as I had always found jelly-coated doorknobs to be, they were preferable to ointment smeared everywhere. It was a revolting experience.

There were few enough options for girlfriends, let alone boyfriends. Thus, with no opportunity for normal social interchange, adolescence was a "no man's land" in every respect.

The movies offered much of the rest of the country relief from the Depression, but not for the people who lived in our town. The nearest theatre was 20 miles away. Young married couples with a car went to the movies, but families usually did not and adolescents had no way to get there. By the time I went to college, I could name the movies I had seen on the fingers of one hand, the number of dates on my thumbs. Not even movie magazines were available for adolescent girls. No one could afford such luxury.

Dr. Berry was a wonderful family physician, but beyond that he was also an accomplished singer. During his years as an undergraduate and medical school student, he had been a member of the Yale Glee Club and was one of the Whiffenpoofs who sang "To the Tables Down at Marey's" as the song about this college hangout goes. Nelson Eddy and Lanny Ross, both of *Showboat* fame and possibly Glenn Miller, were among the Whiffenpoofs of whom he often spoke. Not long afterward, Lanny Ross and his wife also moved to a home near Bangall. Mrs. Ross became my mother's best-paying patron for sewing and alterations. Thanks in large measure to her, I had a $500 college nest egg when the time came.

Everyone regretted Dr. Berry's leaving, but no one wept on hearing of his wife's departure. My grandmother despised her, although she had barely set eyes on her throughout those six years. That was because of an event that happened one day soon after they arrived. Lucia, big-boned and buxom, rang the doorbell with the implied urgency of a fire truck. Before she gave anyone time to answer, she had pushed her knee against the door. Our tricky front door key could obstruct entrance to anyone when treated with such insensitivity.

Frustrated at being delayed in her mission that bore no genuine emergency, she lifted the screen from an open front window and climbed in. As she did so, she knocked over the pipe stand beside my father's chair, spilled the ashes, and stepped on his briar pipe. That evening he discovered his pipe had a small crack in the bowl. That was all I needed to terminate treatment for my drooping head and poor posture.

When my grandmother learned what had happened, she was furious. No one ever violated her premises, certainly no one with such lack of both courtesy and respect for property. We both disliked Lucia Berry intensely, albeit for different reasons. An unlikely alliance was forged between us as we joined forces emotionally against our common enemy.

Upon hearing that Dr. Berry divorced Lucia soon after they left, Grandma joined in the cheers. I had never seen her react this way. Divorce was unheard of among people who had lived in this town all their lives. However, in this case, it seemed like a joyful remedy for obvious ills. Like the briefly shared alliance between Grandma and me, their alliance was an unlikely one as well.

21

Emma Moves on and So Do I

Emma's eyesight was failing by the age of 74, but her hearing was fine. She was seven years younger than my grandmother and still saw to Grandma's every request. Her determined spirit was slightly diminished, but only because there were fewer opportunities for her to exercise it at church and in the kitchen.

Emma spent most of the day sitting in front of one of the sunny windows in Grandma's bedroom. Her chair was directly above the doorbell and when its harsh clang sounded, she answered it as always. It rang a second time before her bowed legs carried her downstairs to the front door.

After a brief struggle with the cranky lock, Emma opened the east side of these carved walnut doors to see a smiling face greet her warmly.

Miss Jordan inquired about her and her state of health, and when she asked for my mother, Emma directed her to the priest's potato patch where we were weeding.

She turned right beside the sign to the rectory of the Church of the Immaculate Conception, a sign that would evoke curious questions as I grew. The well-groomed lawn and gardens surrounding the freshly painted house was the work of Father Norris's devoted parishioners. We share their deep affection for him, as he was our priest too, our priest of the potato patch.

Miss Jordan found us easily, following the narrow road that ran past the house and barn toward the cemetery beyond. My mother looked up from her weeding, startled to hear an approaching car. Dressed for duty, Miss Jordan always wore soft Bass moccasins and her navy blue, button-down uniform. I looked at those pearl-white shank buttons with great admiration. It made her look so professional. Her uniform had long sleeves for both summer and winter that were trimmed with heavily starched white collar and cuffs. These and the buttons were removed each night and attached to a fresh one. Whenever we visited her at home, she wore her own clothes; then my mother called her "Isabel."

Miss Jordan, as I would call her all my life, looked up the rows of well-weeded potato plants and smiled as she addressed each of us.

My mother removed her wide-brimmed straw hat and wiped her forehead with a torn linen handkerchief. She had a puzzled look on her face as she walked out of the potato patch to greet her friend. My memory of this is as clear as if it had happened yesterday.

"Mary, I have some news. I hope it will be great news for you and the whole family."

"Yes. Yes," my mother's voice trailed upward. I was right beside her now and saw that her whole face lifted. In fact, she looked as if she had seen a pot of gold at the end of the rainbow.

"Mary, I learned this morning about a place called Ward Manor. It's a beautiful mansion over on the river north of Hyde Park, near Red Hook. The Ward family who founded the Ward Baking Company in Poughkeepsie, has donated its estate for the care of elderly people without homes." She said it all so fast she was nearly out of breath. I recognized this company as the bakers of my favorite sliced Wonderbread.

My mother slumped to the grass where she stood. No doubt Miss Jordan had Emma in mind. My father dropped his hoe at the far end of the row, not believing his ears. She repeated the news. My mother's face was reflected in his. Relief!

"I suggest you drive over; it's only 20 miles from here. Get an idea of it yourselves before you mention anything to Emma."

"Oh, don't you worry," my father replied with a chuckle. "I know only too well how they can put the kybosh on things. We won't give them a chance."

Miss Jordan needed reassurance that I could be trusted with this secret. Of course, I could. When this conversation took place, I was soon to enter third grade; I was grown up and very reliable. "No problem." My parents knew that I could keep a secret, especially since this solution was as important to me as anyone. That was not hard; the old folks never asked me any questions.

Soon my parents were away for the day, ostensibly on a shopping trip. I rushed home from school, anxious for their return and ran upstairs behind them to hear all about it.

"Yes," they told me, "the good news is that this elegant mansion with a wide, walnut-carved staircase and white marble floor provides a home to 50 elderly people."

During dinner, they presented it, bit by bit, to our old folks, so they were able to accept the idea. The following week, they took Emma over to see the place and be interviewed. She liked it, too.

With the good news came the bad. They were filled to capacity, but as soon as they had her application on file, her name would be added to their waiting list. It was a good thing we had no idea how long the bad news would continue, for we were full of hope.

"How long, Mommy how long?"

"Maybe a year or two."

"Ohhh." As profound as my disappointment was, it could not compare with that of my parents. But each year, hope escalated as the anniversary date of her application approached. She was taken for a review of her health status and to learn where she placed on the long waiting list.

Every year, we were met by the same disappointing news: "Not yet, Emma has a roof over her head. We have to give priority to those who do not."

One time, five or six years after the original trip, my parents decided not to take Emma, too blind now to walk to church safely. They planned to tell the social worker that Emma's eyesight was not as good as last year, but they felt there was no reason to push the point.

At noon, they picked me up at school. I was dressed in my good clothes. That alerted everyone to the fact something important was about to happen. Now I could see the "'mythical mansion" that never seemed to become a reality. My parents ardently hoped that the social worker, in seeing me, might be more sympathetic to the long-standing effects Emma was having on my life.

I was light-hearted and full of hope on the way over, eager to convince them it was time to take her. "Mom, can I tell them how she never lets me sleep on Saturdays? How she opens my bedroom door that won't close and can't be locked?" The bedroom was one step below the hallway; it made her looming presence all the more foreboding. As an adolescent who wanted to sleep late, being awakened by her clattering teeth as she hovered above my head was a most unsettling experience.

"Let your father do the talking. If they ask you any questions, you reply politely, but nothing else. Remember, this may be the year it really counts." I was eager to do anything to speed the process. When we arrived, I could see this was a magnificent mansion.

In minutes, the meeting was over. We trudged back to the car. Our return trip would be different. I pushed the hinged back of the passenger seat forward, climbed in, and dropped into my seat. My hopes dropped, too.

My mother closed her door slowly. Her head drooped. My father turned the key in the ignition and released the hand brake, turning his head from view. He drove well below the speed limit through that long, tree-lined drive. I knew better than to ask questions. I dared not speak. No one spoke for 20 miles.

"Anything you want besides bread?" my father asked when he pulled up to the grocery store next to our post office. All my mother could do was shake her head. What she really wanted had been stored for years behind a dam of tears. The dam held. Had it not, there would have been a terrible flood.

My arm was getting tired from carrying schoolbooks. For relief I switched them with my lunchbox. I was awkward as well as skinny, so the geometry book fell into the mud. I would rather it had been my Latin book, the most challenging and distasteful subject of my freshman year.

By contrast, geometry class was my all-time favorite, but that was because I was in love, in love with my teacher who was also our school principal. He was in love, too, but not with me.

He was marrying a distant relative on my mother's side and we were invited. This was to be a very formal candlelight wedding at the Dutch Reformed Church in Poughkeepsie, followed by an elegant home reception.

This event would celebrate many firsts for me: my first permanent, my first long dress, and my first bra. I was really growing up. For now, this was nearly as good as getting married.

"Get married and move away," had been my only hope of escape from the day I started school. This idea was modified now, but throughout my childhood a strong drive prevailed to grow up and get out.

Indeed I did. College was the first stepping-stone, leading to a career in distant locations, but that was still far in the future.

As I walked along the roadside that September afternoon, I was daydreaming about the blue taffeta dress that my mother was making for the big event. When I rounded the curve to walk beside the hay field, I saw her raking leaves on the long driveway that led to Grandma's two-story, yellow barn.

She beckoned vigorously and called, "Hurry, I have a surprise." I saw the broad smile on her face, but she kept me in suspense.

"Make three guesses, and I'll bet you can't possibly guess what's happened."

"You finished my dress."

"No," she replied, still grinning.

That morning, Emma's niece who lived locally, had picked her up for a visit that would last several days. They invited her every year or so, but it was getting more difficult as her eyesight failed. They had six children, and toys on the floor presented a hazard.

With this in mind, my next guess was that Grandma, too, had been invited for an overnight at Aunt May's. No such luck. Occasions when overnight visits of the two old ladies coincided were rare, and provided us a time of big celebration. It always meant we could have waffles for the evening meal. If they were away for two nights, I was delighted to have the menu repeated.

Making enough waffles to feed five people on the cast-iron waffle iron took forever over the woodstove, but with only three of us, it was manageable and very special.

"No," she said, the grin still undimmed. "One more guess."

"News came from Ward Manor," I broached with hesitation, fearing still another disappointment.

"No, sorry, I only wish you could be right," she replied. Her smile faded. This was a wish we shared with equal intensity.

"I give up."

I was so anxious to hear this surprise I overlooked the clue above her shoulder. The four-foot, square door upstairs in the barn was propped open, a rare sight. This was the only source of light. Now I would learn, it was a source of hope.

"Well, at lunchtime, as Grandma and I were eating, it must have dawned on her how different things would be for her, too, if Emma ever got into Ward Manor."

"Yes, so what did she say?"

"Well, she was silent as usual for a long time. I think she realized she would be quite lonely. Maybe she wanted to find a way to be more at ease when just the two of us would be sharing a quiet, if not silent, lunch."

"Yeah, and then what happened?"

"Grandma started talking about changes. And then, out of the blue, she said, 'Mary, why don't you bring your set of dining room furniture up from the barn?' I think she was surprised to hear herself say it."

"What!" I screamed as we turned to face the barn together in our glee. "Did you call Dad?"

"Oh, no, you know, unless it's a life and death matter, we're never to call him at work."

This development ranked almost that close, we thought, reading each other's mind.

We ran to the barn and up the shaky wooden stairs, devoid of even a guardrail. Once more, as we had done so many times, we looked at every side and corner of the crated furniture, undisturbed from the moment it—and we—were dropped into place. My mother always feared that the squirrels and chipmunks had chewed the leather-covered seats to make their winter nests, or worse yet, ground their teeth on the graceful Queen Anne-style legs.

My mother and I were so energized we might have wrenched the slats away with our bare hands. All their furniture had been crated with strips of rough oak. It was a wonder to me that the furniture packers could get a nail to penetrate it. I had tried to build things from the slats removed from the kitchen cabinet, but it was impossible. Every nail I hit bowed its head without making a dent in the iron-clad wood. We knew we would have to wait, but this time there was promise. There was hope.

It was only Tuesday. How could we possibly wait until the weekend to see the dining room furniture? Purchased when they were married, it was their true pride. Pictures of it tantalized me. The emotions that were tied up in this furniture embodied my parents' life together there in happiness. The words Washington, apartment, furniture, dishes, and love were synonymous.

We hurried to the house to envision how it would all look. I ran upstairs for a measuring tape so we could check the size of Grandma's oak sideboard. We found this elephantine piece of furniture would fit in the pantry we called "Greenland" in winter. Together, we pulled the heavy sideboard out; the wallpaper, lackluster oatmeal at best, was five shades brighter there. Instantly, we realized more adventure, more experiences, more joy would ensue. There was no need to ask if we could replace it; the need was obvious. You might say, it was a "given" in a house where not much was readily forthcoming.

Of course, wallpapering had to be done first. Early Saturday morning we headed for town, more excited than I could ever remember. We chose a soft cornflower blue background with a dainty, white-dotted diagonal and rose-buds placed at intervals within the diamond shapes. Best of all, it matched the china; bringing it up from the barn seemed to be part and parcel of the new thaw. There was no need to worry about her china being broken. She and I, not Emma, washed dishes now.

Of necessity, moving the furniture or even seeing it, was delayed for a month while my mother removed the grimy old paper and replaced it with new. It was her first wallpapering experience, and her skill improved slowly. Not only was it difficult to get the paper straight against walls that were not true, but the paper we selected proved to be especially irksome. Aligning these dainty diagonals required precision. Her skill in cutting dress patterns helped, but she would be glad to return to textiles, a more flexible medium.

As my mother struggled with the wallpaper, Grandma came to watch and silently admired the new look. I think she wanted to praise this work, but failed to find the words. Even so, the change that was evolving was monumental and helped to reduce the enormous barriers and the stress of living in this house.

Emma voiced her strong disapproval. Perhaps her resistance stemmed from fears that when she went to Ward Manor, she would have a hard time envisioning the family in a dining room that was unfamiliar to her.

Never in my memory had the old folks ever entertained divergent views relevant to us. This was truly an exception.

Unlike Grandpa K., whose benevolence was legendary, Grandma had to reach deep into an untapped vein of generosity. Hearing her spontaneous suggestion to replace her own dining room furniture with ours, strained our imagination.

Difficult as this may have been for Grandma, who made this offer of her own volition, it was twice as hard for Emma, who had this change imposed on her. Her whole identity, her whole being, was emotionally linked to the kitchen-dining room routine. Emma had had to give up her kitchen, and now Grandma was surrendering the very place where she had served so nobly for half a century.

In every avenue open to her, my mother tried to bring warmth to the place where we lived. This move by Grandma helped significantly, but I would be graduating from college before I could call this house "home."

Nevertheless, a new look was emerging and the excitement it generated was intense. A few weeks later, on a Saturday morning, my father engaged two husky men to help him uncrate the furniture and move it to the dining room. With this excitement also came courage. After breakfast, I heard my mother approach Grandma for an unheard-of request.

"While the men are here, do you think this might be a good time, Grandma K., to bring our small sofa in from the barn? Barbara needs a place to sit and read in the evening."

My mouth dropped. That would surely beat the straight-back chair I carried in from the dining room each evening. I had never had my own place to sit. Besides, the reading table only had four sides.

I looked at my mother; it was as if she had the strength of Gibraltar.

Grandma offered her first line of defense, saying that there was no outlet on that wall. True. When electricity was installed, one wall plug per room had been allotted; no additions were ever made.

Then, in a kinder voice than I had ever heard my grandmother use toward us, she faced my mother and said, "Yes, Barbara needs a place to sit. I think your couch will fit."

My mother gave her the expected, the formal, and the very sincere, "Thank you very much, Grandma K.," but my grandmother had already turned to walk away. Only I saw the tears of joy in her eyes and that was through the mist in my own.

My mother's mahogany dining room furniture was exquisite against the soft blue wallpaper. The chairs were undamaged. Miraculously, the curved glass china cabinet was intact, as was the slender horizontal mirror over the buffet.

Above it, she hung her favorite picture, a reprint of Jean François Millet's 1857 painting *The Angelus,* which portrayed a peasant couple bowing their heads as a church bell in the distance rang at "eventide."

Although on closer look, these are potato harvesters, my mother liked to think of it in her own mind as the flax growers on the fields of Belgium. She would turn to me and say, "Don't ever forget, you are a Walloon!"

Staring in amazement that Saturday morning at *The Angelus,* she smiled amid tears. Our prayers were already being answered.

By the time I was a junior in high school, Emma's presence had less effect on me. That year I had moved on, going by bus to school in Millbrook, the same school where my parents had met.

Seven years after the first visit to Ward Manor, the call came to bring her. By then she had completed her 56th year in Grandma's household, 14 of them while I lived there. It was Isabel Jordan to whom every member of our family was grateful for locating Ward Manor that provided for Emma's continued care.

Happy, well cared for, and completely blind, she lived there another 13 years before moving on to her final resting place. I, too, had moved on, many times. I would be out of college, through my professional training as an occupational therapist, and commissioned in the army four years by the time Emma died at the age of 96; ironically her death came at exactly the same age as the one she had faithfully served.

In addition to the role Miss Jordan had played in the lives of each of us, as a member of the health professions, she unwittingly became a role model for me. It was on Miss Jordan's navy blue uniform I first saw pearl shank buttons.

Army physical and occupational therapists, dieticians, and nurses all wore identical white starched uniforms, stiff white cap, white shoes and stockings. I often thought of her as I changed buttons nightly on the hospital attire I wore for 20 years.

Emma, nearly blind, moved to Ward Manor where she lived another 13 years, until she died at the age of 96. Ward Manor is currently part of Bard College.

22

Thanksgiving, Christmas: The Worst and The Best

That memorable year I was a high school freshman, a series of awesome events took place. Earlier in the fall Emma had been invited to her niece's home for a short visit and was invited again for Thanksgiving. This was unheard of and my mother's fantasies began to spin.

The following Sunday when Aunt May came, my father asked his sister to join him in the kitchen. With more assertiveness than I had ever heard, he stated his request.

"Emma is going to be away over Thanksgiving. I want you to take Mother this year."

She did not refuse. I know, because I crept along the dark hall to listen. Slowly she responded, agreeing in word, if not in tone.

"I guess we can but she'll have to stay all week," she replied with her customary reluctance.

Once Aunt May stepped over the doorsill between the dining room and living room, her whole being underwent a remarkable transformation.

Instantly, she became the charming, loving daughter that Grandma knew, issuing a gushy invitation. It was as if it were all her own idea, as if she had had to plead for my father's cooperation. Unbelievably, fate stepped in to extend this magnanimous invitation. It would be nearly four months before either of the old folks could return, but none of us knew it then.

Now I was old enough to understand who "Mr. He" was and what role he had played in Aunt May's life. After witnessing the phony quality of this incident, I began to wonder if he had sensed a similar duplicity. Could it have been this trait that caused him to break their engagement? I would never know.

We did not care if her invitation was insincere. All we wanted was to have our own celebration. My mother had worked hard the previous year to earn money for a propane gas stove. Struggling as she did with the old woodstove had made her appreciate how difficult it had been for Emma to bake molasses cookies, pies, and angel food cakes all those years. Surprisingly, after her new stove was installed, my mother too, began to bake molasses cakes, but not because of any breakfast tradition.

She would sell dozens of them to the weekend New Yorkers who also bought eggs and broilers from her. These dollars were earmarked for an electric refrigerator. "Goodness," I thought to myself, imagine all the changes in our lives: Mother's kitchen cabinet, her dining room furniture and new wallpaper, and sofa her family had never seen. Now with a new stove and refrigerator, one that even made ice cubes, life was more exciting every day.

As soon as Aunt May's invitation was sealed, my mother phoned her sister to come for Thanksgiving. Her family rarely visited, as there was no place to sit and chat. In summer, they might sit on the narrow porch or go to look at the garden. The atmosphere in our house was never conducive to chatting, let alone entertaining. But that was changing, too. With her sister's family of five, plus her two brothers and their families, all of whom lived in a 20-mile radius of us, there would be 14 around our table. We could hardly wait to share all the new developments, and I would see my cousins, a very special event.

Grandma went home with her daughter and son-in-law that Sunday in late November, and Emma was picked up the following Tuesday. We were cautious not to reveal a hint of our plans for fear the old folks might not have left.

My mother had shopped early and prepared as much as she could without Emma's catching on. My father seemed just as excited. I heard him whistle as he inserted the extra table leaves that had not been used since their days in Washington. My mother and I set the table with her best damask tablecloth, matching napkins, her sterling silver and, of course, her china.

The evening before Thanksgiving, our little school traditionally put on a three-act play. Knowing how timid adolescence had made me, the teacher gave me only two lines, but even so, I was terrified that I might deliver them at the wrong moment.

For my mother, the performance seemed to last an eternity. This jam-packed auditorium of 200 people was hot and stuffy, but she never unbuttoned her winter coat. In fact, she felt cold.

The next morning, I was out of bed without being called, for this was the day of our first family get-together, a hallmark of thanksgiving for us all. As I rushed down to the kitchen, I heard my father on the phone talking to the doctor who had replaced Dr. Berry. Minutes later, the doorbell rang.

Returning from the third floor, the doctor quickly laid out his orders, the standard protocol to treat and prevent the spread of a dread disease. My mother was to be quarantined for scarlet fever the next four weeks. I was to be moved out. My father was to go into their room only to take her breakfast and get his clothes; the practical nurse would arrive before noon. Mail and groceries would be left on the porch. There was to be no contact with anyone outside.

In our daze, my father and I managed to stuff and roast the huge turkey, which he ate for far more dark days than he ever wanted to remember. I returned the silver to their slotted cases of tarnish-proof flannel.

So much for our dreams, our plans, and our fabulous party; my mother's families not only had to scurry around for other dinner plans, they would neither see her dining room that was fit for a queen nor that the kitchen had blossomed.

News spread fast. By nightfall, the town was in a panic. Already that fall, five cases of scarlet fever had been diagnosed among school children as well as her friend and neighbor, Mrs. White, who sold us milk.

Townspeople feared, and rightly so, that my mother could have spread this infectious disease throughout the packed auditorium. Of course, I had to leave home, but there was no place to go. No one in town with children would take the risk, and her relatives, too, had children. The doctor finally persuaded a couple down the road, past the White's farm, to board me. To make it worse, I had never seen these people; they were too old ever to leave their house.

After my father and I tried to eat a little of the turkey dinner, I trudged down the road to an unfamiliar and scary destination with my books in one arm, a grocery bag of clothes in the other.

Amazingly, no one else contracted the disease but the fear remained. When school opened after Thanksgiving vacation, I was shocked that my classmates would not sit near me. At recess, I was as isolated as a leper.

For a girl as shy as I already was, this was devastating. Adults were fearful and crossed to the other side of the road, eyeing that dreaded red sign of quarantine that spelled fear.

My mother's case at the age of 56 was the most severe our doctor had ever treated. He told the nurse and my father he was not sure he could pull her through. However, there was a ray of hope if my father would agree to it. A new medicine, called sulpha had just come out, but our doctor had never used it. Unavailable locally, he phoned the New York Medical Center and asked that this medicine be sent by train. It arrived the next day. Special arrangements were made with the bus driver from Poughkeepsie to leave it on our front steps with the promise that no one would come out to meet him.

Remarkably, this medicine started to work. Her fever of 102 degrees that had lasted for over a week broke, her delirium and her rash abated, and the most terrible "strawberry tongue" the doctor had ever seen, started to dissipate. The doctor was tremendously relieved, for sulpha was known in medical circles as a very powerful, but highly dangerous drug to administer.

Effective dosages had yet to be determined. In order to save my mother, he feared the high dosage itself might kill her.

With this dilemma in mind, my father had to make that unprecedented decision to proceed. He was faced with not only the possibility of losing his wife, but with raising a teenage daughter in an old ladies' home. It was enough to send him back to his chair beside the living room window and hold his head in his hands.

In addition, he had to bolster me against homesickness and worry, without divulging the life-threatening status of my mother's condition. He had no one to give him support. The doctor and nurse were fully engaged in my mother's survival.

While she was quarantined at our house, I spent four weeks in another kind of incarceration. Mrs. Symes tried to be motherly, but her childless past made this an awkward role for her and an incredibly difficult one for me. I felt so isolated at school, so lonely here. My father's evening phone calls were my only lifeline.

Mr. Symes helped me with first-year Latin but that was a losing battle from the start. My grades had never been good, usually C's and D's, but my mother never complained. She understood that there were contributing factors, and a time would come when I could blossom.

Finally, it was Christmas, the day I had been waiting for. Throughout her quarantine I had crossed off each day on the Symes' greasy old kitchen calendar.

No longer would I have to come home from school to this low, dingy, unpainted house where this couple lived in poorly lit, unkempt back rooms reeking of kerosene and slept in tiny, freezing bedrooms above.

No longer would I have to sleep under smelly featherbeds, only aired, not washed, since they were brought from Europe.

No longer would I have to study Latin with Mr. Symes who approached my homework with the exactitude of a calligrapher, which he was.

Of all the adjustments I had to make, eating was the hardest. As a 13-year-old, I found food generally unappealing, but they served pasteurized milk, which I had never tasted and found offensive. Added to that, the unfamiliar smell and taste of bratwurst and sauerkraut, standard fare for this German couple, made swallowing at all a struggle.

But that was all over now. Christmas Day was finally here, and it would be different from all that had gone before and any yet to unfold. I got up in the dark, and dressed with speed. Despite their firm pleas to wait for daylight, I pulled on my snow boots, grabbed the brown bag of clothes, and was out the door.

The sun was just peeping over the hills toward Amenia. I ran up the country road as fast as I could, past the big meadow to the right between the Symes' house and Mr. White's farm, then along the meadow to my left, home of the woodchuck colony. As through a zoom lens, the house, the long white fence lining the driveway to the yellow barn, and the kitchen door came into sharper focus with every step.

My father had told me to go to the front door and wait. This felt odd; I hesitated at the steps beside the road before proceeding. With unaccustomed eyes, I took a long look at the layered, three-story Victorian house and its white filigree over the front stoop.

It was in my parents' room that all the action had played out over these four weeks. Here, attended by a devoted nurse, my mother survived. I looked longingly at the small dormer windows on the third floor, then to the wide-paned ones of Grandma's second-floor bedroom. Rarely had I set foot in it, but even less so had my mother.

Now, want to or not, she would be sleeping in Grandma's bed. Questions tumbled through my mind.

Has she been moved down yet? What will she look like?

Had the upper floor already been fumigated as my father told me it would be?

Moving slowly up the marble walk, I saw snow banks piled high on each side. Then I noticed a Christmas tree lying on its side by the front door.

I was jolted back to the reality that today was Christmas Day, when everyone would be celebrating in joyful tradition.

The doctor had not yet arrived, so I sat on the top step of the front stoop and looked out at the snow. Ordinarily on Christmas morning, a new sled or skis would be uppermost in my mind. It would be a great day to try them out, but even though "Christmas as usual" would be put on hold, I was not disappointed.

After all, I was home again. It was home when just the three of us were there. The doctor had said it would be weeks before my mother would be strong enough for the old folks to return. I would never want her to be sick, but if it had to be, I felt entitled to enjoy the consequences.

It was so cold that the lower front windowpanes were frost covered, so I had to stand on my toes to look into our lifeless living room. Sitting down again, I leaned against the post that held up the roof, that framed the house, that contained all the recent chaos, suffering, and love. I riveted my eyes on the crest of the hill by the Catholic church.

For more than an hour, I scarcely shifted my gaze or changed position.

Even though it was freezing, I took off my mittens to stroke the glossy spruce needles of the Christmas tree. I longed for the warm affection of Puff and I would have stroked her fur, but she had died.

The sun was well off the hillside when I caught the first glimpse of the tan Chevy coupe; I had memorized every detail of its shape. I screamed to the vacant front of the house in hopes someone inside would hear.

"He's coming. He's by the church. He's by the rectory. He's almost here."

As self-appointed watch guard, I shot up from my steeled position to run and greet him.

"Dr. Mangieri, can I go in now? When can I see my mother?"

More delays, more disappointments, but at least this was defused by the reality of his arrival.

An hour passed while the doctor saw to my mother's needs and was assured that all the requirements of the Board of Health of the State of New York were being met to the letter of the law. When he came out the front door, he tore off the red sign and told me I could take the tree into the living room. He gave firm instructions, however, not to open the doors toward the back of the house until my father had carried out everything that had to be burned.

The living room was as lifeless inside as it had looked through the window. But I was back and that was what counted now. I waited and waited, hearing my father's footsteps up and down the stairs. Finally he came in. He was undemonstrative as usual, but I had never been used to hugs in our family anyway.

He told me he was glad I was home, but he seemed surprised I had arrived at daybreak. Why should he be surprised? I wanted to see my mother.

"When can I see her?" He told me she had been very ill, but she would be stronger soon.

"I want to see her now," I said in a plaintive voice, sensing another disappointment.

This is how it looked when I, a thirteen-year-old, rushed up the road at daybreak on Christmas Day to wait for Mom's quarantine for scarlet fever to be lifted.

Photo taken fall of 1941, of my mother when she was sixty. I was entering my freshman year at Green Mountain Junior College, that later became a four-year institution at Poultney, Vermont.

"As soon as she is bathed and her clothes are taken out to burn, you can go to the top of the staircase and speak to her."

"Why can't I go in to see her?"

"The doctor says you must wait until she is stronger."

"Why? I want to see her. Why can't I see her now?"

As we talked, he mounted the tree in its heavy wooden holder.

He brought the ornaments and lights in their age-old boxes into the living room before resuming his work. I was content for a while to renew an annual acquaintance with my favorite ornaments. The glistening image of Santa Claus in his red suit and white beard smiled from the top branch, as if to share the joy of knowing we would all celebrate more Christmases with my mother.

Several packages had arrived by mail, so I tore off the brown paper to place them at wide intervals under the tree. I wondered; when will he stop and have Christmas with me. The morning dragged like an eternity to me, but for my father, Christmas gifts had a low priority.

I tired of this imposed patience. Out in the front hall, I crept past the double front doors and up the carpeted steps. To my delight, the door was ajar and I caught a glimpse of the person I remembered so vividly.

I dashed up the last few steps, threw open the door and tore in to hug and kiss her. I was stunned. When I threw my arms around her, I just felt bones, nothing but bones.

"Mom, what's happened to your bones and your skin? They didn't used to look like that. ... And what's wrong with your hair?"

What had not fallen out from the fever was no longer brown. Her warmth reduced my shock, but in her weakened condition, she burst into a torrent of tears. The nurse ran upstairs from the kitchen to send me out.

I was satisfied. I had seen her. The only Christmas gift that counted I had already found, and in its own wrapping.

Finally all the bedding was boiled, and her favorite bathrobe and slippers were burned. These were easy. The oil in the feather pillows gave my father the worst time; it would take a week for them and longer for the mattress to burn completely.

Mr. White came to help since he had already been through the same ordeal for his wife weeks before. He assumed that his immunity fortified him, but he tied a bandana across his face anyway.

With everything out of the third floor, fumigation candles were lit and the door at the bottom of the stairs was sealed. Every requirement had been met.

Exhausted, my father returned to the living room and slumped into his chair. Perhaps he had been as overwhelmed as I was to see her condition.

He was quiet and detached as I sat on the floor and opened my presents. He sat motionless, not even lighting his pipe.

I had been back in school two weeks after Christmas vacation. Plans were being considered for the old ladies' return, but that Friday night, I complained of a rough tongue and sore throat. The doctor returned, and once more a red sign went up. Aside from the first week of fever and discomfort, I relished these four weeks.

This time I was on the inside; there were advantages: not having to face the distancing of my schoolmates nor stinky feather bedding and sauerkraut. Most importantly, the old ladies could not come back. For these few weeks, I had the perfect arrangement. We were a family of three.

In mid-February, Aunt May called to ask when she could bring her mother. My father said it was inadvisable to bring her yet, since my quarantine had only just been lifted. He reminded her of an earlier time when Grandma had caught whooping cough from me and then had passed it on to her. My mother and I burst into silent giggles when he suggested it could happen again. My case was so mild, the doctor had allowed him to go back to work, and considering the medical expenses and the cost of boarding me with the Symes, he needed every paycheck.

Most of all, my mother needed more time to get her strength back before resuming the added stresses and cooking for the old ladies. Taking care of me was sufficient for now. Every night, she cooked either waffles or one of her awesome two-inch-high omelets. We never tired of them. Having scarlet fever was worth it. It was, without doubt, the best time I had ever had in this house. What suffered the most was my Latin. The final grade of "C" stood for compassion, but provided a weak foundation for another agonizing two years studying that subject.

In town, rumor had it that since the three of us, Mrs. White, my mother, and I all drank raw milk we must have been infected by one of Mr. White's herd with the same disease. There was no scientific evidence to support this theory, but the rumor had value to quell the town's anxiety. No further cases developed.

When the quarantine sign was removed, I was right there to grab it. It signaled that for a limited capsule of time, this house had been home for a family of three, the only such experience we ever had. This scarlet red sign was hung above my bed in an honored, but unlikely, place alongside the tranquil tones of my favorite painting, Vermeer's *Lacemaker*. These were powerful symbols of unity and peace in a household where unresolved stress reigned supreme.

My mother's near-death experience became a transcending one for her. It seemed as if this benchmark had re-energized her physically and emotionally. She often commented on this phenomenon. Throughout the remaining 25 years of her life, she met each day with gratitude and a positive outlook with which to cope with life's vicissitudes. At the age of 80, she would succumb to breast cancer.[1]

1 When she was diagnosed in 1960, she was the only person I had known with cancer, a vivid contrast to the statistics of today that claim one in eight women will face this diagnosis in their lifetime.

In 1998 I became part of that statistic, but early detection and advances in treatment over the intervening 38 years have been dramatic. The intense, weekly doses of radiation my mother endured produced severe burns up to her ears. Current treatment of 30 days of lighter, more focused radiation has provided my health and survival for a decade.

23

Word of Grandma's Demise

My mother's letter-writing was legendary. She wrote without fail every Sunday and Wednesday night from the time I started college until days before her death. Phone calls were a luxury we rarely engaged in.

So it was in one of her routine letters during my senior year at Syracuse University, that I learned matter-of-factly of Grandma Knickerbocker's death. Her funeral would have been held by the time I received word. There was no expectation that I would return for it. In fact, aside from Christmas and summer vacations, the only time I returned during my four years of college was to celebrate my parents' 25th wedding anniversary.

Leaving for college implied the normal transition to the adult world and career, the breaking of childhood ties. For me, college represented opportunities to develop the close friendships I had never experienced and to pursue the adventure I had longed for. Although I know she missed me terribly, my mother was always supportive of my leaving home. Mutual letter-writing maintained our close bond and helped to mitigate her loss when I left.

At the age of 96, my grandmother's demise was not a surprise. Her good health, hearing, eyesight, and flawless memory lasted until the day she died. She continued to weed her flower beds, walk up and down stairs, and keep an astute interest in the newspaper, her daily radio programs, and her intricate handcraft skills to the end. The last winter of her life, she had moved to May's home. Perhaps the fact that her daughter's house had indoor plumbing was a major factor in this decision.

During her lifetime, my grandmother had never been able to establish emotional closeness with those in our household as strongly as she clearly had with "her" president. During FDR's "Fireside Chats," she would get up from her wicker chair beside the reading table to sit in a low rocker next to the radio. She reveled in his resonant voice and hung on every word this Pied Piper had to say. My grandmother died within a year after Sara Delano Roosevelt and only a few months before the death of the president.

Thus, neither of these women would have to experience the shock of FDR's sudden passing in the spring of 1945.

Shy as a deer in the headlights, this high school senior is nevertheless determined to find a career around inventing.

24

An Inventive Spirit Sparks a Creative Career

With limited funds, mediocre grades, and no clear vision about a career, finding a suitable college was a problem. Compounding the situation in the early 1940s was the reality that there were few career options open to women other than secretarial work, nursing, or teaching.

I had some help from my mother's family. Her brother drove us to Cornell University for my interview at the College of Home Economics. As a Cornell alumnus and former instructor, he graciously offered any possible assistance to ensure my acceptance.

I was overwhelmed by the size of the campus and it was my perception that the other girls also waiting to be interviewed had much better grades. For certain, they were far more sophisticated. An instant flashback reminded me of the young tent-mates from well-to-do city families I had met at Camp Sloane. I knew I did not belong there. Lacking sound scholastic aptitude, I could not have lasted six weeks.

Then there was Vassar College, just 20 miles away in Poughkeepsie.

When Mathew Vassar, businessman and distiller, was establishing the college, my grandfather, like many others in the farming and business communities, made a financial contribution. Grandpa Ham, brought up as a Quaker and one who never imbibed, had to overlook the fact that the fledgling college was funded by a profitable brewery. But he kept his eye to the future, specifically to the education of his three young daughters. My mother the oldest, was accepted, but failed the physical due to glandular tuberculosis.

Grandpa Ham's contribution had not been forgotten. As a result the Vassar College Alumnae Association offered me a four-year scholarship. Full tuition at Vassar for four years was an offer that I could not disregard, especially in view of our limited resources. But the Alumnae Association may also have seen this as a means of between easing the divide between "town and gown."

The Dean interviewed me. It did not take long. Her height and ample size, stiff posture plus intimidating voice made her look like a puffed pigeon.

Discussion of my math grades made her even more aloof. She implied that if they had to take me, in view of my alumnae scholarship, perhaps I should major in history. That did it! A polite "thank you" and I was out the door.

Good fortune has sustained me many times throughout my adult life.

Such was the case when someone suggested I consider Green Mountain Junior College in Poultney, Vermont that later became a four-year institution. This turned out to be the ideal college for me. It was small, and the campus setting reflected the beautiful New England atmosphere. More importantly, the faculty was concerned not only with our formal education, but also with our social maturation and careers. Green Mountain was the mecca I sought. I was comfortable there and found other students who were as timid as I when they arrived. I enrolled in home economics but had no interest in learning to cook.

I nurtured a hidden agenda to eventually design kitchen equipment, the only option I saw to exercise my drive to be an inventor. I was ahead of my time for I would have excelled in designing today's gidgets and gadgets. But then, there was no call for my inventive spirit. Cooking classes were shrouded by my childhood antipathy of the kitchen, and sewing classes were a bore.

At Green Mountain, I found ceramics and interior decorating to be my most enjoyable classes. It was the instructor for these courses who started me on my career path. He told me he had heard of a profession where crafts and activities were used to rehabilitate persons with injured limbs. Unfortunately he mistook the name, as many people do, calling it physical, rather than occupational, therapy.

I investigated physical therapy and found nothing that drew on my skills or interest, so I dropped the idea. Only when I transferred to Syracuse University to complete my degree did I learn the difference. Immediately, I went to the nearby Syracuse Neuropsychiatric Hospital to see its department of occupational therapy. Like most hospitals, it was short staffed due to the war. The occupational therapy director offered me the opportunity to work as a volunteer. I eagerly accepted and volunteered one morning a week throughout my junior and senior years.

Excited that I had found the career I would follow, I returned for Christmas vacation in my junior year, ready to drop out of Syracuse. I planned to transfer immediately to the Boston School of Occupational Therapy, which then required only two years of college for admission.

My mother quickly informed me that I was not to leave until I had a college degree. She said after that, I could do anything I wanted, as soon as I earned the money to pay for it. Another delay, but hope was in sight.

Then, a watershed event came about through my father. A conscientious, daily reader of *The New York Times,* he sent me an article that said the Army Surgeon General's Office in Washington, D. C., was seeking college graduates with degrees in either home economics or fine arts, to be trained as occupational therapists. I wrote immediately for an application, even though I was more than a year away from graduation.

On entering my senior year, I met other students in my applied arts theory and design courses who also knew about the program. These classes were my all-time favorites, and for the first time, A's appeared on my report card.

The bombing of Pearl Harbor had occurred during my freshman year. By late 1944, our troops had been fighting in theatres of combat throughout the world for three full years. The Allies were hopeful that the war in Europe would soon end. For me, there was a downside of this promising news. Rumors were circulating that the Surgeon General's Office was canceling further training courses. My heart sank.

When I came back for Christmas as a senior in 1944, I told my father about the rumors and implied that there would be no need to apply. My father's words were clear and memorable: "You don't know that. There's been no announcement."

Then, suddenly, we were jolted back to the reality of war and its continued ravages of life and limb. News of the December 16th break in our lines at the Battle of the Bulge, in Belgium, flooded the airwaves by Christmas Day, and dominated the newscasts well into January.

The War Emergency Course for occupational therapy was not canceled.

From among the nine students at Syracuse who applied, only one other girl and I were accepted. Her father, a local orthopedic surgeon, had connections to the Surgeon General's Office; most of us felt that this had given her an unfair advantage. However, it was her father's contacts with people in the SGO that had lent strong credibility to the cancellation rumors. Now with the setback of the Battle of the Bulge and prospects of even greater casualties beyond, it seems feasible that this single battle caused the SGO to reverse its decision. One more training class of occupational therapy students would be conducted. This was the one to which we applied, and to which I was accepted.

Most applicants had better grades throughout their four years of college than I. I am convinced that my "ticket" was the letter of recommendation from the occupational therapist I had worked under as a volunteer. She indicated that not only did I have the aptitude, but I had maintained my composure while psychiatric patients were undergoing electric shock treatment. Although not part of my normal volunteer duties, due to staff shortages members of the occupational therapy department were sometimes assigned to assist in this procedure. Thus, she advised, I should be able to handle the impact of whatever war injuries I would encounter.

She was right. I would see horrendous war injuries to arms, legs, and faces. Also there would be amputees and spinal cord injuries to treat, plus men burned in armored tanks whose faces defied recognition. Later, there were those in need of rehabilitation following poliomyelitis. Indeed, my experience as a volunteer had helped prepare me for the impact of what I would face. I was ready.

But just waiting for the news from the Surgeon General's Office was agony for this anxious band of seniors. One day in March, I was astonished to see three envelopes in my mailbox, a record number. The long business envelope was a magnet for my eyes. I was so excited, I could hardly read. The letter informed me that I had been accepted for the War Emergency Course in occupational therapy.

Under a Civil Service appointment, I was to report on June 1st to the Milwaukee–Downer College for Women in Milwaukee, Wisconsin, to start training. With my appointment came a stipend of $100 a month for room, food, and bus fare. That was more money than I had ever seen. I was ecstatic. Call it luck, call it good fortune. Often throughout my career I have met requirements by "the skin of my teeth."

So it was that: (1) I had located an occupational therapy program to observe and confirm that this would be my chosen profession, (2) learned of the SGO program through a newspaper clipping, and (3) discovered this program was not canceled as rumored. But there were other factors at play as well.

I had the right degree, and luckily I met the age requirement of 21 years by a mere two months. Suddenly I recognized I was in the right place at the right time only because I had been moved up from first, to second grade the winter we lived in Florida. No one could have guessed that this decision fourteen years earlier would have such far-reaching consequences.

The Day of the Three Envelopes was memorable for other reasons.

Each of the other letters brought word of someone who had been killed in action. One, a high school classmate, was killed when the 4th Marine Division stormed the beaches of Iwo Jima.

The other, a glider pilot in Europe, had been transferred to the infantry when reinforcements were desperately needed to resist the Germans at the Battle of the Bulge. He survived the battle, only to be killed three weeks later in Saarburg, south of Luxembourg, as General George S. Patton's Third Army advanced toward the Rhine. Between the overjoyed response to my course acceptance and the distressing news of my friends who were killed in action, my emotions were truly on a roller coaster.

I was so eager to start my studies for occupational therapy, graduation could not have come soon enough, but world events that spring intervened to capture our attention. The nation was stunned and saddened by the unexpected death of President Franklin D. Roosevelt on April 12, 1945. Regrettably, he never saw the efforts of his wartime presidency reach conclusion. A mere 27 days later, hostilities ceased in Europe. This time, the whole nation was on an emotional roller coaster.

Graduation day finally arrived, but even during this momentous day, reminders of the country's three-and-a-half-year intense ordeal were never far away. The chancellor opened the ceremony with the announcement that someone was listening to a radio off stage, and if news of V.E. Day or Victory in Europe came, the graduation ceremony would be interrupted immediately to announce it. We watched. We waited. No one came forth, but the level of anticipation was electrifying.

However, a friend and classmate created a poignant reminder of this devastating war. She had returned for her last semester after dropping out to marry and have a child. Here she was, in a sea of black caps and gowns, carrying her six-month-old baby who had lived with her at her sorority house.

Matching the baby's pink organdy dress was a corsage of tea roses from her in-laws. Her husband, a B-17 pilot stationed in England, had been killed over the Ruhr three weeks before their baby was born.

The chancellor's voice cracked when he read her name as she walked across the platform to receive her diploma. Then he took the little girl into his arms, as if to baptize her, and said, "I hold in my arms, an honorary member of the Syracuse University Class of 1967 with full scholarship to the college of her choice." As everyone stood to applaud, I doubt there was a dry eye in the audience.

Excitement for me that day was intense. I had my degree and the prospect of professional training, but there was more. Strange as it may sound, for the first time in my life, I could happily say I was going "home." Our house was no longer a powder keg. It was truly home for the three of us. Grandma's bedroom was the new home of my parents' furniture, a welcome change from those cramped third-floor quarters of the previous 20 years.

No news of the war's end was announced before we started back that day. Our old car had no radio, so whenever we stopped, we eagerly asked for word. However, the following day, May 8, 1945, marked V.E. Day and relief. Having free access to Grandma's radio now, our attention was riveted on every word.

I reveled in being home, but it would be for a brief three weeks. Then I would leave for the adventuresome world beyond.

In retrospect, I can envision how very proud my father must have been for me to receive a college degree, something he had longed for all his life.

More than that, he knew he alone, had played the pivotal role, not only in discovering the SGO program, but in urging me to persist toward that goal despite rumors to the contrary.

Again I feared that our course might be canceled, on news of the end of the war in Europe, but my good fortune held. Sixty-four women from across the country, between the ages of 21 and 55, assembled at Milwaukee–Downer College for Women. It was one of a number of colleges providing this accelerated professional training.

Here were teachers, artists, grandmothers, and recent college graduates.

The older students brought maturity and life experience, but returning to the classroom and keeping up the pace was brutal. With two semesters compressed into four months, many dropped out.

We studied hard in classes six days a week and late into the night, trying to master everything the instructors pressed on us. There were classes in anatomy, then neuro-anatomy, kinesiology, and dissection, plus lectures about how to treat orthopedic and psychiatric patients. In addition, there were the craft classes. They were usually a breeze for art and home economics graduates; on the other hand, artists typically struggled through the science classes.

We commuted to school as straphangers on the crowded busses, all the while quizzing each other from our index cards about the origins, insertions, and innervations of muscles. I loved every minute of it. My former teachers would never have believed my grades that put me near the top of the class.

There were no dorms for us at the college, so we searched for housing anywhere near a bus line. An upstairs bedroom with a hot plate served as an apartment. A few of the older students had cars, but 12 gallons of gas a month on an "A" ration card for civilians did not go far. The stress level was high; out of the 64 who started 50 finished.

Those who completed this rugged, four-month curriculum were assigned to eight months of occupational therapy clinical training in army hospitals throughout the country. Our class, the last of perhaps 25 War Emergency Courses, trained about 1,000 occupational therapists in all.

Clinical training brought little homework, a welcome relief from the heavy academic workload of the previous months. Better than that, we were surrounded by hundreds of young men, a vivid contrast to my college years where the male student population had been quickly decimated after Pearl Harbor. Although there was a firm rule forbidding us to date patients, we sometimes suffered convenient memory loss. At the completion of a successful eight months of clinical training, we were eligible to sit for the National Occupational Therapy Registration exams. If we passed, we became fully qualified as professional staff members.

How fortuitous to have discovered this profession, which dovetailed so closely with my interest and aptitudes. Here was the career I had searched for, a career that allowed my inventive spirit and problem-solving skills to flourish. My enthusiasm for designing or adapting equipment never waned. In addition, modalities of the day, ceramics, weaving, or woodworking often required precise adaptation to meet the individual needs of a patient's rehabilitation. It was both challenging to motivate the patients and rewarding to see them engage in activities designed to ease their trauma.

During the war, dieticians and physical therapists were eligible for reserve officer commissions because, in many cases, they were serving overseas. Since servicemen were brought back for rehabilitation, occupational therapists worked in the 67 stateside army hospitals as civilians under Civil Service. After I became a registered occupational therapist in 1946, I continued as a civilian staff therapist.

In 1948 Congress established the Women's Medical Specialist Corps. This legislation made it possible for dieticians, physical and occupational therapists who met professional, physical, and emotional requirements to obtain regular army commissions. In 1956, as men joined these professions, the name was changed to the Army Medical Specialist Corps.

Distinct differences existed between a reserve and a regular army commission; each had its advantages. A regular army commission provided job security, essential for career officers, plus retirement in 20 years with its assured income and health benefits. Reserve officers served in wartime for the duration, and beyond, but were subject to a reduction in force at the discretion of the army when fewer personnel were needed. Thus, they were denied opportunity for continued employment until retirement, important to family men.

When our corps was formed, it offered women for the first time in their professional careers, the same opportunities and benefits as men: job security, health benefits, and retirement. However, women faced constrictions unique to them. As with anyone in service in time of war, they were "frozen" for the duration. This created a problem for female officers who married and wanted to leave the service to be with their husbands and start a family. Because of the legal commitment of their commission, they could not be released unless they became pregnant. Just such a freeze occurred within the second year of our being commissioned, with the advent of the Korean conflict.

Qualifying for a regular army commission involved a comprehensive process. Detailed applications were accepted during a narrow, three-month window. Six months later, screenings were conducted.

For a week, we underwent physical examinations, psychological testing, and rigorous interviews. A total of 50 women, including applicants for the Army Nurses Corps and the Women's Medical Specialist Corps were screened at Fort Dix, New Jersey, one of a number of such locations throughout the country.

What I feared most was that I was too thin to meet the weight requirement. The morning of our physicals, another occupational therapist, aptly named "Tiny," and I ate as many bananas as we could hold, but I still fell short. The kind nurse who weighed me understood that literally more than my weight, my career hung in the balance. She winked at the last pound, saying, "Looks like 96, don't you think?" I collaborated in a heartbeat, as this enabled me to meet the minimal requirement for my 5'7" height. I was thrilled once again to squeak through by the skin of my teeth.

Although I was thin, I was never anorexic; I had just grown into a taller version of that skinny little kid I had always been.

Throughout the week, one by one, each of us met the Screening Board, that we soon renamed the "Murder" Board. Sitting alone in a wooden armchair, I looked out at the eight foreboding officers who comprised my board. Virtually sitting at attention in a semicircle were the medical, dental, and administrative officers, plus an occupational therapist sent from the Surgeon General's Office, and lastly, a line officer who was a West Point graduate, now an infantry major.

Over the next hour or more, they had as many opportunities as they wished to engage me in a fast-moving dialogue, posing a wide range of questions. Their strategy was for someone at one side to engage me intently in one line of questioning, while another officer at the opposite side prepared to shoot his questions. Sometimes I was caught off guard at the sudden shift to a totally different set of queries. My voice was steady, but my hands shook.

The only question I remember came from the infantry officer who, out of the blue, asked what I would do if I became a prisoner of war. I knew all the pat answers: divulge name, rank, serial number, and nothing else under the Geneva Conventions. I knew that initiating a plan of escape was expected, especially of officers. But this man was concerned with issues beyond the conventional. "What did one bring to the situation to sustain oneself emotionally under such stress?" This was indeed a frightening prospect. As a young therapist of 24, it had never occurred to me to think such a thing could happen, but suddenly the possibility became real. I have forgotten my answer, but I had the strong impression he was speaking from personal experience.

Surprisingly, I had already seen POWs firsthand. More than a thousand German POWs, reportedly captured at El Alamein in North Africa, were held behind barbed wire within a garrisoned compound at the Newton D. Baker Army Hospital at Martinsburg, West Virginia. I had been assigned there as a civilian student for my clinical training; similar compounds had been set up at locations throughout the country. Most of army hospitals then carried a patient load of 1,000 to 3,000 servicemen and women. With the acute labor shortage, these POWs filled the need for manpower, augmenting the hospital workforce in the laundry, the kitchen, and various hospital departments.

Among these prisoners were field-grade officers ranking major and above. Some were trained engineers and physicians. Others had served as the commanding officers of these enlisted men when they were captured.

Imagine the indignation of these elite, arrogant Nazi officers as they were stripped of their rank and herded together with their enlisted troops. Humiliation followed, as their heads were shaved and they were issued gray uniforms affixed with huge black P W letters front and back. While our armed guards were marching them to and from their assignments the prisoners were required to maintain total silence and keep their eyes to the floor.

They had endured the early weeks of captivity including intensive stateside interrogation, but compared to what our POWs were experiencing in enemy hands, we felt these men were being treated ever so humanely. I often wondered what must have gone through the minds of our patients who were seriously burned and maimed. Conceivably they could have been injured at the hands of these healthy, rigorous Germans who walked in their midst. Regardless of the American soldiers' feelings, I never heard of any physical altercation initiated by the patients.

Rules were very strict. Absolutely no verbal, or eye, contact was permitted with any prisoner. Infractions were met with a court martial for members of the armed forces, and immediate dismissal for civilians like us. The one exception was the person in each department; in ours it was a staff occupational therapist who spoke German. Even as a civilian, she served under the Commandant of the POWs and in our department, she alone gave the prisoner his orders.

The purpose of sharing the following observations of German POW's is that it opens a tiny window of history known only to those involved at the time, and virtually unknown to the public then, or now.

Empty troop ships returning from Europe brought these prisoners to various east coast ports, including Philadelphia. There they were taken to their next destination by train with covered windows, often under cover of darkness. Travel by night precluded the prisoners' knowledge of the terrain. It also prevented Americans from learning of their location, or even their presence in this country. There was concern lest German sympathizers try to free them, or angry Americans attempt to kill them.

For many thousands their first destination was to an armed garrison hidden in the Pennsylvania mountains some 40 miles north of Gettysburg. This government-owned compound had been built for the Civilian Conservation Corps, a program developed by FDR during the Depression to provide thousands of young men with work on roads and in forests.

It was here in 1943, that German and Italian prisoners of war who had been captured in Africa were screened, interrogated thoroughly, and then moved to their next location. Some were used as translators and located near Washington. Others served in army hospitals in the east and Midwest.

After the war, when no longer needed as a POW compound, this CCC camp underwent yet another transformation. Privately owned at the time, it was used by various churches in the Washington area to hold weekend retreats for young adults.

I learned of the colorful wartime history cited above while attending one of these retreats in the early 1950s. By that time, I had been commissioned several years and was stationed at the Walter Reed Army Hospital in Washington, D. C.

At various times throughout my life, there have been recurrences of unlikely associations. So it had been with knowledge about some POWS, and so it would be again when I was sent overseas.

In 1955 I was assigned to the 98th Army General Hospital in Neübrueke-am-der-Nahe in Germany, some 45 miles east of Luxembourg. This tiny village was composed of six houses, a post office and the local beer hall called the "gasthaus."

At the 98th, I came to know Dr. Müeller, one of the German contract orthopedists who shared with me his experience as a POW. Captured in North Africa, he had been confined for two years in a prison compound at an army hospital in Battle Creek, Michigan; there he was assigned to the surgical pavilion. As a result of his experience, he was inspired to attend medical school when he returned to Germany.

While I was assigned to the 98th General Hospital it provided the medical support for the men and their dependents at the enormous U.S. Artillery post at

Here is a new 2nd Lieutenant, all 96 pounds of her. This photo was taken during a visit to see Ora and Flora Porter at their home in Oswego, New York, 16 years after the winter in Florida when I was moved up a grade. This enabled me to meet the critical age requirement for occupational therapy training in the War Emergency Course by two months.

This is the passport photo of my parents when they came overseas to visit. My mother, then 75, lived to the age of 80, my father to 90.

Baumholder, 15 miles away. It was through Dr. Müeller that I learned this post was where General Erwin Rommel, known as the "Desert Fox," for his shrewd military tactics, trained his Afrika Corps. It was here that Dr. Müeller and presumably the POWs I had observed during my training, had been prepared for combat in North Africa and were subsequently captured.

In reflecting on these events, a mystery developed, but there is a very plausible explanation. My memory seemed clear that we were told that most of those POWs in West Virginia had been captured at El Alamein. During my research for verification, however, it became apparent to me that the Americans would not have taken prisoners there. It was the strident British General Bernard Montgomery and his troops that had fought Rommel's troops in that famous battle to protect the Suez Canal. I realized one plausible explanation. The British would have been hard pressed at that time to feed more people in their beleaguered kingdom. Therefore, the German POWs whom they captured in Africa, were brought to the United States on returning troop ships to prison camps here that held more than 400,000 prisoners.

Some soldiers captured in the Italian campaign were also brought here. But after D-Day, German captives were primarily kept on European soil and put to work in the supply chain far behind the lines. Exceptions were those whose background knowledge could be used by military intelligence; they were sent to England.

Seven years before I went overseas, I was undergoing my required interrogation before the Screening Board, but that was not the only questioning going on at that time. Plenty of questions were being asked about me around my hometown as well.

Once while I was home on leave my parents related how concerned our neighbors were to have the FBI at their doors investigating my past.

Although the neighbors were directed to keep the incident secret, that did not stop our town's rumor mills. After three people realized that they had all been questioned about me, speculation took over.

My former fifth and sixth grade teacher, Becky, the eternal queen of gloom and doom, asked my mother what kind of trouble I was in. I am sure espionage, or sedition, headed her list. My mother explained that the background check was part of the security clearance I needed to receive my commission. The teacher shook her head, looked down toward the floor, and said in her depressed monotone, "I never thought Barbara would ever make anything of herself." This became our family joke as I advanced in my career.

Having met the requirements to be commissioned a second lieutenant, I was sent to Fort Sam Houston for basic military training for women officers. I survived those six weeks that included lectures on medical, administrative, and military procedures, plus marching drills. That was the easy part. Belly-crawling under barbed wire amid a few scorpions scampering from the scorching heat near San Antonio, Texas was more of a challenge.

In 1948, 34 officers were selected to pioneer the Regular Army Occupational Therapy Branch originally named the Woman's Medical Specialist Corps which also included a Physical Therapy Branch and Dietician's Branch.

We were commissioned sequentially by age. As I was next to the youngest, I ranked 33rd. My serial number, J-33 is so short it would come as a surprise to anyone who has been in service.

In time, our ranks rose to about 100 officers, and included men by 1956, at which time the name was changed to the Army Medical Specialist Corps. The Occupational Therapy Branch has remained a very small, proud, and close-knit group.

During my 20-year career, I was assigned to various army hospitals throughout the United States and overseas. I also served as a faculty member and Assistant Chief of the Army School of Occupational Therapy at the Medical Field Service School, Fort Sam Houston, Texas. This school was accredited by the American Occupational Therapy Association in 1952. During the three years of its operation it trained perhaps as many as 45 to 50 2nd Lieutenants for the 12-month curriculum prior to their going to army hospitals for eight months of clinical training.

My first two years in Civil Service as a staff occupational therapist were credited toward my retirement. Thus, I was able to retire in 1966 with the rank of major, after only 18 years of commissioned service.

In 1964, I was named among 22 to become a Charter Fellow of the American Occupational Therapy Association, and was a member of the World Federation of Occupational Therapists from its inception. In 1992, I concluded a professional career that spanned 46 rewarding years.

The significance of this photo is that it shows the caduceus of the Women's Medical Specialist Corps, the only one in silver ever issued by the Army. This caduceus with black letters "W" superimposed on the "S" was worn from 1948–1956. Men were then joining the occupational therapy profession for the first time, thus the name was changed to the Army Medical Specialist Corps and designated by a gold caduceus and a black "S."

Of the original 34 officers granted a regular army commission in the Occupational Therapy Branch of the Women's Medical Specialist Corps, the author was the only one who served 20 years, to reach retirement.

25

An Emerging Fifth Freedom

In 1949, as a newly commissioned second lieutenant, I was selected by the Army Surgeon General's Office to attend the six-month graduate program for post-polio rehabilitation at the Georgia Warm Springs Foundation, in Warm Springs, Georgia.[1] I was the only army occupational therapist ever given this privilege and I was surprised to receive an opportunity such as this so early in my career.

My civilian roommate and I were also the first occupational therapists accepted for the program at this center, known worldwide as the premier location for the rehabilitation of poliomyelitis.[2] Patients came from all over the United States, Canada, and foreign countries.

This experience also opened a window through which I was able to witness first-hand, another side of history about the world's most prominent polio victim, but I could not have recognized this at the time. When historian Hugh Gregory Gallagher revealed the full extent of the late president's disability in his 1995 book, *FDR's Splendid Deception,* the public was shocked.

I, too, was somewhat, but not entirely, surprised. Immediately, I began to reflect on my own observations; this unique point of view emanated from my experience at the Georgia Warm Springs Foundation four years after the president's death. Now I began to recognize unexpected insights about this man. I realized how his life experience was completely controlled by this crippling disease, thereby enabling him to perceive what drastic changes in society were needed for those who were also afflicted with serious physical disabilities.

Before I proceed, I must set the stage by which readers of today can grasp the devastating nature, trauma, and fear of the nearly forgotten disease of poliomyelitis, or polio as it is commonly referred to. It is important to understand its paralytic outcome and the rehabilitative measures that emerged to meet the multitude of the needs of polio patients. Even more important is the need

1 This currently is named The Roosevelt Rehabilitation Institute.

2 This disease was originally called "infantile paralysis," for its devastating outcome to children, but adults were affected by the polio virus, up to fifty-five years of age or more at onset. This virus was transmitted by minute droplets, expelled through the respiratory system.

to recognize the way our rigid social climate negatively impacted lives of the disabled at that time.

The initial, acute stage of polio required three weeks of isolation in a hospital. Children were especially traumatized by being taken from their parents immediately upon diagnosis. They were placed in an isolation ward among other children, who were often screaming in pain and fright. Parents were devastated, and worried that they might never see their child alive again. This dreadful period imposed emotional isolation for the victim when love and support of the family was needed most.

Not only could children not see their parents, but they could not even see the faces of the nurses and doctors who wore scary masks and sterile white hospital gowns. Symptoms included the sudden onset of a raging fever and brutally painful muscle cramps that were partially mitigated by the Sister Kenny method of applying hourly hot packs. Hot packs became unbearable in the stifling heat of summer, since air-conditioning was unknown.

Nurses tried valiantly to prevent the patient's joints from tightening during the acute phase when they were in isolation. Nevertheless, elbow, hips, and knees would usually require continued, painful stretching over the following months. Only when the joints were mobile could opposing muscles that had been stretched and weakened by the disease have any chance of recovering their function. If improvement was to take place in these paralyzed muscles, it normally occurred within the first three to six months.

In the rehabilitation phase that followed the period of isolation, physical therapists were charged with the painful stretching of these tight joints three or four times a day. It was difficult for them to inflict such pain on adult patients, but imagine how hard it was as therapists to treat tiny infants and children who began to scream whenever they approached the crib.

To instill in the parents how imperative it was for them to continue this painful routine when their child was released from six months of rehabilitation, must have been torturous for therapist, parents, and child.

Stretching to maintain joint mobility was equally important for adolescents and adults. Unless the patient's legs could be straightened, it would be impossible for them to be fitted with long-leg braces with knee-locks. Their hips would also require stretching, so they could stand upright to walk. In order to use crutches the elbows had to be straight and arm muscles strong enough to do so.

It was not uncommon for the respiratory muscles to be paralyzed, requiring the patient to be placed in a body-length respirator called an iron lung. In addition to the fright of being in an isolation ward, and in an iron lung, the added fear of possible power failure of this electrical device during thunder storms was overwhelming. At such times, an aide stood by, so that if the power failed, he could manually pump the handle at the far end to maintain a stable breathing rhythm.

Whenever the power failed, hospital staff and maintenance crew alike ran to take up position at one of the many iron lungs of patients who were out of isolation. Imagine a patient's inherent fear, knowing his or her life was totally dependent on others. Day or night, death was but a breath away.

In time, some of these patients with "bulbar polio" as it was called, would recover. For others, like a local grade school acquaintance of mine, this was a life sentence. Patients could have bulbar polio yet have no paralysis of other muscles. Some fully recovered. Most tragic were those bulbar polio patients who had no paralysis of other muscles, but might never walk again, so dependent were they on an iron lung.

One of the most mystifying aspects of polio was the fact that pregnant women were much more susceptible during the first and third trimesters, but they were unduly immune during the second. A former college roommate contracted bulbar polio while she was pregnant with her fourth child. She told of the sleepless nights during those many weeks she spent in an iron lung. In a large room filled with many, each one had their own distinct, noisy, juxtaposed rhythm. She recovered and had no apparent physical weakness thereafter, only to succumb to the post-polio syndrome with its incipient muscle weakness, in her elder years.[3]

If a pregnant woman contracted polio in her third trimester and delivered her baby while she was still confined to isolation, the newborn would be rushed out before the mother had barely seen it. Although the infant's exposure to the virus would have been brief, it was placed in an isolation unit for newborns primarily to protect other infants, or to allay their parents' fears.

Growing up with the fear of this disease, during the severe polio epidemics, is still vivid in my mind. In summer, children were prohibited from playing with others outside the home or from going to the local swimming hole. It was feared that chilling of the body brought on the disease. Sunday school picnics and family outings were canceled. Movie theaters might be closed, as they were considered to be too risky. Often, fear reached a point of hysteria.

Some summers, there were no epidemics. Other summers, an epidemic would rage in one region of the country while another region would be relatively unaffected. Outbreaks were particularly prevalent in cities where people had close contact. When the doctor arrived at the apartment of a child suspected of having polio, the police were called and the child was taken immediately to the nearest hospital isolation unit.

When someone sneezed they might inadvertently spray the immediate area with droplets of the virus. No one could tell when a person might suddenly develop chills, high fever, and painful muscles. Within a day, their limbs and/or the respiratory muscles could be paralyzed.

Paralysis was spotty, but there was a predilection for certain muscle groups: those that brought the thumb into position to grasp a pencil or spoon; the deltoids at the top of the shoulder that lift the arm; the muscles of the trunk that stabilize the shoulder for arm movement; and the large muscles of the hip and leg.

Post-polio victims who were dependent on crutches or a clumsy wooden wheelchair were rarely seen in public. For them, there was little or no access

3 According to Gallagher's account, in the year preceding the president's death, he became very depressed by an awareness that the level of his remaining muscle strength was steadily declining. Could it be, this was the onset of the "post-polio syndrome," we have only recently come to recognize?

to the outside world and in rural areas, at least, they were often sequestered in a back room of the house. Teachers were assigned from the public school to tutor these children. If children we knew became afflicted and could no longer attend school, we might never see them again.

After experiencing physical and psychological isolation during the acute phase, the social isolation polio victims now faced was inordinately cruel. So fearsome was the specter of this disease, the public could not face its devastating consequences with compassion. The considered opinion of the times was that it would be too upsetting to the public to see them in a crippled state.

In 1919 when FDR succumbed to polio, the public equated physical disability with weakness of character and an inability to perform. In a climate such as this that forced disabled children and wheelchair-bound adults from public view, anyone with a promising future was faced with a heart-wrenching dilemma. According to Gallagher, since Roosevelt was at the beginning of an avowed legal and political career, his family and his political advisors decided to hide the extent of his disability during any public appearance.

Throughout his years of public life, photographers were forbidden to take a photo or direct a newsreel camera on him that showed the president in his wheelchair; reportedly only one such photo exists. Likewise, out of respect for the man and the Office of the Presidency, ethics of the times kept photographers and newsmen from revealing that they had ever observed his dependence on one.

FDR first came to Warm Springs in 1924, five years after being stricken. At his instigation, he and several blacksmiths fashioned a set of crude, long-leg, wrought-iron braces, hinged at the knees. These were attached to a sturdy, padded, metal waist band, hinged at the hip. Supportive devices such as this were previously unknown. This heavy, iron prototype that enabled him to stand also became an important breakthrough that benefited countless other polio victims. Due to the climate of our society, the president never would have wanted credit for this contribution.

Gallagher revealed that later his stainless steel braces were artfully hidden by a coat of black paint. These were attached to his black shoes, beneath extra-long pants that covered his shoes when he was seated. Despite his acknowledged dependence on crutches to walk, he discarded them for political reasons. Only carefully staged images of his arduous, tempered gait were given public view. His right hand gripped the cane he ground into the floor, while his left hand could be seen clutching the elbow of the son who was usually responsible for this, Franklin, Jr.

Another significant contribution of FDR to polio rehabilitation was also unknown until it was revealed by Gallagher. Long before Roosevelt was president he and his personal physical therapist at Georgia Warm Springs Foundation, Miss Alice Lou Plastridge (Converse) RPT, developed a standardized, five-step grading system to measure any change in muscle strength. This system started with "O" for a totally paralyzed, flaccid muscle, ranging to "N" for normal strength, with "P" for poor and "F" for fair, as "F-" and "F+," to indicate the intervening levels of strength. At the Warm Springs Foundation, patients were re-tested by their physical therapist at monthly intervals to determine progress and the potential benefit from continued rehabilitation.

Although there was little reason to hold out hope for further improvement so many years after the onset of his polio, the president remained relentless in his efforts to regain muscle strength. Throughout his life, he exercised his weakened legs in the buoyancy of a warm pool. At Warm Springs perhaps this was done to inspire others, as much as for himself.

Whenever possible, newly afflicted patients who were lucky enough to be accepted for treatment and rehabilitation at the Georgia Warm Springs Foundation were transferred there shortly after they were out of the isolated, acute phase. The rehabilitation phase was as intense physically as the acute phase had been painful. Training of a patient's paralyzed muscles to maximize their function, fell to both the physical and occupational therapists. Each therapist was carefully trained to identify and test the level of muscle strength in accord with this grading system. The foremost goal of the patient's therapy was to balance the power of opposing muscles over each joint. It was my very good fortune to be trained in muscle testing by the Director of Rehabilitation, Miss Plastridge, the physical therapist who achieved worldwide acclaim for her contributions to polio rehabilitation.

Physical therapists were responsible for upper and lower extremity muscle exercise. The earliest phase of this treatment might include one or more pool sessions daily as well as additional periods of exercise and stretching in the physical therapy clinic or at bedside.

The rehabilitation pool of naturally warmed spring water had a flat floor for about 20 wooden tables, called "plinths"; each was positioned inches below water level. Varied heights accommodated patients from toddlers to large men. A rubber pillow supported the head. Therapists and patients were clad in bathing suits to carry out the prescribed program. The warm water was relaxing, making it somewhat easier for the patient to endure the painful stretching of tight muscles and joints. The water's buoyancy often enabled slight movement in an arm or leg that was too weak to move otherwise. Pool time was an emotionally uplifting part of the day. When even slight progress was evident in a patient, it was a time for all to rejoice.

Physical therapists were also responsible for training their patients in the proper use of long-leg braces, of crutches, in gait training, and methods of adapting to life in a wheelchair.

Whereas physical therapists could support a specific joint and isolate movement of muscles or muscle groups to stimulate and strengthen them, treatment was more complex for the occupational therapists to apply properly. They were required to observe and palpate the muscle "belly" as the patient worked on appropriate craft activities that were selected to improve the strength in weak hand and arm muscles. Occupational therapy activities included hand-weaving, light woodworking, leatherwork, and any activity that could be properly directed to strengthen those muscles. Most of the polio patients were too paralyzed to do more than the most modified forms of these crafts, a challenge to therapist and patient alike.

I was excited to be working with the brace makers at Warm Springs, pioneers in this newly developing field of rehabilitation for the specific needs of polio victims. I learned how to design and fit the newest type of lightweight, aluminum hand braces that were originated there. These metal braces were lined with soft doeskin for gentle support of the patient's wrist and finger joints to prevent the stretching of weak muscles into useless, frozen positions.

These Warm Springs hand braces became the foundation upon which to attach functional, assistive devices. I soon recognized how I might apply my inventive aptitude to provide a modicum of independence for my paralyzed patients. For instance, I devised a way to secure a rubber-tipped pencil to the hand brace so that a patient with fingers too weak to use the keyboard of an electric typewriter could now do so. This usually required that they be supported at the wrist and elbow by doeskin arm slings suspended from above their wheelchair by lightweight springs or rubber IV tubing to promote a horizontal, lofting movement that also stimulated shoulder muscles.[4]

People with established careers as physicians, lawyers, executives, and professors had their own special requirements if they were to continue any aspect of their life work. Our challenge as occupational therapists was to conceptualize and create functional devices for their specific needs. In addition, many patients needed to have a pen, spoon, or toothbrush secured to their hand brace for maximum independence in their normal daily living activities. Each assistive device was customized to best meet the needs of the wage earner, housewife, or child.

One of the most significant elements of the Warm Springs routine occurred every Monday. The medical staff, therapists, brace makers, and the four or five physical and occupational therapy graduate students gathered while the Medical Director, Robert Bennett, M.D., reviewed as many as 25 cases during teaching rounds. One by one, the physical therapist presented her patient in a wheelchair or stretcher to summarize findings of the current muscle test. Dr. Bennett noted this, their hand and leg bracing, and whether or not there was improvement in the patient's wheelchair function and ambulation skills. The occupational therapist then cited the status of the patient's independence in daily living needs through adapted equipment for the upper extremities.

---

4 The folding Everest & Jennings wheelchair of steel tubing with a leather seat was newly available at that time, now that the need for metal in the wartime munitions factories and urgent post-war civilian needs had been met. This timely innovation had been inspired and designed, in part at least, by Mr. Jennings, an engineer who allegedly had come to Warm Springs for his own polio rehabilitation.

Arm slings were suspended from a right-angled 3/8-inch metal rod secured to the uprights of the wheelchair. These rods extended three feet above the chair, and protruded forward several feet, so that cuffs for the wrist and elbow could be suspended at the proper position to elevate the patient's arms about 45 degrees.

This was an anxious time for the patient and each of the therapists. They had dedicated hours to arduous, and often painful, therapy; strong bonds developed. It was especially sad when the therapist had to report that a plateau of improvement had become evident in the past two months. That usually signaled a termination of treatment at Warm Springs. With only a hundred beds, others were eagerly waiting their turn.

After each case was reviewed, Dr. Bennett would dictate a note for the patient's chart. Sometimes a brief discussion followed, or he would offer some perspective on what procedures they were doing now that differed from those of a year or so before. He often indicated trends he was recognizing, and he might cite the most recent research on prevention of this disease that was reported in medical journals, but the results were still years away. These weekly sessions of five to six hours were exhaustive, but they were by far the most comprehensive learning experience I ever had over an occupational therapy career that spanned 46 years.

The new functional braces developed here gradually gained universal use for polio patients throughout the country. Later, patients with arthritis and various neurological conditions, such as multiple sclerosis, benefited as well. It was exciting to watch these cutting-edge developments at Warm Springs. Therapists and brace makers from Tuskegee Institute came to learn how to duplicate the Warm Springs bracing methods and apply these to the hundred or more polio patients being treated there. Therapists and staff members from the Leprosy Colony in Carville, Louisiana, arrived to see the advances in leg and hand bracing that might be beneficial to their patients. Contractures of the wrist and fingers were a paramount problem for leprosy patients, so hand bracing helped to stabilize the joints and slow the decline of function.

During those six months I was privileged to study at the Georgia Warm Springs Foundation, I observed bits of history from which I was later able to develop my insights. Changes that Roosevelt could only have dreamed of, are now part of our society, a part of our history. Changes that I consider can be directly attributed to him have required half a century to materialize. Only through distant hind-sight can we recognize the profound acumen he possessed that made his dream for the handicapped a reality.

Allow me to describe what always impressed me about the enduring warmth and deep affection for the president that radiated the halls and grounds at Warm Springs. The late president had loved being there for many reasons. This facility offered warm rehabilitation pools and the best care available anywhere. He also enjoyed being there because he could relax in this close-knit social structure among fellow polio victims.

The most remarkable tribute to this man of winning charm was the fact that many patients who were being treated there during the times he visited were fully aware of the degree of his paralysis. Like members of the press, they too kept the condition of this wheelchair-bound leader confidential. They were imbued with such awe and respect for his indomitable efforts to regain muscle function that they never betrayed his trust. They were also grateful to him for making therapy at Warm Springs known and available to them.

Unknowingly, I was witness to this prevailing phenomenon of confidentiality about the president's condition. It is possible that some degree of secrecy may have arisen out of the wartime need for national security, although by 1949 when I was there, this factor alone would have been irrelevant. I recognize, in retrospect, how the wonderful staff of doctors, therapists, and brace makers were so protective of FDR's image that they, and the people in the town surrounding this "mecca" on the hill, kept the extent of the president's paralysis sealed from the public long after his death. Throughout my training there, nothing of it escaped the lips of the brace makers, or his personal therapist, with whom I shared my childhood experiences about living near Hyde Park, since she told of having visited the president there at various times. After reading Gallagher's book, I was able to appreciate the depth of their loyalty. Only now, 63 years after his death, am I able to recognize what an enormous impact our long-standing president had in shaping attitudes of our society.

When I left Warm Springs in July of 1949, I was assigned to the Walter Reed Army Hospital in Washington, D.C. I was challenged immediately with putting to use all that I had learned during my training in rehabilitation. We were then in the midst of a summer polio epidemic and, at the Walter Reed Army Hospital, there were numerous wards of post-polio patients. All of the servicemen and women from the army and air force whose home was located east of the Mississippi River were brought for treatment to Walter Reed, while those from west of this location, were flown to the Letterman Army Hospital in San Francisco. These patients were past the acute, infectious stage, out of isolation, and while some were in iron lungs, they could be safely moved by air. Service personnel and their dependents, including wives and children from infants to adolescents, were brought here for treatment. It was most shocking to see whole families, afflicted at the same time, be transferred together to Walter Reed for rehabilitation.

The sudden and devastating nature of polio is exemplified by one of my most memorable patients, a full colonel in the air force. He was a flight commander, leading his squadron from Hickam Field in Hawaii to Travis Air Force Base in Sacramento, California. This handsome, healthy-appearing 6'2" officer told how he climbed into the pilot's seat in Hawaii, but by the time they landed in California, he was shaking from chills and unable to move his pain-ridden arms and legs. The pilot's seat had to be removed from the floor of the plane so he could be lifted out, never to walk another step.

At Walter Reed, it was crucial to provide these patients our very best care. It was also incumbent upon me to train as many occupational therapists as possible in the principles of hand bracing and the design of assistive devices.

Summers then were very different than anything one can envision today. We were still years away from the discovery of the vaccines by Drs. Jonas Salk and Albert Sabine, which would eradicate this frightful disease. Epidemics affecting more than 150,000 people annually between June and October continued for the

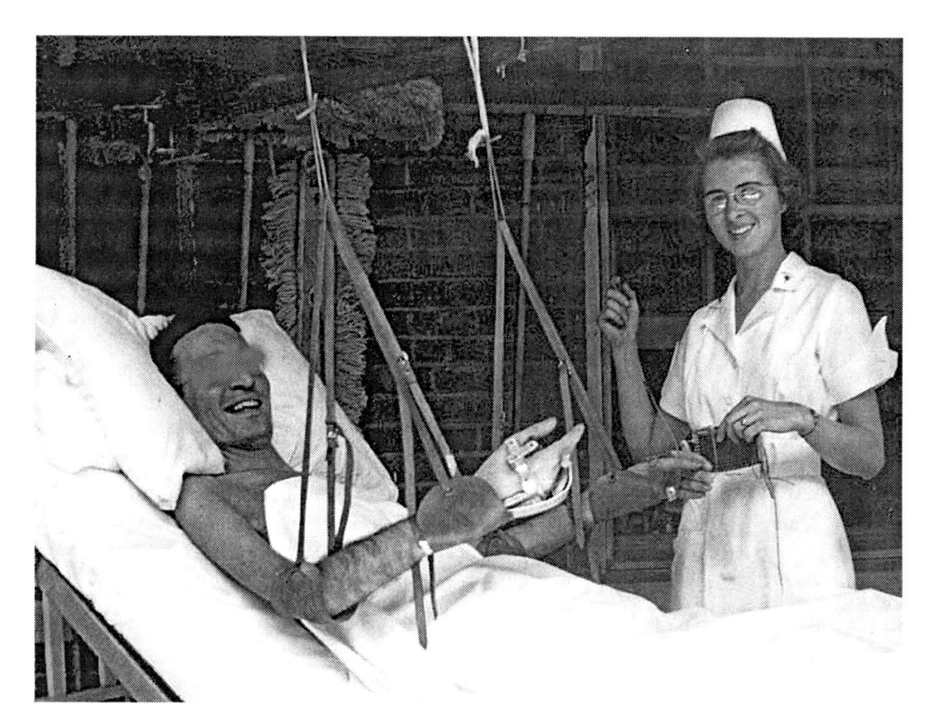

Many service men and women and their dependents who had polio were treated at Walter Reed Army Hospital. Arm slings and hand braces were patterned after those at the Warm Springs Polio Foundation, Warm Springs, Georgia. This is where the Army sent me to train for six months in the rehabilitation of victims of this devastating disease. The occupational therapy goal here was to motivate the patient to mobilize his remaining muscle function.

next four years. School openings in September were sometimes delayed until after the first frost, when the epidemics subsided.

The Salk vaccine came into use in 1953, and within a few years, all of this was changed. Fortunately, polio epidemics are history. No longer do children or adults who would otherwise have been afflicted face possible death, excruciating pain, long rehabilitation, or the need for assistive devices.

During his presidency, Franklin Delano Roosevelt helped to relieve poverty-stricken citizens in the Great Depression and led the free world in wartime. The public could not be informed at the time of those earlier contributions to polio rehabilitation, such as the leg braces he designed, or the muscle-grading system he helped develop. From my perspective, there was another little-recognized but far-reaching achievement, one of historic proportions.

Having had to cope with his own severe limitations, he not only recognized the needs of the physically-impaired for urgent change in our society, he set about to inspire it. So subtle and so obscure was his approach, it is truly remarkable that he would be able to alter attitudes that were so firmly entrenched. He alone could do this by virtue of his own condition, his empathic point of view, and his position in the eyes of the world. The enormous impact of those dramatic changes he set in motion can be recognized only in retrospect.

Legendary was his rapid response to the economic needs of those in the bread lines, who had lost everything to the Crash of '29. What was less apparent was that within the first year of his presidency, FDR set about with equal determination to address the needs of others who were afflicted with poliomyelitis. With his winsome personality and passion he introduced what would later become the *March of Dimes*. This was the first, full-scale, public, fund-raising charity. It was celebrated each year with great fanfare on his birthday, January 30th.[5]

He often came to the Georgia Warm Springs Foundation to celebrate this event; newsreel photographers were welcomed by his broad smile. There he sat on a simple wooden chair, surrounded by dozens of adults and children in wheelchairs, while others stood in their long-leg braces, supported by crutches. Each was championing his or her fight against the resulting paralysis of polio. They were grateful to their friend and president for his support and humble acceptance of their plight. Here, for the world to see, his smile implied that the public should accept their condition, as well. The press loved it, and so did he. Every theatre carried impressive newsreels of these events, and the public flocked to see them.

Adroitly deflecting public awareness from his own disability, he focused their attention on an endearing cherub, chosen each year as the "poster child," to highlight this fund-raising campaign. Life-size pictures of a pink-frocked little three-year-old stood in "dwarf-size" long-leg braces and crutches, smiling into the eyes of those who hastened to add their dime to such a commanding cause.

Through the *March of Dimes*, Roosevelt enabled people, who could barely spare a dime during the depths of the Depression, to feel good. They graciously gave what small sum they could for those who were obviously in greater need. It was their earnest hope that some form of prevention could come about to protect others in the future. In my opinion, it was FDR's vivacious inspiration for this compelling public concern that helped to forge our character as individuals and as a nation to be a "giving" society. Whether for polio or cerebral palsy, for earthquakes far and wide, hurricanes, floods, or tsunamis, people of this country have been recognized for their human concerns and their gracious giving to those in urgent need.

What a lasting legacy this is.

Contrary to popular belief at that time about the innate weakness of persons who had a physical disability, the president demonstrated he was neither weak in character nor unable to perform the duties of his office due to polio. He enabled the public to acknowledge this by his forthright leadership and infectious charm. Consequently, people were able to follow his lead in molding society's attitudes. More than anyone else, FDR helped to change the world's landscape for the

5 The initial fund-raiser for polio, called The President's Birthday Ball, was held in Washington and other cities on January 30th, 1934. Large, annual fund-raising events like this continued until 1937. It was then, that a year-round campaign for contributions was solicited from millions of small donors, urged to give just a dime. It was aptly re-named the *March of Dimes*.

disabled. He evoked a climate of acceptance about disability, unknown at that time. Out of this environment, legislators slowly implemented laws that required public access for the physically-impaired. Employing the handicapped became an enlightened business mantra professed by many, practiced by some.

The president's four freedoms of World War II called for freedom of speech and expression; the freedom of every person to worship God in his own way; freedom from want; and freedom from fear. I have labeled the unseen seeds of this enduring and profoundly life-changing legacy a "fifth" freedom. This promotes freedom from prejudice for physical, emotional, and intellectual impairment and public access for the handicapped to employment, recreation, educational opportunities, and civic engagement that the able-bodied take for granted.

As an occupational therapist, I feel privileged to have witnessed the fringes of history that helped to institute positive attitudes toward the disabled. As president, Franklin Delano Roosevelt set the climate of acceptance for freedom from physical and societal barriers, so the handicapped could lead a full and productive life as he had done as leader of the free world.

26

Just Desserts: Just Dazed in Vermont

It was a stifling hot day in August 1971. In silence and without one tear, I pulled the kitchen door shut for the last time and turned the old, nickel key. This was the same key my family had used for more than 75 years since Grandpa acquired this house. Called a "skeleton" key, it, or others like it, could possibly have unlocked any house in town.

As a young child, it was difficult to understand the issues involved in the previous owner's $1,200 unpaid grocery bill and Grandpa's absorbing his mortgages in exchange for the house. In my creative mind, I envisioned Grandpa walking down the hill from his store carrying a large bag of groceries in each arm. I thought Grandpa had gotten a pretty good deal.

My father lived another ten years after my mother's death in 1962. He resided in Florida, first for the winter, later full-time. At the age of 86, he made a full recovery after two hip fractures six weeks apart. Several years before he died at nearly 91, he decided the house should be sold.

The time was right for me as well. I had retired from the army and opened my private practice in occupational therapy in Princeton, New Jersey, in 1966. This was the first free-standing occupational therapy practice in the United States, meaning it was unaffiliated with any institution or physician's practice. It also served annually as an observation clinic for students in the occupational therapy curricula at Columbia and New York Universities; the Universities of North Carolina and Florida sent their graduate students for three-month clinical affiliations.

This practice was dedicated to clinical research and the treatment of children and adults with learning disorders. In 1980, the text, *An Holistic Approach to the Treatment of Learning Disorders*, was published, and has been used in occupational therapy curricula, and by clinicians, in various English-speaking countries. Recently, it has been translated into Dutch.

Having my own practice allowed me to schedule the time I needed to close the house. I returned to Bangall to spend several weeks sorting items for the auctioneer and preparing the property to be put on the market.

There was some advantage to being an only child. There would be no quibbling of siblings, nor re-opening of long-buried jealousies. On the other hand, I faced this enormous task alone. I sorted, made decisions, and cleared nine rooms, cellar, and attic, plus the barn and outbuildings during the humid, hot days of August.

The dark, rickety door opposite the third-floor landing of my childhood years opened into an unlit, still-scary attic. Under the scorching slate roof, I unpacked rows of roll-top trunks mothballed for generations.

I sorted through dust-laden junk that had escaped discard. Antique collectors were attracted by old coffee grinders, tea canisters too rusty to use, and mildewed maps of our area that were drawn generations before my grandparents were around.

Items such as these were cherished by people whose lives were never entwined in them. Most vivid was my distaste for the multiple sets of gold-trimmed Lenox washbowls, pitchers and commodes; our attic produced enough for a vintage hotel.

Memories flashed. It was these that had caused me the greatest embarrassment when I brought home a boyfriend who took indoor plumbing as a given. The ecstasy of antique dealers over these relics equaled the humiliation they had heaped on me.

Since the house had been undisturbed for several years, wasps, flies, spiders, and bats enjoyed one continuous jamboree and death march in this creepy, shuttered attic. Any creatures still alive resented my intrusion, whether in the attic, the dirt-floored cellar or the outbuildings. Inadvertently touching a soft-bellied bat was the scariest.

As I pulled the kitchen door shut and locked it for the last time, I gladly closed this chapter of my life as well. I hung the key in its accustomed place for the auctioneer. He would pump value into the remaining furnishings of the Knickerbocker house, in silent testimony to a long-past Victorian age.

Exhausted, I slumped into the driver's seat of my royal blue Edsel and backed the fully loaded car out of our driveway for the last time.

Boxes, some fragile, were packed in the trunk and on back seat. As I started back to Princeton, I drove cautiously along the peaceful, winding Taconic Parkway and began to relax. I had the satisfaction that not only was the job done, but that it had been done in ways my parents would have appreciated.

Suddenly my thoughts were interrupted and I slammed on the brake. The entire load was thrust forward; boxes flew and a bookcase cracked me on the head.

Dazed and saddened, I pulled over to the shoulder. What should I do now? It would be the last opportunity to carry out my plan to annihilate that dreadful remnant of childhood. As distant in time as my association with those dessert plates had been, the emotional compactor in my stomach churned in an instant.

How could I have overlooked them on my final sweep through the house? They were sitting on my mother's enamel-top table beside the kitchen door. Under the sweltering August heat, I reflected on the number of times I had mentally rehearsed my final act.

I had often pictured picking up those six dessert plates, locking the door for the last time, and carrying them around to the desolate concrete steps at the back of the house. Chosen with the care and planning of one about to commit an execution, this would be the perfect spot to demolish them.

These plates epitomized our lives and evoked a kaleidoscope of my childhood. Slowly my pulse returned to normal, my mind to a more rational point of view. I convinced myself I had seen the last of them and reluctantly rolled the car into the southbound lane.

Memory of those dessert plates faded from my conscious thought. I was living a richly creative and rewarding life. I was fully absorbed in developing my occupational therapy practice, designing and patenting therapeutic equipment, and conducting ten years of clinical research for my textbook.

Then, in 1976 I married a Princeton psychiatrist and psychoanalyst with whom I had been stationed in the army. I shared the tremendous joy and satisfaction of helping to raise his two fine young boys through adolescence and into adulthood.

As a family, we often vacationed in Vermont and by the mid-1980s, we moved there from New Jersey. My husband resumed his private practice and was a clinical professor at Dartmouth Medical School across the Connecticut River in New Hampshire.

Our move to Vermont put us closer to my younger stepson, Daniel, who was graduating from the University of Vermont and later finished medical school there. My older stepson, Mark, was living in California, after completing law school.

One weekend, during the fall foliage season, our friends, Betty Ann Affleck and her companion Harry Mayerovich came from Montreal to visit. Their weekend hobby was going to garage sales, flea markets and antique shops. Since they were unfamiliar with our area, I drove them around to places they had circled in the local newspaper. We visited several before they were lured into an antique shop. I followed in quiet accord. The musty, dusty barn held tables, cabinets, and chests of antique relics.

As I walked through, I tried not to look at what was a revolting sight for me, a throwback to the long-buried life I had lived. I stepped over a dilapidated hatbox and nearly fell into a child's wooden wagon as I was trying to call Harry's attention to an old accordion that I knew would interest him. Assuming they had seen all they wanted to, I turned to leave. It was then that my eyes dropped upon an unforgiving sight. I was jolted into the past. Was what I saw, what I thought I saw? It had to be.

The owner approached saying, "Those are just desserts, no more to match that pattern." I counted them and thought silently, "Yep, that same damn six!" Some had chips my fingers had never touched, but those plates were unmistakable.

I put down the dusty plate. My palms were sweating. I feared I could not make it to the door, but the fall air restored me. By the time our friends reached the car my wave of nausea had subsided, but I was still trembling.

Now I faced another dilemma: should I go back and buy those plates? Here was one last chance to demolish them.

I sat quietly in the car, in a distraught, yet pensive, state. After a few moments, I turned the key. Gradually, I was able to relate to our friends what had precipitated such a strong visceral reaction. Those dessert plates carried a heavily endowed history for me. In brief, I explained how we had moved to Bangall at the time my grandfather died and my father lost his job.

Although my parents had shouldered their full responsibility for two decades, there was no assurance that Grandma's house would be left to them. She was prone to write frequent codicils to her will, predicated on who was in or out of her good graces. These hand-written documents may have had no legal value, but one could never be sure. Neither could one count on Aunt May who might lay legal claim to anything written in her favor.

When Grandma's will was read, my parents realized the property would be theirs. Unwilling to risk investing their meager funds in home improvements until then, they could now make plans to install running water. It had been a long wait for a bathroom.

Betty Ann turned toward me with a puzzled look to say, "But what about those plates?"

"Betty Ann, when I saw them, the Christmas of those plates flooded my mind. It was the year I was eight years old and the first Christmas my father had a job." I hesitated. When I regained my composure, I told her the story.

> Presents were scarce every Christmas. From Emma there would be still one more pair of her knitted wool slippers, just like the tasteless, yellow and gray striped pairs that we had collected in previous years and scarcely worn. From my grandmother, I would receive yet another white linen handkerchief, edged by the tatting she did with great skill, despite her aging fingers.
>
> By now I had been conditioned to expect no more. My sixth birthday had prepared me. The frosted angel food cake, Emma's standby, was no different from all those birthday cakes she had made over the years, but her present was baffling.
>
> "A duck on a string, Mom what do I do with this?" I asked in undisguised disappointment.
>
> "It's a pull toy," my mother said, her voice reflecting the same feelings. She already knew Emma's perspective had not changed from the time I had arrived as a toddler and disrupted her life and her household.
>
> By this time, there was no longer the magic of Santa Claus, but the strange reality of gift-giving in our family did not escape my attention. I never saw my father give my mother a Christmas gift until I was in college. "Why not?" I asked timidly.

"Christmas is for children. Long ago we agreed that you should have the gifts, not we. When there's more money that will be the time for gifts."

The lifeless, gray flannel men's pajamas I would see my mother sew in the fall would be dutifully wrapped. As I handed out the gifts, I noticed with sadness that sometimes it might be the only one my father would get, aside from my own handmade calendar from school.

Until my father had a job, his income was non-existent. In Washington, my father had worked hard, and they had invested their small savings in the stock market. Like most people, they were poorly informed and lost much of it before they moved back to Bangall.

My mother often reminded me how lucky we were to have a roof over our heads and three meals a day, but she never articulated our painful reality. Here was the stark contrast between bare financial existence on the one hand, and a live-in cook on the other who served meals, with sterling silver and china on damask linens. Even to a child, this seemed odd. Speaking of china, we had china galore. There were full sets of Lenox, Haviland, and Limoge, and enough silver for a hotel dining room.

No one entertained, so Emma never touched the pieces of fine china, nor rustled them in her dishpan or their numbers would have been depleted fast.

Sitting near the Christmas tree that particular morning, I handed out one gift at a time to prolong the experience with a minimum of gifts. I carefully lifted a box and read the label. "Here, Mom is one for you. The tag says: 'To Mary, from Emma.'"

She unwrapped it with the measured suspense expected of us all in anticipation of what could be coming into view next.

"Oh," she tried to exclaim with grateful surprise, but only the surprise came out. "Dessert plates...for the table."

The tan colored plates trimmed with depressing maroon, bilious green, and black were unforgettable, perhaps a Woolworth special.

Each year, Christmas morning was special for reasons that exceeded the joy over my gifts. I was allowed to sit on Grandma's living room floor for a period of time, amid all the Christmas paper as if we had had five times as many presents. This became my symbol of joy at Christmas.

That night, I crept close to the door of my parents' third-floor room. I could tell that my mother was on the brink of tears as she pleaded with my father. Then they discussed something I had never heard before.

"I know Grandpa K. made a life-long promise to Emma of $25 a month, but here we are, only just now having any money at all and you feel you have to honor your father's promises. That's just ridiculous!"

"Well, Mary, Emma hasn't been paid since we came here to live. I feel a promise is a promise. She's entitled to be paid whenever I can. It won't be every month, but once in a while I'll have to give her the salary she's expecting."

"...And what does she do with it?" she said, "buy more china. The last thing we need in this house is more china. Ugly dessert plates at that." I heard my mother's voice crack.

My father replied, "I'd have to agree, those dessert plates are pretty revolting."

Here he was, caught between the desperate feelings of my mother and his own characteristic dedication to keep a promise, one he had not made, but felt duty bound to honor.

The obvious needs of his own family pressed hard upon his mind. Even though he earned only $35 a week, he knew my mother was trying to put away a little each month. She viewed college for me as a must, and her nest egg from selling eggs and chickens or from her occasional earnings doing restoration sewing, grew ever so slowly.

Whereas Emma's duties were now confined to housecleaning, she still envisioned the kitchen as her domain. Thus my father tried to resolve the conflict over this divisive issue with light humor.

"Yep," he asserted, "Emma is sure hooked on desserts. If we were down to our last cracker, she would want to make it into a dessert...And then serve it to us on those dreadful plates."

This drew a muffled chuckle from my mother, even through her tears.

A few days after our friends returned to Montreal, I began to reflect on what had happened. I pictured the red barn with the "Antiques" sign outside. My decision had been correct. I no longer needed to slay the dragon to obliterate that dreadful symbol of my past. My life as an adult has been greatly enriched with all the joys and opportunities that were sparse in childhood. I was happy too, that someone else would be serving their desserts on those memorable plates.

27

Letter to Grandma "K."

Summer '03

Amid flowers in my garden, I'll stay all day.
It's here in Vermont, I write to you, Grandma "K."[1]
During the big "D" Depression,
your little "d" depression went unrecognized.
Could we have done more about it, had we realized?

You kept yourself contained, unexposed, like living in—
inside an egg from our Plymouth Rock hens.
We couldn't reach you, felt rejected when we tried.
I was frightened. I thought you didn't like me inside—
because I was a child.

I kept out of sight and was ever so quiet.
I listened, I watched, and learned all I was able,
by creating my home under the living room table.
From silence and strain, peace could quickly erode.
Your house seemed like a powder keg about to explode.

And yet, beneath your shell there must have been
a person I wanted to know.
To write you now makes me sad enough to cry.
I want to cry out to you, to ask
for answers unspoken, to understand at last.

Who was the person Grandpa knew and surely
must have loved, when both of you were young?
What happened that made you close the door
and bolt it from within? In your Victorian house,
was there a well-locked secret amid three floors?

Or, did your intellectual yearning seem so demanding
to incite your withdrawal, your anger notwithstanding?
Did your brilliant mind haunt you, demand more instead?
Did Wordsworth, Shelley, Shakespeare, and Keats
gratify you more than Grandpa's gracious treats?

1 Grandma Knickerbocker

Were you deeply jealous of this merchant's goodwill,
idolized by townspeople, of whom he never thought ill?
Was it his warmth, his good humor, his generosity to a fault?
Those traits were so human, you were unable to relate.
What made life rich for him, was hard for you to contemplate.

When he died, wasn't there some way to have grieved your loss,
some way to have expressed it beside your austere façade,
and your cloistered aloofness from public promenade?
Was it our very presence that reminded you,
of impending closure, on your life's journey, too?

Instead of personal warmth for me, you placed your affinity
with public causes, to the Democratic Party,
In defense of our country with a big "D" Democracy.
Maybe you also applauded democracy with a little "d,"
for those beyond the rigid, frigid walls in which we lived.

I've been thinking of you, Grandma "K."
Amid flowers in my garden, where I spend the day.
I remember your garden well, the one beside
the lilac bush that shaded from the road
the square, old outhouse, primitive and cold.

With the same regularity of your coming downstairs
to listen to news at noon about foreign affairs
would be the annual appearance of California poppies.
Tangerine petals cupped stamens of black
on plants big as our washtub, each year they came back.

They peeped over the mound of our well-cut lawn,
visible from the house and the roadway beyond.
Bachelor buttons, straight-stemmed and blue,
flowing clusters of white daisies shot up, too.
How they loved the hot sun and showers in the afternoon.

It is here in my garden, in Vermont, Grandma "K.,"
I am closest to you, and for the first time, I can say
I feel your presence in my life—with joy.
I use your garden tools, the narrow rake, the trowel,
whose splinter-free handles helped grind your hardened soil.

I found the "claw" hand rake with the handle Grandpa extended—
attached with sturdy wire, now rusted, from years untended—
so with more ease, your frail arms could reach,
from that tiny, five-foot body reach, out—
if not to human beings, to close generations of garden weeds.

I remember how, with sweat pouring down your tissue-paper
cheeks, you would work hard, with bare hands to dig, to rake
throughout the steamy summer mornings, without a break.
We worried you might overdo, you and the heat, both ninety-two.
But our concern was for naught—you scarcely noticed 'til noon.

It seemed to me, when you weeded your garden,
you were closest to enjoying yourself. You were unguarded.
Perhaps it was therapeutic for you, as it is for me,
close to mother nature's magnetic force to be.
That unseen force—now pulls us together from far, far apart.

You never allowed us to share your experience,
to witness serenity, or real joy in your life.
If only you could have, it would have eased our strife.
Permission to enjoy ourselves, as grandchild, son, and daughter-in-law—
to share more of our lives with you—required a deep spring thaw.

I longed for a more traditional, affectionate relationship
as grandchild to grandparent, but our love stayed un-kindled.
Now I feel some heritage through my garden flowers.
I, too, grow California poppies, and hollyhocks that tower
above bachelor buttons and wild, white daisies like yours.

I am content when I grasp the tools you used so long,
those tools we might have shared, if you had cared.
I can be closer to you in my garden than ever
I could have been, watching from the sidelines, for never
would you speak as you worked in your garden—alone.

These tools are a legacy that bind us, among those
very few things I preserved from your house, because
this was always your house, your home, never ours, never mine.
Now we can share those flowers your tools help to blossom.
This bond makes it better for us both, better for my mind.

I am, with all the best wishes I can find,

Your distant relative, and granddaughter,

Barbara

Part II

Gold commemorative coin to celebrate the tercentenary of the arrival of the earliest settlers, the Walloons in 1623–1624.

Commemorative stamps of the tercentenary of the Walloon settler's arrival in 1623–1624.

Flax to Freedom

It is the flax
that's grown in fields
that's pulled in clumps
that's retted in pools
that's cracked to open
that frees the strands
— for spinning.

It is the heddle
that lifts the thread
that parts the warp
that moves the shuttle
that carries the woof
that is beaten firmly
— into cloth.

It is the loom
that women use
that weaves the linen
that makes the sails
that powers the ship
that carries the refugees
— to freedom.

Barbara Knickerbocker Beskind
— 1995

History Revisited, History Revised

The focus of Part II is to define the origin, culture, and identity of the Walloons, and clarify parts of their history. The Walloons are descended from the early Belgic tribes located south of the River Waal, from which they derive their name. The language of the Walloons evolved from early Latin, together with the French languages of the Middle Ages. French continues to be spoken throughout the Walloon provinces of Belgium today. In the Flemish provinces, the language is Brabantish, akin to Dutch.

Part II also challenges the date cited on the 1924 tercentenary stamps and gold coin that celebrate the Walloons' arrival on Manhattan Island. Presumably the date 1624 was drawn from the writings of the de Forrest family in 1900 and 1914, and/or Riker in 1904.

Walloon historians Griffis and Bayer, writing in 1923 and 1925 respectively, claim these first settlers arrived May 20, 1623; so does Martha Lamb, prominent historian of early New York. They presumably drew on the work of historian John Romeyn Brodhead and his research of the Dutch West India Company archives in Amsterdam that was published in 1853. Mystery and confusion over this date remains and warrants further research.

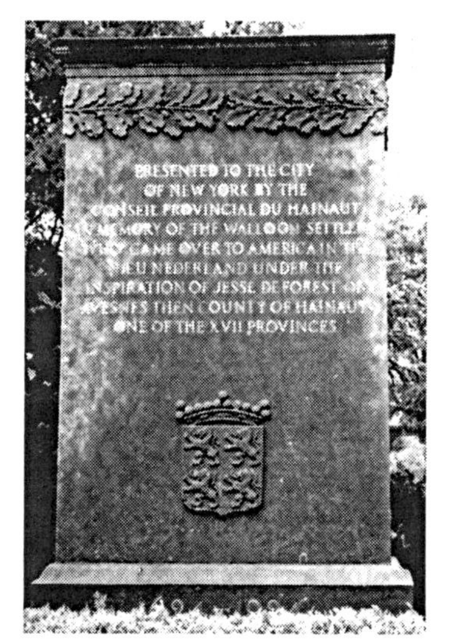

The Walloon Settlers' Monument, at Battery Park near Castle Clinton, was dedicated in 1925.

Part II also serves to clarify the identity of these original settlers. The commemorative stamps and coin identify them as Huguenot–Walloons. The Walloon Settlers' Monument in Battery Park, erected by the New York City Department of Parks and Recreation in December 2001, refers to them as Belgic–Huguenots. Research into history of the Reformation, when the Walloons fled Spanish oppression at the hands of the Duke of Alva, indicates neither is correct and these names may have been coined in America. They were known at the time as Walloon Reformists, but events transpired that soon obliterated this label in history. The ground-breaking role of

This 2001 plaque explains the history behind the Walloon Settlers' Monument dedicated in 1925. Significant errors are contained in the text.

the Walloon Reformists that was crucial to the formative years of the Protestant Reformation has been obscured as well.

For centuries, Walloons had been loyal Catholics. They were known in Europe for their innovative minds, minds that could be readily inspired by a neighboring activist Martin Luther, in his daring step in 1517. As early as the 1530s some Walloons entertained ideas for worship that were less restrictive, but they had no intention of abandoning the church. Neither did they disavow the Holy Scriptures, for which the church could have punished them as heretics.

After more than three decades of trying to get church authorities to accommodate to any significant change, they were so frustrated, that they took matters into their own hands. By August 1566, as strident iconoclasts, they set about in rampant disregard to destroy all statuary, crosses, and any vestiges of religious symbolism in some 400 Catholic churches and convents throughout the region. As a result, King Philip II of Spain sent his Duke of Alva to quell these ardent, reform-minded Walloons. Increasingly they saw their cause expanding: they sought relief from Spanish oppression in civic matters, as well as rigid religious doctrine.

John Calvin's teachings matched their cause and beliefs. Guido de Bray, a devoted follower of Calvin, and a Walloon pastor, became their foremost leader. The

French Huguenots were better organized Calvinists at the time and were warmly welcomed as proselytizers by these Walloons. They spoke the same language and could easily help to spread the word of religious reform. Courageous Huguenots often crossed the French border into the adjacent Walloon provinces of Hainaut and Artois in disguise, under the cloak of darkness. Walloon Reformists rose up against the Duke of Alva in the Revolt of 1567–69 throughout the four Walloon provinces of The Netherlands. At that time, all 17 provinces were under control of Spain and the Papacy.

There also remained many Walloons who were loyal to the Catholic church and were staunchly aversive to the Calvinists who revolted, labeling them "protestors." The name "protestant" evolved from this and other protests in Europe; obviously that name has survived.

The events surrounding the arrival of the first Walloons in the New World, especially those who settled the tip of Manhattan Island, needs serious study with attention to historical accuracy. The 2001 plaque to commemorate these Walloon settlers cites an erroneous date: Jesse de Forrest appealed to the British-controlled Virginia Colony for permission to create a Walloon refuge in 1621, not 1821. Verification of other details about Jesse de Forrest remains controversial.

For years, Jesse de Forrest had vehemently advocated forming the Dutch West India Company hoping it could provide transportation to a haven he wanted to develop for himself and other displaced Walloons. He was discouraged by the slow process. The charter was finally signed on June 21, 1623. Despite claims to the contrary, the best research to date indicates that he was not among the original Walloon settlers on Manhattan Island. Much later, however, three of his children arrived in adulthood and carried out significant roles.

According to his own journal, Jesse de Forrest had sailed for Guiana, lured by gold, silver, and the highly cherished dyewoods he hoped to sell on his return to Leyden, to the Drapers Guild, of which he was a member. His journal, dated 1623, was translated from French to English in 1914.[1] This document is of interest because it brings into controversy whether the Walloons arrived in 1623 or 1624, as will be explored in Part III. Regardless of which year is accurate, Jesse de Forrest died four months after his arrival on the shores of South America.

My purpose in researching these events is to try to clarify some of this confusion of the names, dates, and circumstances when the first Walloons arrived. I also draw attention to relevant events and people whose notable accomplishments have long been overlooked, or whose history may have been recorded differently.

For instance, the Walloons did not join the Dutch, as the above-mentioned plaque specifies. However, having sailed on a Dutch ship, from a Dutch port, to a Dutch territory, it is understandable that many would believe the passengers

1 de Forrest, Mrs. Vol. II, 1914

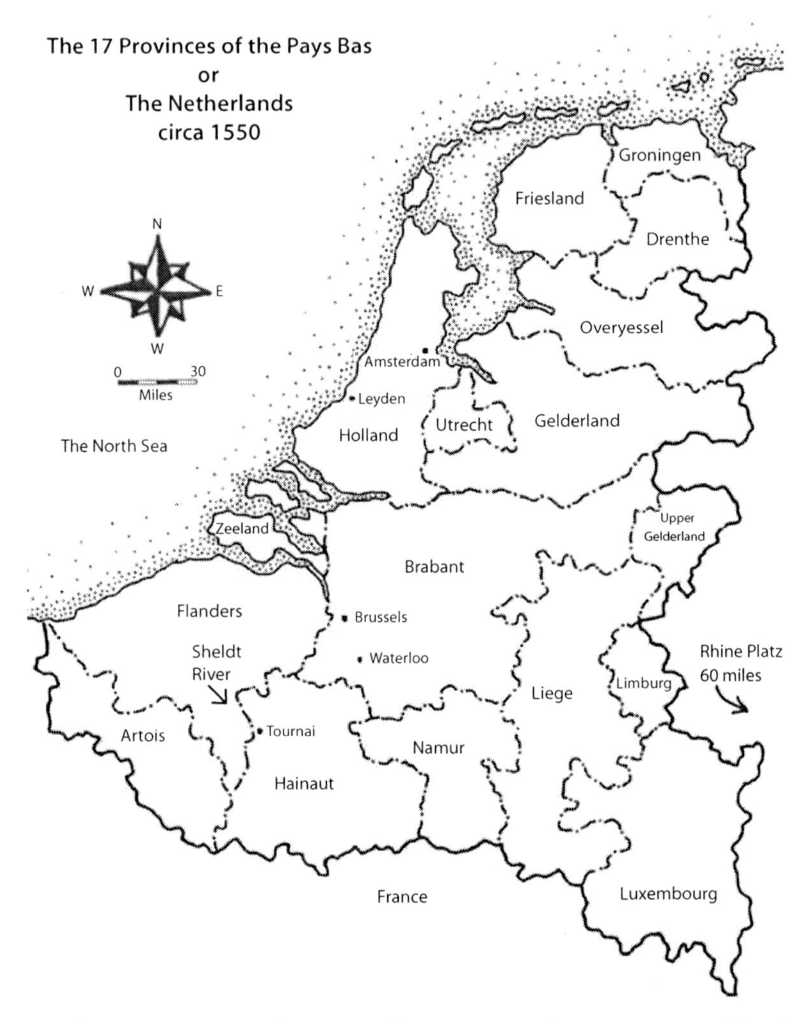

were Dutch. Not one was. All were Walloons, except for one or more Flemings, as people of Flanders were called. A minority of Flemings had fled this Catholic stronghold for their reformist beliefs. Cornelius May, for whom Cape May, New Jersey is named, was Dutch. He was sent over for a one-year tour as the Director of the Dutch West India Company.

Ships of the Dutch West India Company flew their flag and officers had authority to act on the government's behalf. The ships and operations were financed through private and municipal stockholders among five cities in Holland and Zeeland. By contrast, the *Nieuw Nederlandt* which brought settlers to the Dutch territory needed independent financing.

The 2001 commemorative plaque in Battery Park fails to mention the name of Willem Usselinx, a Walloon born in Antwerp, whose tireless endeavors over many years urged the creation of the Dutch West India Company. Since funding

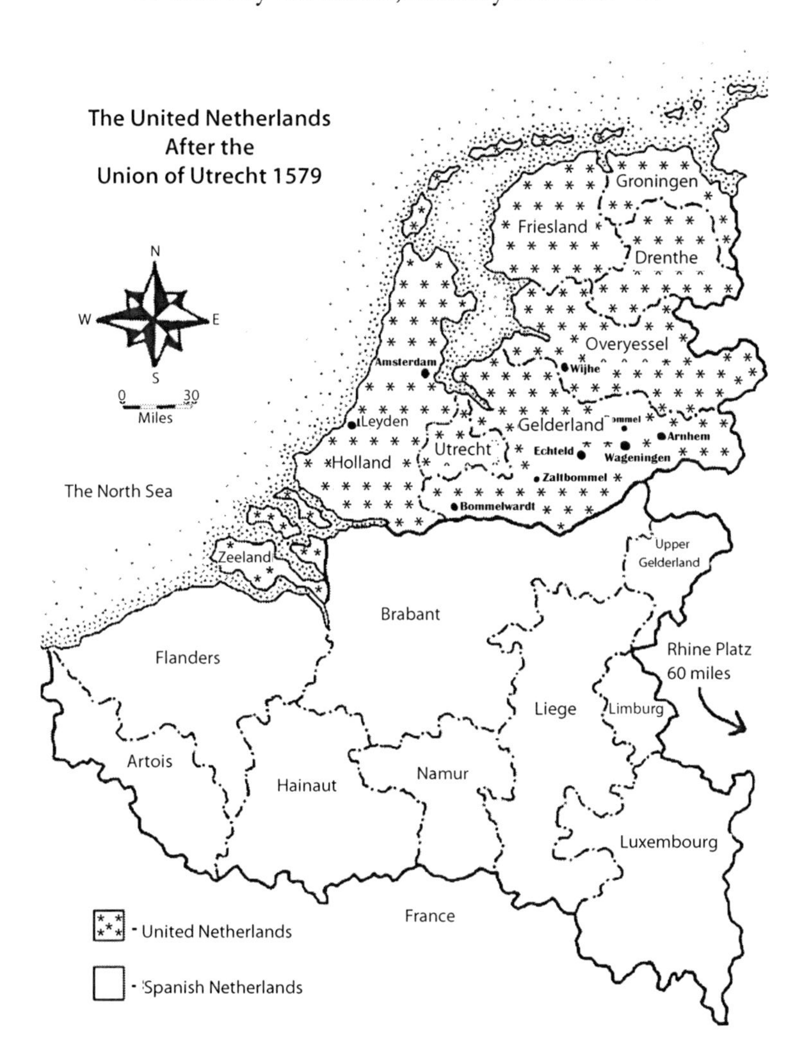

was unavailable through this organization, to build a ship in Amsterdam to transport the Walloon refugees, he sought out private individuals to finance this risky undertaking.

Many who responded to Willem Usselinx's request were Sephardic Jews whose ancestors had fled the Spanish Inquisition in both Spain and Portugal. Until the Union of Utrecht in 1579, Jews in The Netherlands who had converted to Christianity under duress in Spain, continued to call themselves "New Christians." By 1593, they were no longer known as "Crypto-Jews," or "New Christians," since they were guaranteed freedom to worship openly in the Dutch Republic. Sadly, the plaque at Battery Park omits any mention that they were principal stockholders, or how the significance of this had a direct bearing over events that would unfold on Manhattan Island three decades later. This history is clarified in Part III.

The chapters that follow, in Part III, mainly evolve around a personal, humanized history that promotes understanding of events interwoven over a period of eight centuries on three continents: Europe, and North and South America. Although this story is told within the structure of my family's genealogy, documentation of the surrounding historical events is provided, insofar as possible, in footnotes.

Part III

Part III

Introduction

Part I of *Powder Keg* has focused on the many aspects of history that touched my life and helped to shape it. Events of World War II clearly impacted the direction of my professional career.

Part II provides information about the origin, the culture, and the identity of the Belgic Walloons. It cites errors that clearly need to be corrected, dates to be challenged, and pertinent facts that are omitted in the history provided the public in Battery Park at the tip of Manhattan Island.

Part III illustrates how history impacted the lives of two of my distant ancestors, Adrian Vincent, a Walloon on my mother's side, and Harmon Jansen (van Wye) Knickerbakker, a Dutchman on my father's side. In the chapters that follow, I have presented the history surrounding their lives, as a foundation upon which their personal stories unfold. This perspective of our past promotes an appreciation of the present.

Here I offer an expanded glimpse of their lives and times, as I envision them from my study of maps, a broad literature search, and personal experience. I often traveled the lowland terrain while I was stationed in Germany for two years with the army, not far from the border of Luxembourg.

A trip in 2007 helped me envision history of the 1600s that had taken place in the harbor and on the docks of Amsterdam, and at the Dutch West India Company Headquarters, the Jewish Synagogue and diamond district not far away.

A more extensive trip in 2004 brought to life parts of my family history. I toured cities and towns where the two men mentioned above, and even their ancestors presumably had lived. I traveled from the River IJssel in the Oberyessl Province of The Netherlands, ancestral origin of the (van Wye) Knickerbakker family, to the Hainaut Province in southern Belgium. The city of Tournai had been the origin of my Walloon ancestors as the Reformation evolved, and this area had been a part of The Netherlands known as the Belgic Lands.

I looked. I listened. I tried to imagine how life had been then, as I strolled across the cobblestones of the city square in Tournai that crystal clear morning in the spring of 2004. Although it had been 450 years since my Walloon ancestors' feet had trod the soil of Hainaut Province, I felt a distinct resonance in my body. Then, suddenly, it seemed that my feet were jolted from under me! The sound was as intense as if 100 canons had been fired in unison.

The peal of bells, large and small, reverberated from every building in a cacophony of sound loud enough to shake their very foundations. From the bell towers, those deep booming tones and shrill accents rose above the tiled roofs and over the flatlands as they had for centuries, carried by the strong sea breeze from the west. They pealed for what seemed forever, that Sunday morning, calling worshippers to service. The deafening sound caused babies to cry, children to clasp their ears, and tourists like me to duck into buildings.

Belgians have always been renowned carillonneurs, admired by Belgian youth like today's sports figures. Boys often aspire to be the bell ringer that all will someday hear, ringing the bells from the five-towered, stone Cathedral of Notre Dame in Tournai. When it was built in 1150, large bells were newly emerging on the stage of history. Forged of iron and brass, tonal quality slowly improved and their size increased.

Bell-ringers' schools sprang up across the Belgic Lands. Could it be that some of the youth I watched that Sunday morning were descendants of the early bell-ringers? Could their ancestors have attended the famed bell-ringers' school of Master Jef Derijn in Mechlin, some 50 miles north, along the River Scheldt and home of the famed Flemish painter Peter Paul Rubens?

So energized was this climate of the mid-1500s that word about a reformation pealed loudly from the belfries to forge a faith in their souls as strong as the metal of the resounding bells. It was in Tournai, on the River Scheldt, that Walloons of the Hainaut Province met in secret, fomenting a hotbed, a battleground, a powder keg of protest against Medieval Catholicism. It was in Tournai, the Reformists' Revolt exploded in 1567. It was in Tournai, and other Walloon cities, that the people rose up to fight for religious worship free of Catholic doctrine, and representative government free of Spanish rule. It was in Tournai, that my family roots were found in the flax fields beside the River Scheldt.

Medieval Belgian blocks had been rounded into cobblestones by the wheels of history. Those same cobblestones under my feet were now worn by cars, motorcycles, and the grinding of metal-wheeled delivery carts. They had been smoothed over the centuries by struggles of peasants and laborers, by struggles of nobles and kings, and in our recent past, by struggles of nations. Artillery pieces of two world wars had rolled through these narrow streets and across the town square, leaving their scars.

Growing up, I had always heard that my Walloon ancestors had left their beloved Belgic homeland because of oppression in the Spanish-controlled Netherlands. Until I started to review this history, the question had loomed in my mind as to how Spain and The Netherlands, so far from each other, so different in their cultures, had ever become connected. Drawing on my rich imagination, I wondered if I could go back as an historical observer, timeless, silent, and unseen? Could I watch this history unfold? Could I hear it? Could I sense it as a first-hand observer?

How, as a writer, could I imbed myself into those lives, lives being lived so distant in time and place? My solution was to inaugurate a new style of writing ancestral material. I have identified this as the *first-person historical omniscient*. It is with this perspective that I bring to life the lives of two ancestors in old Europe and witness their early years in America.

1

A Walloon Heritage: Adrian's Story from Tournai to Nova Belgica

(1567–1634)

The Historical Background

The religious environment of the Belgic Walloons in the 1500s:

Walloons throughout the Belgic Lands had been devout Catholics for centuries. Then, after Luther's protest against the church in 1517,[1] news spread across the border to their provinces nearby. Innovative ideas began to resonate in the minds of these people who were known in Europe for their strong-willed nature and their drive to explore new ways of doing things. So it was in their worship of God.[2]

Before the 1530s they had no intention of abandoning the Catholic church, but gradually they began to question the need to relay their prayers through the saints. They sought alternative, direct, and interactive ways to worship.

At the end of the 15th century, as the Renaissance was drawing to a close, there was a great literary outburst at the Theological Division of the Sorbonne.[3] It was here that crucial seeds of change germinated, to stimulate the emerging reformed movement.

The names Luther, Zwingli, Calvin, and Knox easily come to mind among reformist leaders. Unsung heroes and certain external forces of the late 15th and early 16th centuries that helped to advance the early days of transition have gone largely unrecognized. These people and the prescient forces at work are identified here:

(1) *The ground-breaking role of the reform-minded Belgic Walloons* is brought to light.

They shared the bond of a common language with French-born John Calvin[4] and were drawn to the tenets of his beliefs expressed initially in his "Institutions of the Christian Religion," that he wrote in 1536.

---

1 Bainton
2 Wilson
3 Griffis
4 Griffis

(2) *The risk-taking role of the French Huguenot proselytizers* who came into the heavily-controlled Catholic Belgic Lands helped mobilize and spread Calvinism among the Walloons.

(3) *The visionary role of Guido de Bray,* the Belgic Walloon preacher, espoused the broad concepts of civic freedom, a cogent outgrowth of Calvinism.[5]

(4) *The unrecognized role of Clement Marot,* and his contributions, unwittingly propelled this movement. As Professor of Hebrew at the Sorbonne he translated as many as 30 of the psalms from Hebrew into French in 1540; in 1541 he set them to music.[6]

During those early decades of exploration between 1530 and 1566, those Walloon Catholics who treasured conformity within the church, sat side by side with other Catholics whose imaginative minds were stirred by excitement for change. These reform-minded Walloons envisioned incorporating more openly expressive ways to worship within Catholic doctrine.

Having translated the psalms in 1540, Marot recognized how much the French people loved their music, and then put these psalms to music, in song. These songs were carried to the reform-minded Walloons who then began to sing them in the fields, in their homes, and at church.[7] Some of the Walloon Catholics who remained loyal to the traditions of Rome may also have enjoyed hearing them sung in their native language during services.

Whereas preachers often addressed noblemen and the well-to-do merchants about ideas that challenged the church, the peasants converted themselves. Peasant life was so difficult they relished any form of relief. Expressing their faith and joy through song in the language they knew, caused the word of the reformed movement to spread across France and the lowlands with uncommon speed.

This was a startling departure from the long-obscured, detached message in Latin. Latin was known only to the priests, who could scarcely have provided a translation for these curious worshippers. Now the Walloons, whose intellect had been aroused, demanded more answers, more expression, more freedoms. They were determined to have the refrains of music from the psalms rung from the bell towers as well.[8]

The vibrant sound of bells that rippled these refrains from church belfries provided an even more powerful and infectious vehicle to carry the message. Thus Clement Marot, by his work, had provided an unwitting, unexpected, unspoken catalyst of the Reformation, perhaps equal in outcome to Luther's daring stand several short decades before.

In 1561, Guido de Bray, a devout follower of John Calvin and a preacher, documented his own beliefs. It was written two years after Calvin had prepared his French language *Confession of Faith* in Geneva. Guido de Bray's 25-page

5 Griffis
6 Griffis
7 Griffis
8 Griffis

Belgic Confession of Faith was written in Poitiers, France when he was but 21 years of age.[9]

Whereas the *Belgic Confession of Faith* paralleled Calvin's in many respects, this was an independent composition that addressed the timely issues unique to followers within the Walloon provinces. Guido do Bray had immediate and long-range goals for formulating his *Belgic Confession of Faith* in 1561.

First, he wanted to disprove the rampant charges of the Catholic church that these reform-minded Walloons were heretics, punishable under religious law because it was thought they were not following the Holy Scriptures. Since the scriptures were indeed central to their Calvinist beliefs, de Bray adamantly refuted this charge in his written document.

Second, it was his ultimate religious goal to unite all Christians of the reformed faith into one, through love, charity, and mutual service.

Third, and a more imperative reason that Guido de Bray had for documenting his belief was his hope that this would protect the reform-minded Walloons as they sought altruistic, non-militant methods of redress for their grievances.

It was with faith and considerable naiveté that Guido de Bray sent a copy of his *Belgic Confession of Faith* to King Philip II the following year, in 1562. In so doing, he fully expected to legitimize their stand on religious expression free from Rome, and civic rights freed from Spain. No reply was forthcoming.[10] Four years later, after more than 30 years of evolving their beliefs, the reform-minded Walloons felt the time had come to challenge Catholicism by taking matters into their own hands. In a united front, on a dark night in August 1566, they entered some 400 churches and convents throughout the Walloon provinces and parts of Flanders. With iconoclastic zeal, these ardent, provocative reformers destroyed every vestige of symbolism of the Church of Rome.[11]

Their actions precipitated the two-year War of Revolt (1567–69). These Walloons were called "revolters," by the Spanish authorities and "protestors," by loyal Catholics. The Walloon Catholics were understandably enraged at the devastation of their church property and sacred symbols. This outrage instilled revenge of neighbor against neighbor in a fury that mirrored their Spanish rulers. Tragically, this also set the climate for them to accept what was about to unfold around them, the nearly-obscure Second Spanish Inquisition.

Along the River Scheldt about half the Walloon population vehemently supported a revolt against Spanish oppression and Medieval Catholicism. An equal number of Walloons, and most of the Flemings from the coastal provinces in Flanders, were strong supporters of the Church of Rome and loyal to Spanish rule. Feelings on both sides escalated to become deeply entrenched.

French Huguenots were better organized Calvinists and were unimpeded at that time, in their religious practices. The revolutionary-thinking Walloons warmly welcomed them as proselytizers of the reformist doctrines. However, in this climate of terror and suspicion clandestine preachers had to be smuggled

9 Griffis

10 Griffis

11 de Forrest, Mrs.

across the border into the provinces of Hainaut and Artois in the dark of night. So it was with Guido de Bray, who often stayed in France for his own safety and returned to Hainaut in unsuspecting disguise.

Many years of peaceful, civil protest had brought no change, but when the Walloons' frustration escalated, their drastic actions that night in 1566 brought a direct response. Philip II ordered the Duke of Alva to assemble his troops to quell this rampant revolt.

As they were preparing to leave Spain, Philip II instructed the Duke of Alva to institute an inquisition against those "revolters" in the lowlands. Ironically, this was exactly 75 years after the Jews suffered their own inquisition that forced them to leave Spain.

Torturous blood rightly coursed through Philip's veins, since he was the great-grandson of Ferdinand and Isabella. In 1492 they had directed Torquemada, the Inquisitor General to carry out their commands against the Jews, forcing them to become Christians or leave.

The Duke of Alvarez, as he was called at home, arrived on Walloon soil in 1567. He had landed in Italy and come north with 10,000 troops referred to as the "blackbeards."[12] Supposedly he intended to come by way of Geneva to confront Calvin, but choose another route that may have been easier for troop movement.[13]

The Duke of Alva lost no time instituting the orders of Philip II. This, the Second Spanish Inquisition, lasted for 12 years (1567–1579). It fully qualified as an "inquisition" because an atmosphere of espionage and spying on family, friend, and neighbor was encouraged, holding out hopes their own lives might be spared torture and death.

Three hundred and seventy-five years later, another inquisition of Jews and their persecution would be repeated by a modern-day demagogue. And now, regrettably, in our generation suspected incidents of questioning under torture are yet to be disproved.

Factors that enabled the reformed movement to escalate and expand in the 1500s

Factor number one: Characteristic tenacity of the Walloons had been forged over centuries.

Persistence in overcoming difficulty was characteristic of the Walloon people. It was central to the very being of Guido de Bray. These origins also contributed directly to the rise of the reformed movement. Responding to oppression by the Spanish rulers, he conceptualized the principles of his over-arching document of reform in the *Belgic Confession of Faith*. This Calvinist preacher had a leading role in galvanizing them as "Walloon Reformists," an identity they would soon lose as they fled during the Second Spanish Inquisition.[14]

12 Bayer
13 Bainton
14 Griffis

Guido de Bray, child of the Borinage, was born in the small city of Mons east of Tournai, a hotbed of protest on the River Scheldt. Ironically, he was born in 1540, the same year that Clement Marot translated the psalms.

With tenacity, Guido de Bray avidly pursued his ultimate goal: to unite all people of the reformed faith. Because he aggressively promoted freedom of religious expression, and even dared to sing the psalms in public, his own dedicated life came to an early end.

It was on the scaffold in Mons, at the age of 28, that Guido de Bray was put to death in 1568.[15] Sadly there could be no public display of grief, or those believers would have met the same fate. Three hundred years after Guido de Bray died, Vincent van Gogh would bring to light the character of the potato eaters and the misery of the coal miners here in the Borinage.

History of the area indicates this was the "Saltus Carbonarus," or the "coal forest," of Roman times, the "coal fields," of Walloon times,[16] and the "coal pocket," of World War II, the site of two months of frenzied combat around the nearby city of Namur.

Factor number two: *Songs conveyed the reformed message broadly.*

By translating the psalms and putting them to music, Clement Marot provided a dramatic and unexpected result. This stimulus addressed the needs of peasant and nobleman alike. Excitement spread across France and the lowlands like a prairie fire.[17]

Factor number three: *Spanish oppression forged the will of the Walloon Reformists to attain religious and civic freedoms.*

There were unintended consequences of Spanish oppression. It served not only to define and forge the concepts of Guido de Bray, but it mobilized the reformed movement throughout the Walloon provinces. The stark, painful reality of their oppression made the peasants especially willing to follow this leader who coupled religious freedom with personal freedoms and political will.[18]

Factor number four: *Walloon Reformists carried these concepts of freedom with them.*

These principles circumscribed in the *Belgic Confession of Faith* so inspired his fellowmen that as refugees, these Walloon Reformists carried the concepts of faith and freedoms with them when they fled.

Although Walloons were migrating to Holland and England as early as the 1530s to find a less restricted climate, from 1544 to 1585 there was a constant stream, at times, a flood, especially by 1567 and after.[19]

In their diaspora, the Walloons at the time of the two-year revolt fled not only to France, Holland, England, and Ireland, but farther away, to Sweden, where there is still an identifiable community. Others traveled to Russia and some

15 Griffis
16 Riker
17 Griffis
18 Griffis
19 Griffis

arrived in South Africa, perhaps by way of trading ships of the Dutch East India Company sailing to the Orient in the first decade of the 1600s.

Its successor, the Dutch West India Company was formed in 1623; Walloons then settled along the coast of Brazil and, after 1630, on the island of Recife. They often brought a copy of the *Belgic Confession of Faith* with them, as they did when they came here to the Dutch territory.

The reformed movement consolidates to become an established church (1561–1621)

In the years shortly after the *Belgic Confession of Faith* was written in 1561, border cities such as Valencienes and Walloon communities along the River Scheldt, Tournai among them, became hotbeds of the emerging Reformation. The idea of forming synods evolved around the warm hearths.

These synods were attended by small groups of men from throughout the Walloon provinces who came together to make unified decisions based on the needs of the people each represented. This provided a template for civic representation as well.[20]

Of necessity, synods in 1563, 1564, and two in 1566, were held in secret.[21] Out of the concepts fostered by Guido de Bray, these Calvinists evolved a vision that could address their strivings for civil governance as well as less restricted ways of worshipping.[22]

Twelve years after the end of the two-year revolt (1567–1569) came the Union of Utrecht in 1579. This created the Dutch Republic in the name of the Seven United Provinces. While it gave them political independence from Spain, it did not prevent continued fighting in Leyden and elsewhere. There was sparring on the high seas as well.[23]

Not until their Twelve Year Truce with Spain (1609–1621), were the Dutch people finally able to take a respite from their war-like concerns to attend to the rapidly expanding reformist movement throughout their provinces.[24]

Furious debate ensued for years over the drafting of the *Articles of Faith* they would follow.[25] In 1574 the Dutch had asked their pastors to follow the *Heidelberg Catechism*. Debate centered now on whether they would continue to do so, or adopt the *Calvinist Confession of Faith* brought from France, or the *Belgic Confession of Faith* that was practiced by the widespread proliferation of French-speaking Walloon churches in their midst, that then numbered 70.[26]

The final decision was to adopt the latter. Foremost in their minds perhaps, was their recent experience with Spanish religious and political oppression, but also Guido de Bray's vision for uniting all people of the reformed faith. So it was that the *Belgic Confession of Faith* became the doctrinal foundation of the

20 Riker
21 Griffis
22 Griffis
23 Riker
24 Brodhead
25 Brodhead
26 Brodhead

National Dutch Reformed Church there.[27] It is followed to this day throughout the Christian Reformed Churches in America. The principles and language of this document became the initial template and signature contribution to representative governance that are firmly ensconced in the United States Constitution.

Walloon historian, Eliot Griffis, credits Guido de Bray and his *Belgic Confession of Faith* as contributing toward the creation of a Republic in The Netherlands and in the United States as much as many great men.

Development of the Dutch West India Company, chartered in 1623

First, the Dutch East India Company was formed in 1603 to sail to the Orient for tea, silks, and spice. Because the route was long, and was fraught with pirates and stormy seas around the Cape of Good Hope, they were eager to find a shorter, safer route. Officials in Amsterdam were convinced a route by way of the North Sea, the Arctic Ocean, the Barents Sea, and the ice-choked route between the Arctic island of Nova Zemyla and the coast of Siberia was feasible. To this end they engaged Henry Hudson who had made two prior, but unsuccessful, attempts. Although he failed to achieve this goal again in 1609, he did provide the Dutch their claim to the territory where the river he discovered would subsequently carry his name.

The Twelve-Year Truce between the Seven United Provinces and Spain ended in 1621 and soon their animosity resumed. Not wanting to irritate the Spanish as this truce came to a close, the Dutch government was reluctant to respond to various Walloons, namely Jesse de Forrest and Willem Usselinx, both of whom were agitating for the formation of the Dutch West India Company. They were in hopes of finding a refuge from the overcrowded Provinces of Holland and Zeeland to which they, or members of the previous generation, had fled.

The charter of the Dutch West India Company was established in September of 1622, but not finalized until June 21, 1623.[28] This was a commercial enterprise that was given the authority to act on behalf of its country to manage the territories and/or make further conquests. The company was comprised of five chambers throughout major cities of Holland and Zeeland. Amsterdam was the largest and it supervised the funds for all the chambers.[29]

Additional funding was provided from the state for vessels directed toward the conquest of Spanish and Portuguese holdings. Being authorized to act on behalf of the Stadhuis in The Hague, they sent out ships with 2,800 troops as soon as the company was founded, to take Bahia, a Portuguese possession on the coast of Brazil.

The commercial goals of the Dutch West India Company centered on the nefarious and bountiful slave trade from Africa which had been established by the Spanish and Portuguese, had been franchised to the English, and would be

27 Bayer
28 Brodhead
29 van Rensselaer, Mrs. Schuyler

exploited by the Dutch. Their main interest was to provide labor for the coffee plantations they were acquiring in Brazil.[30]

In addition to the lucrative slave trade, and trade route for furs and tobacco here, plus spices in the Caribbean, they were principally interested in conquests on land and at sea. South America held more allure than North America, because of the deposits of gold, silver, and jewels.

This company was not concerned with the development of colonies.[31] They were simply bringing settlers to the New World to hold the territory to which their country had already laid claim, and thus prevent the Spanish from gaining control.

The passenger ship *Nieuw Nederlandt*

Turning from the conquests and exploits of the Dutch West India Company, we trace the challenging voyage of the *Nieuw Nederlandt* that sailed under the flag of the Dutch West India Company. It was a ship of 260 tons, built and equipped in 1622–1623 to transport 100 passengers to the Dutch territory. They would be "planted," as the term was used then, in four locations, to secure the territory for the Dutch between that which the English held in the Virginia Colony to the south and its New England colonies to the northeast.[32]

Many, perhaps most of these passengers, were unable to pay for their passage. Thus they were indentured in servitude to the company for years, the length of time depending on the size of the family. At the end of five, or even ten, years for some, they received a plot of ground as their own. Single white males and blacks from the Congo, were at that time usually indentured for seven years.[33]

The *Nieuw Nederlandt* came by way of the Azores, across the Atlantic to Guiana, and up through the Carribees, as the Caribbean was then called, to arrive in the Dutch territory. This ship, like others in the Dutch West India Company, was allowed to leave port as early as March, a few months preceding the formal signing of the company charter in Amsterdam in June. It would appear to have been May 20, 1623 when passengers arrived in the spacious harbor at the tip of Manhattan Island. However, the year cited here is at odds with the tercentenary celebration year cited as 1624.

Here-to-fore small groups of Dutchmen had sailed up the Noordt River that Hudson discovered, to trade with the Indians and return home with precious furs to sell. But it was the Walloons who were the first settlers; they brought families, flaxseed, and farming tools.[34]

The Dutch territory of Nova Belgica/Nieuw Nederlandt

The Dutch territory known from history books as Nieuw Nederlandt actually was not given that name until three years after these Walloon settlers first arrived. In 1626, the territory was given the status of province, with an official seal and rights that were equal to each of the Seven United Provinces of the

30 Pool, 1930
31 Brodhead
32 Brodhead
33 NOVA Program on Slavery
34 Bayer

homeland. The formal Latin name on the maps of the time cite this territory as "Nova Belgii" or "Nova Belgica," meaning "new lowland," the designated name that endured for decades, after it had been officially changed to Nieuw Nederlandt.[35]

The Walloons called their tiny settlement Nova Belgica also.[36] That name was changed to Nieuw Amsterdam in 1630, but was not in common usage until 1640. [37] This was the same year the territory became a colony.[38]

The role of Willem Usselinx

For many years before the Dutch West India Company was chartered, one man, Willem Usselinx, had worked tirelessly to promote the concept, and he is generally considered to be its founder. Usselinx, a Walloon, was born in Antwerp in 1567 the same year Alva first set foot on Belgic soil.[39]

Usselinx had fled the Spanish oppression with his family when he was a young child. Possibly, it was an underlying dream of this dauntless visionary that the militant endeavors of the new Dutch West India Company might reclaim his Belgic homeland, now officially the "Spanish Netherlands." This dream might have been shared by other displaced countrymen as well.

In 1622–23, apparently there was no funding available to provide for a passenger ship to the New World. Therefore, it became a goal of Willem Usselinx to raise sufficient private money to do so. Among others in Amsterdam, he approached the members of the Sephardic Jewish community of diamond cutters whose families had brought these skills with them to Amsterdam when they fled Spain and Portugal.

There may have been a number of reasons why it appealed to them to become stockholders in this venture.[40] For one thing, these Jews may have felt an empathy and compassion over a shared history of pain, torture, and exile committed by a common enemy. Additionally, these diamond merchants may have viewed this as a way of gaining greater participation and interaction within the established mercantile community of Holland.

If these Jewish stockholders also knew that one of the underlying goals of the Dutch West India Company was to capture Spanish ships and territories, this could have served as a powerful incentive.

As principle stockholders, they helped to finance not only the construction, but also the passage for a number of Walloons on the *Nieuw Nederlandt*. Although the profound influence by Usselinx in this endeavor seems verifiable from numerous sources, it is curious that his famed biographer, John Franklin Jamieson, makes no mention of it.

35 Brodhead
36 Wilson
37 Griffis
38 Griffis
39 Jamieson
40 Costobel

Church Bells from Puerto Rico

In 1625 the Dutch made an expedition to the Carribees as the Spanish-held islands were called. In this interaction on the island of Puerto Rico, a set of church bells was confiscated by the company crew.[41] These were brought back as bounty to Nova Belgica, to grace the tower over Francois Molemacher's gristmill on Slyck Steeg, that became the first place of worship in the Dutch territory.

Capture of the Silver Fleet

Vessels of the Dutch West India Company were soon charged with a highly lucrative mission. They were to search the seas for the famed Silver Fleet, known to carry its annual cargo of silver and gold from mines in Mexico and Peru back to their Spanish ports.

It was in 1629 that 28 ships of the Silver Fleet, loaded with precious cargo and anchored in Havana harbor, were discovered by the Dutch ships commanded by Admiral Heyn. He gave irony a new twist by commandeering these 28 ships and their cargo. To the Dutch, the act was one of valor, but now the Spanish saw it as piracy.

With courage and daring Admiral Heyn led the captured Silver Fleet, commanded by the Dutch, and sailed into the Amsterdam harbor. All but two ships of the captured Spanish fleet made it.[42] This amazing cargo of 140,000 pounds of silver and gold was then worth 12 million guilders. The captured booty repaid private and municipal stockholders amply and filled the company coffers handsomely. One could hardly believe this, in view of its continued lack of financial and military support for the fledgling settlements of the Dutch territory.

The confusing role of Jesse de Forrest

Jesse de Forrest, who was brought up in a reform-minded home in Avesnes, France, came to Leyden as a young man around 1609. He became an outspoken leader and controversial figure there, in his effort to re-locate Walloon refugees to the New World. It is an accepted fact that he petitioned the English for permission in 1621, to take 100 Calvinist families to the Virginia colony, but this was denied. A similar request to the Stadhuis in The Hague in 1622 was also denied.

For years, Jesse de Forrest had been a challenging, frustrated advocate of founding the Dutch West India Company. Presumably the Dutch chose to delay establishing this enterprise at the immediate conclusion of the Twelve Year Truce (1609–1621) in order to avoid agitating their adversary, Spain.

Confusion, and even mystery, surrounds the role of Jesse de Forrest, and this period of history is central to establishing the accurate date that the first Walloon settlers arrived on Manhattan Island.

Family accounts about this man, in the two books listed in the bibliography, adhere to the date of his departure from The Netherlands as 1623. Diaries he wrote in Guiana that were translated from French to English in 1914, also cite the date as 1623.[43]

41 van Rensselaer, Mrs. Schuyler

42 van Rensselaer, Mrs. Schuyler

43 de Forrest, Mrs.

According to one report, in the summer of 1623, the *Pigeon* was outfitted in Plymouth, England for a sea voyage, presumed to be the one that went south to the Canary Islands, where it met another sailing ship, the *Mackerel*.[44] Together they sailed west to the shores of South America whereupon, the *Pigeon* headed to Guiana, while the *Mackerel* continued along the coast of the Americas until it reached the mouth of the river Hudson had found. Reportedly it wintered there at the northernmost end of the river, anchoring off Castle Island, where Albany now stands. The date of the arrival was December 12th, but it is the year that remains in controversy.

If the *Mackerel* arrived December 12, 1623, as the de Forrests claim, that would put the arrival of the *Nieuw Nederlandt* the following May, 1624, the date cited on the commemorative coin and stamps. However, if one relies on the logs of the Amsterdam Chamber that were researched, and the report published, by John Romeyn Brodhead in 1853, the *Mackerel* arrived at Castle Island December 12, 1622. Therefore, on its homeward voyage down river that spring, it would have come across the *Nieuw Nederlandt* at anchor off Manhattan Island in May of 1623, not 1624 as is cited.

How the date of such a clear-cut, historical event could be so shrouded with controversy and confusion adds to the mystery and invites further research. Understandably Jesse de Forrest and others were eager to explore the deposits of silver, gold, and jewels that could be found there, but of special interest to him, were the dyewoods, because he was a dyer of fabric. He had been accepted into the Draper's Guild in Leyden, prestigious because only their members were permitted to dye fabrics in color that brought a higher price than black.

Being driven by financial stress at home, he may have joined, or promoted, a venture to South America. The red extract of the pernambuco trees was in great demand, and he may have envisioned making his fortune by selling this to members of the Draper's Guild when he returned.

To add to the confusion, the *Pigeon* returned from its voyage to Guiana, leaving three men behind for a year, as the Captain had been ordered to do. Sealed orders from the Dutch officials, he was instructed to open only days before the ship's return, indicated Jesse de Forrest would be one of those three.

According to most records, his family was destitute to the point that liens had been placed against their furniture and his dyer's cauldron for unpaid rent.[45] Sadly, his wife and ten children never reaped any benefit of his earnest efforts, nor did they ever see him again. He died of heat stroke in October, four months after he arrived.

Further confusion arises about the story of Jesse de Forrest's life from the historian of this time, James Baird, who claimed in 1855 that this Walloon, his wife and five children were passengers arriving among the initial settlers aboard the *Nieuw Nederlandt*. If this were true, most likely there would have been some reference, or record, of this adamant and highly vocal promoter having made his mark. No such records have surfaced, but subsequent accounts clearly indicate his brother and three adult children arrived within the first 10–15 years of the

44 de Forrest, Major
45 de Forrest, Mrs.

founding of this settlement. Several children settled in Haarlem, as it was spelled then, and one of the daughters returned to Holland.

Reconciling the arrival dates regarding both the *Mackerel* and the *Nieuw Nederlandt* as derived from family accounts, the personal diaries of Jesse de Forrest, and the official records of the Dutch West India Company remains a challenge. Understanding the confusing circumstances behind this mystery is even more daunting.

Adrian's Story from Tournai to Nova Belgica

(1567–1634)

One sunny Sunday morning in 1560, in my role as unseen historical observer, I slipped into a pew midway down the main aisle of the enormous Church of Notre Dame in Tournai. I wanted to be surrounded with sound from every direction. Soon the lusty voices of song burst forth, reverberating from the stone columns and the vaulted ceiling, and causing the revered stained glass windows to vibrate. As the sun shone through those colorful jewel-like panes, the Walloons sang in the language they knew. They were so thrilled to be active participants in the services, their energy was palpable.

But these earth-shaking changes were not enough for the industrious Walloons. They took it upon themselves to challenge the role of the saints, customary intermediaries in their prayers. They became so audacious they believed they could bypass these saints, and the Virgin Mary, and take their pleas and their gratitude directly to God in prayer.

Out in the flax fields I overheard them quietly discussing it all. "Why," one asked, "if we can pray to God directly, why do we need the statues anyway?"

On that dark night in August, 1566, I sensed something dreadful was about to take place.

Trembling in horror, I watched them lop off the head of the Virgin Mary they had previously worshipped so reverently, right there in the Church of Notre Dame on the town square in Tournai. I shuddered as they destroyed the religious relics and statues of saints before going on to shatter the precious stained glass windows that told of parables and the miracles-of-old the saints had performed. There would be a heavy price to pay for these unprecedented acts of contempt and violence throughout the Spanish-controlled land.

The clatter of the loom in the corner of the kitchen was stilled. The beater, the treadles, the harnesses no longer moved as the dark-haired maiden swiveled around on her wooden bench. From farms around, like-minded neighbors and relatives gathered, and waited quietly, at the home of Adrian-the-Elder. The year was 1567.[46]

Without a rustle of sound, the door flew open. Noordt Zee winds ushered in a chilling sight. I heard deep gasps and, like the other women, I, too, was frightened. I sat there, silent and unseen, on the bare, cold floor next to a young boy and his little sister. They kept silent, as well.

Adrian, now seven years old, was proud he could till the flax fields beside his father and his grandfather. Beside him sat three-year-old Yvette, clutching the thatch doll that her grandmother had made for her last winter, shortly before she died. This dark-haired little girl was anxious to grow tall enough to look over the half-door, on those rare sunny days in summer, when her mother could open the upper half. The overhanging thatch roof protected the doorway during the rainy, foggy days that pre-dominated much of the summer.

As if by pre-arrangement, no knock, no sound preceded the Catholic nun who entered and turned to close the door. Before the gasps of terror had subsided, this figure with dark, flashing eyes that peeped out from a black woolen shawl, unfurled the disguise—amid sighs of relief and admiration. Even by candlelight, the adults all recognized the young Calvinist preacher as Guido de Bray, a Walloon and one of their own faith and persuasion.[47]

I watched Guido de Bray warm himself at the hearth after a cold journey by boat on the darkened River Scheldt after he greeted those gathered in the crowded kitchen. This highly respected young man brought troubling news: the fearsome Duke of Alva had already arrived in Italy by boat. He and his men were headed north, a frightening specter. On hearing this, every man and woman in the room gasped. Mothers clutched their babies as if this Alvarez of Toledo were already at their doorstep.

As I sat there beside the well-behaved children, I was troubled. I sensed ever so clearly this could be one of the last religious services this highly-revered man might ever conduct, and that it would definitely be the last time anyone in this room would ever see him. With joyful devotion he led the long and fervent prayer; then he read from the psalms in the French accent of the adjacent Namur Province. Guido de Bray concluded the service by leading the worshippers in those popular, new songs in subdued voices they shielded from outsiders' ears.

After the neighbors left the warm kitchen of Adrian-the-Elder, I watched from the cold floor as the tall, slender gentleman slumped to his knees. He ducked his head under the split-log mantle that held the wooden feeding board, a carved children's mug, and a pewter tankard. In deep reverence, he closed his eyes and said a fervent, silent prayer in front of the dying embers. His stance embodied the pain of friends and neighbors as they trudged home with heavy hearts. I tried to envision the enormity of this news on everyone.

---

46 The story I have constructed here begins three generations before the Adrian Vincent on record sailed from London on the *Mary and John* in 1634. It depicts how Adrian-the-Elder and others might have experienced difficult and very significant events at the time of the emerging Reformation.

47 Guido de Bray is presented here with as complete a factual history of his ministry, beliefs, and achievements as is available from Griffis, Bayer and others. However, the fictional aspect of his arriving at the home of Adrian-the-Elder is presented here to capture the fervor and feelings of the times.

As soon as the children were asleep, the young Vincent families gathered closely, deepening their feelings with every breath as the three sons and their wives contemplated the wrenching moves they were forced to consider. They were saddened to leave families, to leave friends, to leave the countryside of Bruegel's paintings, but leave they must, if they were to preserve their lives and their faith.

In the days to come, as the young boy watched his parents act in unusual ways, he had many questions. But questions were not encouraged and answers would not be forthcoming. It would be risky to divulge plans for their departure. One could never be sure of underlying attitudes and suspicions of those nearby, who might readily take revenge into their own hands.

I had seen this elderly man bring the little boy to the town square in Tournai many times before, but on this Sunday, I could have sensed something special about their interaction, even if I had not known. The boy's expression was more strained and he held his grandfather's hand tighter than usual.

This bright, sunny morning, the gray-haired man with swarthy skin, so tall, so erect, and still so muscular, turned toward the seven-year-old and squeezed his hand in reassuring love. I strained to hear him over the sound of the bells, as he said in rapid French, "Remember, Adrian, Walloon blood courses through your veins." The child looked up at his grandfather and then down again, puzzled and frightened.

As the sound of the pealing church bells died down that morning, he continued: "You may not remember those bells of Notre Dame, nor the cobblestones beneath your feet, but you must never forget, 'You are a Walloon.'" It was eerie to hear these exact words of my own childhood. Even in my timeless, unseen role, I was shaken.

In hushed tones I heard the old man explain to his grandson, why he was sending his three sons and their families away, and why he would stay to fight. In silence he reminded himself that, when circumstances forced him to do so, he would go underground with his own beliefs, and rejoin the church as a nominal Catholic. I could hear his voice tighten with emotion as he spoke again, commanding the child not to reveal a word. Clouds began to roll in from the Noordt Zee and gray skies soon blocked out the sunshine.

The gray-haired old man and little boy turned to leave the town square of Tournai, but I lingered. As the rain began to fall over The Seventeen Provinces, my mind wandered back to the time in history when these lowlands had been ruled by France and were then called the "pays bas."

Centuries before Caesar's time, rain had fallen on the Belgic Lands south of the River Waal, flowing west from the Rhine to the Noordt Zee. Walloons lived below the River Waal and had met Caesar's legions there with ferocity. These early Belgic tribes had protected their lands, their coal fields, and their independence from Roman conquest. Now they were compelled to protect it once again.

As I stood there, I wondered how much of their history had been handed down. Did these Walloons of Hainaut Province and elsewhere in The Seventeen

Provinces know how their land had come under the Holy Roman Empire in Maximillian's time? More urgent matters loomed before them now. Matters of personal survival and their fight for religious freedom and political independence were foremost in 1567.

But they must have wondered, as I did growing up, how The Netherlands, so clearly Dutch, had ever come under Spanish rule. Who were Philip II and his father Charles V, and his great-grandfather Maximilian I on his father's side? How were they ever to become connected with Ferdinand and Isabella on his mother's side? I needed to know. I needed a foothold on the history of these times, when Spain and The Netherlands seemed intrinsically bound. I began my own search through maps, through books, through travel.

As the rain intensified, I ran to catch up with the grandfather and his young namesake as they trudged along the east bank of the River Scheldt to the flax farm, land their family had tilled for generations. I heard him tell the boy how he had implored each of his sons to carry the name Adrian into successive generations and to be strong in keeping the faith for which so many Walloons were fighting.

Cautiously he kept from telling the child what he feared most, that many of these revolters, or "protestors" as they were labeled by the Catholics, would die for their fervent beliefs.[48] This Two-Year Revolt (1567–1569) would propel the action that clearly became the Protestant Reformation and the Walloon Reformists, as they were now called, would flee by the hundreds to places where they could worship as they believed.

Wanting to overhear the conversation, I walked side by side with this dark-haired little boy, as his grandfather turned toward him to explain what was happening, but again imploring his silence. Some Walloons, he said, would head south, as would one of his own sons. They would pack their donkey cart with spindles and spinning wheel, with heddles and floor loom dismantled for the trip, until they could find refuge among kindred Calvinists, the Huguenots of France. I could foresee that in the months to follow, they would find a new location in the Normandy countryside 90 miles west of Paris, where they would settle and name their new town Tournai for the one they had left behind. There, in Tournai, France, I knew they would be safer for a time, but being in the minority, their Walloon identity would be obscured and they would become absorbed as French Huguenots.

Generations later, I would be stunned as again, the descendants of the original Walloon Reformist refugees, now Huguenots, were forced to flee because as Huguenots they now were severely oppressed in France. The Edict of Nantes which had provided them protection from the Catholic church, was revoked in 1685.[49] This oppression was fully sanctioned by the Church, commanded by the priests, and conducted by the "dragoons," dreaded hoodlums of revenge.[50]

48 Bayer
49 Bayer
50 Brodhead

"Some of the Walloons," I heard him tell his grandson, "will trek east, first crossing the hills and valleys of the Walloon provinces of Namur and Liege before climbing the long, sloping hillsides to the friendly and safe grounds of the Protestant German Palatines."

It would be in the Rhinephaltz of the Palatines in Germany, and Wesel in particular, where thousands of these Walloons would flee as Alva arrived to take up his post as their Military Governor and Spanish oppression escalated.

It was in Wesel where Pieter Minuet's grandfather had fled, and where his father had become a Walloon minister before Pieter was born.[51] Then, in the mid-1600s, thousands more refugees from Huguenot France would arrive and the identity of those Walloons would become obliterated by the sheer numbers of newcomers.[52]

In the 1690s, when people from the town of Die Pfalz on the banks of the Rhine emigrated to the west bank of the Hudson, they named their village New Paltz for the place they had just left. Here in America, the Walloons and the Huguenots would soon be known simply as "Huguenots" and the identity of the Walloons among them would again be lost.

Trudging back toward the farm, the little boy pressed the old man as to where he and his family would be going. I did not hear his response. I knew, however, that little Adrian could not fully comprehend that he would never again see his grandfather, nor would his feet touch the ground of his homeland.

Catholics, and those Walloons who for their safety, rejoined the church in order to remain, saw the emigration come to a standstill by the early to mid-1580s.[53] Sadly they also saw the serious depletion of their technological expertise. Their economy, their land, and their spirit were devastated.

This depletion would continue to be felt until 1830, when Belgium became a sovereign nation following intermittent alignment with The Netherlands. When this 19th Century drive for independence began, it was not in the Flemish provinces but in the Walloon provinces, just as it had been by those ardent, reform-minded Walloons 300 years earlier.[54]

Early the next morning at river's edge, I watched this erect gentleman suddenly age as, with tear-filled eyes he knelt down to hug his grandson for the last time. He looked into the boy's frightened eyes and whispered softly in his ear, "Adrian, my boy, always remember you're a Walloon." Then I saw him turn and, with shoulders slumped, he walked back to the farm to face his remaining years alone.

Adrian sat down in the bottom of the boat at his parents' knees. Beside his mother, sat little Yvette clutching her prized possession, the thatched doll on her lap, just the way her mother was holding the baby. A number of families of the neighborhood, Walloon "protestors" all, settled into the flat-bottomed riverboat as it pushed off from the dock.

---

51 Griffis
52 Griffis
53 Brodhead
54 Griffis

Adrian's mother, I noticed, was shivering beneath her woolen shawl, as she wrapped it firmly around the baby on her lap. This shawl was an heirloom from her grandmother, woven years earlier at the time these floor looms were first created in the Walloon provinces. The Walloons of Hainaut, Liege, and Namur were at that time, Europe's most technologically advanced.[55] In fact, it was the skills that Walloon émigrés carried to Holland, England, and Ireland that helped these countries eventually emerge from darkness and take part in the Industrial Revolution.[56]

Headed north, their trip along the Scheldt took several days. I averted my eyes from the tears that spilled down their cheeks as the women took one last, long look toward the shoreline. In some places they saw tiny pale blue blossoms of the flax fields they were leaving behind sway with winds from the Noordt Zee. Other fields had been ravaged and burned by those whose religious ideas were at strong variance. The largest exodus, of more than 100,000 Walloon Reformists, occurred in the weeks and months before Alva arrived.[57] Over a period of the next 12 years, those Reformists, who had stayed behind to fight, suffered the pain and torture of the Second Spanish Inquisition.[58]

But, back on the River Scheldt, I watched as their riverboat arrived in Delfshaven, several miles south of Rotterdam. They unloaded a treasured sack of flax, their spinning wheel, a dismantled loom, and a few other possessions into a small boat that plied the canals from Rotterdam to Delft by the Vliet waterway, to reach Leyden, the mecca in Holland for Walloon refugees.

Several generations later in 1608, the Separatists from England would also congregate in Leyden and live there for 12 years before the healthiest members among them were selected to make their historic "pilgrimage." These Separatists who became our Pilgrims, loaded their boats at the Rapenburg Canal and headed south along the inland waterways to Delfshaven where they would board the *Speedwell* and later meet the *Mayflower* in England.[59]

It was fifty years before that, when the young Vincent family first settled in Leyden among other Walloon refugees of the Hainaut Province. There were many French-speaking Walloon churches there, for the newcomers. Throughout Holland, at this particular period of the mid-to-late 1500s and well into the mid-1600s the 70 French-language Reformed churches served the estimated 500,000 Walloon refugees. The cities were filled beyond capacity; food was scarce, prices rose, and jobs were few. It is understandable that not all Hollanders welcomed this influx.

They made it especially difficult for these émigrés to join the prestigious Draper's Guild for dyers.[60] The fact that those who were not accepted could only

55 Bayer
56 Lamb
57 Bayer
58 Riker
59 Brodhead
60 de Forrest, Mrs.

dye cloth black, seemed sadly ironic, since the early Walloon refugees of the 1530s had introduced looms to Holland for the Dutch to weave cloth.[61]

Seven-year-old Adrian found his Dutch playmates fun to play with. These little tow-heads, whose hair was so different from his own, introduced him to their game of marbles using soft clay rolled in smooth balls, baked like bricks, and called "knickkers." They played their games on the fine-grained, white sand beside the cobblestone streets. They had fun, even though initially they had little understanding of each others' language beyond the essentials of their game. I noticed Adrian was visibly saddened to leave his new playmates, when his father found it necessary to move once more.[62]

They packed their meager belongings and boarded the small boat that took them by way of the Rapenburg Canal and inland waterways back to Delfshaven. There, this young Walloon family would board a ship to carry them to England, where they were welcomed for their skillful knowledge of loom design and weaving. Already, by 1550, a Walloon chapel had been built in the crypt of Canterbury Cathedral to honor these early émigrés and provide a place for them to worship.

Two generations later, the boy whose grandfather had said goodbye on the bank of the River Scheldt, now went to the docks near Henley, on the River Thames.[63] In silence and unseen, I was saddened to watch this historic moment for the family unfold. The grandfather first said "goodbye" to his son, Adrian, and then to his grandson, Jon. He did not hug them as his own grandfather had done in farewell to him as a child on the river bank in Tournai. Grown men shook hands, but any further show of emotion was not customary.

Adrian would soon sail from London on the ship the *Mary and John* while the grandson, Jon, and his wife, Annetje Jans who kept her family name as was traditional, went with him only as far as London. Adrian's name alone appears as a passenger on the *Mary and John*. It seems feasible that they followed at a later time.[64] That did not stop the gray-haired man from saying his farewell with the familiar phrase. I heard him whisper close to Jon's ear, "Don't ever forget you are a Walloon."

When Adrian sailed on the *Mary and John*, in the spring of 1634, he came as a private citizen. He was ready to start life anew, in the tiny Manhattan Island settlement where the first Walloons had arrived ten years earlier, and called their new home "Nova Belgica."[65] However, he could have had little understanding of what they had endured.

---

61 Griffis

62 Whereas public records about Adrian Vincent cannot be documented prior to 1634 when he arrived on the *Mary and John*, family history indicates they had originally come from Tournai to Leyden. Extensive research, however, that was done in 2004 by Jeremy D. Bangs, Ph. D., of Leiden, reveals no evidence that the family was there long enough to show up in the "chimney" tax records of the time, nor become members of the French-language Walloon churches, a more significant indicator. Thus, I have concluded they, like many other refugees, soon moved on from this vastly over-crowded Dutch city, to England.

63 This setting on the River Thames has been arbitrarily chosen for its accessibility to London.

64 On the Costello Plan of property ownership in Nieuw Nederlandt in 1660, there are six plots owned by Adrian Vincent and one of these was occupied by his son Jon Vincent, and wife Annetje Jans. It is possible that they met and married in America, but, since no marriage records are apparent, the story is constructed this way.

65 Griffis

A decade earlier, as a silent, unseen observer, I had watched the original, weary Walloon settlers, who arrived May 20, 1623, on the *Nieuw Nederlandt.*[66] It was sunny, but a cold blast of air rolled off the bay. I was so stunned to see the sight before me, I was scarcely aware of the discomfort of the cold, jagged rocks where I sat. A clatter of voices rose as dozens of Indians raced past me to the water's edge.

Others had already paddled out in their hollowed-out bark canoes to the "wooden island" floating before us. Never before had they, nor I, laid eyes on a ship that large. It was many times the size of the 90-ton *Halve Maane* they had watched 17 years before, when Henry Hudson and his crew had sailed past and then continued up the Noordt River for 150 miles.

Suddenly there was even more excitement. One French vessel, and possibly two were in the channel, beside the island at the "narrows." With bated breath, I stood there on shore wondering what would happen. Were these ships of war? Were they about to challenge the Dutch claims on behalf of the rulers in France?

The *Nieuw Nederlandt* had scarcely a firearm on board, and no one trained to fight. Everyone on shipboard must have been terrified to see this new danger. Their recent ancestors had been accustomed to dangers face-to-face in the homeland they fled, and they themselves had endured the frightening storms at sea, but now to face unknown, potential hazards of war single-handed was just too much.

With the ice now gone, a Dutch sailing ship, the *Mackerel,* had headed down river, to return to Holland with its full cargo of tobacco and furs. Upon arriving at the southern tip of Manna-hatta, as the Indians called it, the captain was surprised to see the *Nieuw Nederlandt* anchored there. The three-banded, blue, white, and orange flag, emblem of the Dutch West India Company, was flying from its masthead.

It was with some anxiety, the captain and crew noticed the French vessels beyond and promptly brought four or five cannons up on deck. I stood there on shore in virtually a frozen posture, and heard the cannons fire a "signal of understanding" to the French vessels to leave. I watched as, far in the distance, the *Mackerel* escorted the intruders through the narrows and out to sea. This unanticipated incident allowed the Dutch to retain control of their territory, but narrowly, you might say.

I was so fascinated at the unexpected sight of this "floating island," I joined those 30 families on shipboard, in my unseen role. I heard them discuss plans to raise tall stalks of flax for the fancy collars and lace cuffs so popular among the burgers and merchants of Rembrandt's Amsterdam. Manna-hattin, the spelling they would adapt, had a less viable growing season.[67] Their flax would grow no higher than eight inches; marketing plans would vanish.[68]

66 Brodhead
67 Lamb
68 Griffis

Brought ashore by canoe-sized skiffs lowered from the deck, these Walloons were surrounded by cinnamon-skinned, brightly painted, and scantily clad natives. As they headed toward shore, their tiny boat rocked up and down in the waves. I heard screams of fright from the little girls and whoops of excitement from their brothers. I watched the weary, frightened women hold their treasured linen sacks of flaxseed shoulder high to protect them from an unexpected wave.

The little boys squealed at the jelly-like feeling in their knees after that long voyage on rocky seas. My ears became instantly alert when I heard them speak in French, the same French accent I had listened to so intently in the town square in Tournai.

Not one passenger aboard the *Nieuw Nederlandt* was Dutch; all were Walloon except for one or more Flemish reformists[69] whose original language, the language of their rich literature, was Brabantish.[70]

Except for one young child whose descendants claim was aboard, not one of the passenger's names was recorded. Only the name of Cornelius May, the Director of the Dutch West India Company survives, because Cape May on the New Jersey shore bears his name.

Before the ship left Amsterdam, the officials of the Dutch West India Company had designated where each family would be "planted." The eight families designated to settle the tip of Manna-hattin waved from the pebble-strewn cove, sad that they would never see each other again.

Then the *Nieuw Nederlandt* unfurled its sails and cast off, to deposit other families along the South River, later named the Delaware. The four couples, who were married on board, were planted there as well. The largest group, of 12 families, would settle the uppermost reaches of the Noordt River, Hudson's discovery. Still other families from this ship would settle the Fresh River, now called the Connecticut, near Hartford.

Here was the perfect match-up of profound needs of each party engaged in this history-making expedition. The Walloons needed a new place to settle, to worship freely, and to have a land, a country, to call their own. The Dutch West India Company saw the need of those survival skills for which the Walloons were well known: ingenuity, inventiveness, and a renowned persistence in overcoming difficulties. So it was, these early descendants of the Walloon Province of Hainaut were the first settlers of the Dutch territory that continued for many decades to be identified as "Novi Belgii" or "Nova Belgica" on Dutch maps.[71]

This tiny band of Walloons, it would seem, named their tiny settlement on Manna-hattin Island, Nova Belgica as well, perhaps in honor of their lost homeland. Thus, the settlement of Nova Belgica, within the province by the same name, became the forerunner we know as New York, New York.[72]

69 Griffis
70 Bayer
71 Wilson
72 Griffis

The seal of New Amsterdam.

The 1653 Seal of New Amsterdam

The present seal of New York City.

Seal of the City of New York, 1664
and adapted in 1929

The Indians were friendly, and some even let the newcomers till their cleared patches of land. I watched, as the young boys set to work planting the flaxseeds, so treasured a crop in Europe but so disappointing in America.

It was painful for me to see them struggle as they built shelters, similar to those of medieval origin, to protect each family from the snow and gales that winter would bring across the broad harbor. I admired how the Walloons—armed only with their simple farm tools, bare hands, and determination—devised their initial shelters by first digging three or four feet down into the ground. Then they lined the walls and floor of these dirt "wells" with rough-hewn logs. Above it they built the sides and a roof with bark slabs and tried to thatch it.[73] Their make-shift thatch of twigs, weeds, and cattails was a far cry from the hollow-stemmed stalks piled a foot thick, to shed the rain and shield homes from the Noordt Zee breezes.

After digging for days, often an unforgiving rock loomed several feet beneath the surface. Then the 12-foot square hole would have to be abandoned, only to start again with no better promise. Despite their attempts to lay out an orderly row of houses, as they were accustomed to, those plans were frustrated by both rocky, and swampy, terrain.

These shelters precluded building a fire inside, but when the deerskin they hung over the narrow entrance was pulled aside, the scent of roasted chestnuts from the fire outside often rushed in. I was as excited as they to see this nourishment stem pangs of hunger and warm their souls. In the pile of rocks surrounding the small fire, warm ones were rolled into the well at dark, carried out cold in the morning.

Starvation that first winter was barely avoidable. They might not have survived had it not been for the deer and wild game the Indians shared, fish from the bay

73 Wilson

and the crop they found beneath the butternut, chestnut, hickory, and walnut trees on "Nut Island." This tiny island in the harbor was later purchased by a governor, hence it became Governor's Island.

Here in Manna-hattin, besides the unforgiving rocks beneath the soil, the peril of storms, and near-starvation over the winter, the settlers faced new hazards the following summer. They soon discovered the makeshift thatch dried from the wind and caught fire easily, so unlike the thatch at home, which was kept moist by the wind-blown fogs from the sea. Sadly, some lost their meager possessions and that of greatest pride and value to them, confirmation of church membership back in their French-language Walloon churches in Holland. By good fortune, their copy of the cherished *Belgic Confession of Faith* survived.[74]

It was not until 1626, three years after their arrival, that funds were approved in the Stadhuis in The Hague, to build Fort Amsterdam.[75] Its walls were constructed of rock and sod which would need replacing in a few years. Within the fort a structure was built for the director and quarters for the soldiers and sailors serving in the Dutch West India Company. In contrast to the Pilgrims, the Walloon settlers lived outside the fort; their location at the tip of the island offered them an added measure of natural protection. By contrast with other early settlers in America, the Walloons did not build log cabins. Rather, they constructed wind-blown timber mills for lumber to build their houses. Timber mills were not seen in New England until much later and derived their power, not from windmills, but from water-driven paddles along a millstream.

The first eight families planted here waited in desperation the following year for the shipload of livestock they had been promised. The livestock were loaded onto the *Mackerel* heading back to Manhattan Island, ironically, to help in the survival of the Walloons, just as it had previously figured in the salvation of the Dutch territory.[76] In fulfillment of the promise, it sailed on time, but unexpected events intervened.

After leaving the dock in Amsterdam, it sailed north through the Zuider Zee to the island of Texel. There the captain picked up a "pilot" to guide his ship through the treacherous straits. Past Texel, they emerged into the Noordt Zee, and headed south along the coastline, with a full load of livestock. Sadly, this ship was overtaken by pirates off the Dutch shores of Zeeland.

The next year, Pieter Hulft, one of the directors of the Amsterdam Chamber of the Dutch West India Company, privately outfitted another ship designed specifically for livestock. A special deck was constructed with individual stalls, covered with three feet of soft sand to protect the heaviest animals.[77] On this latter day Noah's Ark, the stalls were kept as clean as any in Holland.

74 Griffis
75 Griffis
76 Wilson
77 Wilson

Safety measures and food were provided these prime cattle, horses, sheep, and pigs with the care and concern equal to that accorded royalty. Below deck there were tanks constructed to carry enough fresh water for the two-month voyage. This time, an armed yacht was sent by the Dutch West India Company to accompany them. It carried additional grain and fodder for the animals, plus 45 Walloon settlers, more farming tools, and seed.[78]

This monument commemorates the establishment of Fort Amsterdam at this site in 1626, now Battery Park.

As we sailed from Amsterdam up the protected Zuider Zee, the water was calm. The customary mooing, braying, and blatting arose from this sea-going barnyard. But when the ship edged through the Texel straits and into the Noordt Zee, things changed. The protests intensified as we sailed down the coast to the English Channel, known to seamen throughout the ages as unpredictable and unusually rough. This Noah's Ark could have championed a string quartet, the Belgian stallions on bass, the roosters striking the high notes, with the sheep and cows standing in for the viola and cello. By the time we hit the Atlantic, every voice was heard.

The pitch of this 300-ton ship seemed to drop into a trough so deep, I wondered, standing there on the bow, if it would ever rise to see the skyline again; it did, pausing a moment before dipping once more in its endless, predictable, unsettling rhythm. Amid-ship, the port-to-starboard roll that was added to the pitch from bow to stern made it an even more unsettling experience. The chickens and roosters caged in the fantail flew from one part of their cages to another in a ceaseless effort to find some spot to regain their equilibrium. There was none. The hens stopped laying eggs and the roosters crowed in alarm at midnight as powerfully as they did at dawn.

Of the 102 head of livestock on board, only two died en route, which can be credited to expert planning, and the devoted care they received. The animals included the black and white breeding cattle from Friesland we know as Holsteins. The breeding stock of heavy, chestnut-colored Belgian work horses, needed for timbering, stood 17 hands high.

78 Wilson

Francois Molemacher bought one of the lighter-weight horses. In 1626, he built a horse-driven gristmill on Slyck Steeg. This was a deeply rutted, muddy road in spring, remarkably bad even by standards of those days and was equally dusty all summer. Slyck Steeg was a dog-legged street that ran east off the Herre Gracht.[79] It would be renamed Mill Street by the English and later changed to South William Street, the name it carries today.

The bells, confiscated in Puerto Rico in 1625 were mounted in the tower over Molemacher's gristmill, to call worshippers to service there and continued to do so even after the congregation built a small barn-like structure on Perel Straat.[80] The latter was on the north side of the street between the Herre Gracht, which became Broad Street[81] and the street a block to the west the English would name Whitehall.[82]

Eight years after Francois Molemacher's gristmill had been built, the ship out of London, the *Mary and John,* slowly sailed into the harbor. I stood at the fantail of its gently rolling deck, all-seeing but unseen. I looked over the side and saw a bouncing bark which Adrian Vincent must now climb down to if he was to complete his journey to the New World. Before he stepped from the deck, down the shaky, crude, hemp ladder to the bark below, he looked out at the shoreline. His ears caught the faint sound of bells in the distance. He could not know that the bells ringing that Sunday morning from the tower in Molemacher's gristmill on Slyck Steeg would be virtually the spot where he would spend the rest of his life. He would buy six plots facing the Herre Gracht. The lot at the corner of Herre Gracht and Slyck Steeg would become the location of his tavern.

The Dutch West India Company was poorly managed. Soon the Amsterdam Chamber became disinterested and was an inadequate supporter of this tiny settlement. Thus, in need of funds, they offered lots for sale. Records indicate the price of each lot was a mere $9.63, an unheard of bargain in our minds, but considering Pieter Minuet had bought the whole island for $24, inflation seemed already in effect.[83] Perhaps it was the availability of land as well as this bargain price for real estate that lured early settlers.

City maps from 1649 as well as the Costello Plan of 1660 show the exact location of Adrian Vincent's six lots.[84] Whereas Adrian Vincent's lots were purchased for the whole sum of $57.78, its value in 1674 was listed at $1,500.[85] Now, as the location of the present-day International Telephone Company at 75 Broad Street, its worth has increased exponentially.

---

79 van Rensselaer, Mrs. Schuyler

80 The Dutch spelling is used for street names to correspond with that used at the time these events took place.

81 de Forrest, Mrs.

82 Griffis

83 Todd

84 Utrecht-born Jacques Cortelyou was named the official surveyor of Nieuw Amsterdam of the Nieuw Nederlandt Colony and was charged with documenting the owners of businesses and residential property in 1660. This precise map of streets and plot owners was inadvertently misnamed the Costello Plan because of the name of the town in Italy where it was found, and where it remains.

85 Jamieson

The entrance to the International Telephone Company is on the corner of Broad Street and South William Street. According to the Costello Plan, this is the exact location of the tavern that belonged to Adrian Vincent.

It seemed that French was the language most of the people spoke then, except those few Walloons like Adrian who had been brought up in England, and had arrived with him from London. It was in the mid-1630s, that the Dutch first began to populate the settlement. This was mainly due to a promotional tract written by Johan de Laet in 1630 to protect his own investment and that of the Dutch West India Company. The passengers must have been aghast to discover it was such a primitive place, but few left. What family would want to endure a return trip?

The property belonging to Francois Molemacher ran between 20 and 28 Slyck Steeg, a dog-legged street. The previously mentioned gristmill was located at

20–22.[86] This location and the artifacts discovered at the second gristmill at 28 Slyck Steeg are of historic importance.[87]

As an unseen historical observer, I watched people gather for worship at Molemacher's first gristmill. It was built in 1625, and the second floor was large enough for 50 people.[88] I sat in the back row on a hard, hand-hewn bench. Initially, two caregivers of the sick, who were supplied by the Dutch West India Company, were responsible for reading the scriptures and conducting their prayers from the wooden desk in front that served as a pulpit. Then in 1628, with the insensitivity characteristic of the Dutch West India Company, but in keeping with company policy for managing affairs of the territory, a Dutch-language pastor of the Dutch Reformed Church of Holland was sent over. His name was Jonas Michaelius.[89]

In my timeless, unseen role I watched with both reverence and empathy as history unfolded before my eyes. More than 60 people crowded in as Jonas Michaelius served The Lord's Supper for the very first time in the Dutch Province of Nova Belgica, August 11, 1628.[90]

There were also humorous moments for me, watching this ill-equipped pastor stumble through the scriptures in the native language of these Walloons. Composing the prayers in French was even more challenging to him. Perhaps for that reason, the sermon was brief. In time, his French from the pulpit became more fluent. The faith of the congregants never faltered, but any confidence they had that the Dutch West India Company would care about their own needs had been shaken, as it would be time and time again.

Their needs changed as the settlement grew. The tiny, barn-shaped church they constructed on Perel Straat would be renamed decades later "Old Kirke" by the English.

Within the first few years of construction, these Walloons would find Indian raids during services were a distinct risk. They decided to build a church within Fort Amsterdam. Until then, the growing congregation of this little community of Nova Belgica returned to Molemacher's mill, where sometimes multiple services had to be held on Sunday.

The Church of Saint Nicholas, as the congregation named it, was constructed of stone. This feature plus being inside the fort afforded members greater safety. The original Dutch Reformed congregation of the gristmill on Slyck Steeg, and the Olde Kirke, and subsequently the Church of Saint Nicholas, later became the Marble Collegiate Church of New York. This church can be rightfully proud of the continuous records of births, deaths, marriages, and church membership that has been maintained since 1638.[91]

It is almost certain then, that Adrian Vincent, and his family on the Herre Gracht, coming from a devout reformed past, would have initially at least,

86 van Rensselaer, Mrs. Schuyler
87 The practice of religion in pre-colonial America is described in the following chapter.
88 Jamieson
89 Bayer
90 Valentine
91 van Rensselaer, Mrs. Schuyler

worshipped around the corner, at the Molemacher's gristmill on Slyck Steeg. I was overjoyed as an unseen witness of my family history to find the names of Adrian's son, Jon, and his wife, Annetje Jans, were among the first recorded members of the Church of Saint Nicholas and that infant Hester Vincent was baptized there.[92]

It is very possible that generations earlier, in Tournai, Adrian-the-Elder had given his three sons a mandate to perpetuate the name in successive generations. The assumption seems plausible, because records show that two more men by that name arrived within three decades. A variation in the spelling of their names presumably reflects their sojourns in France or England.

In addition to the Adrian Vincent already cited, who arrived on the *Mary and John* in 1634, Adriaen Vincian arrived on the ship *Draetvat*, meaning—"Dry Keg"—June 2, 1657.[93] Then, another Adriaen Vincian, who is clearly identified as a flax farmer from Tournai on the River Scheldt, Province of Hainaut, arrived on the ship *Hope* on April 8, 1662 with his wife and children, ages sixteen, twelve, and five years. These details are documented in the genealogical research prepared by my mother, Mary Ham Knickerbocker, and others, for its 1959 publication.

No record of property ownership of the family of Adriaen Vincian, who arrived on the *Hope* in 1662, appears on the Costello Plan since it was prepared two years prior to his arrival. However, it seems clear that he and his family resided across from the original Vincent lots on the Herre Gracht, very possibly between Bridge and Stone Streets.

92 The Vincent Family Genealogy

93 The name of the passenger on the ship the *Mary and John* from London, England, in 1634, was spelled Adriaen Vinchent.

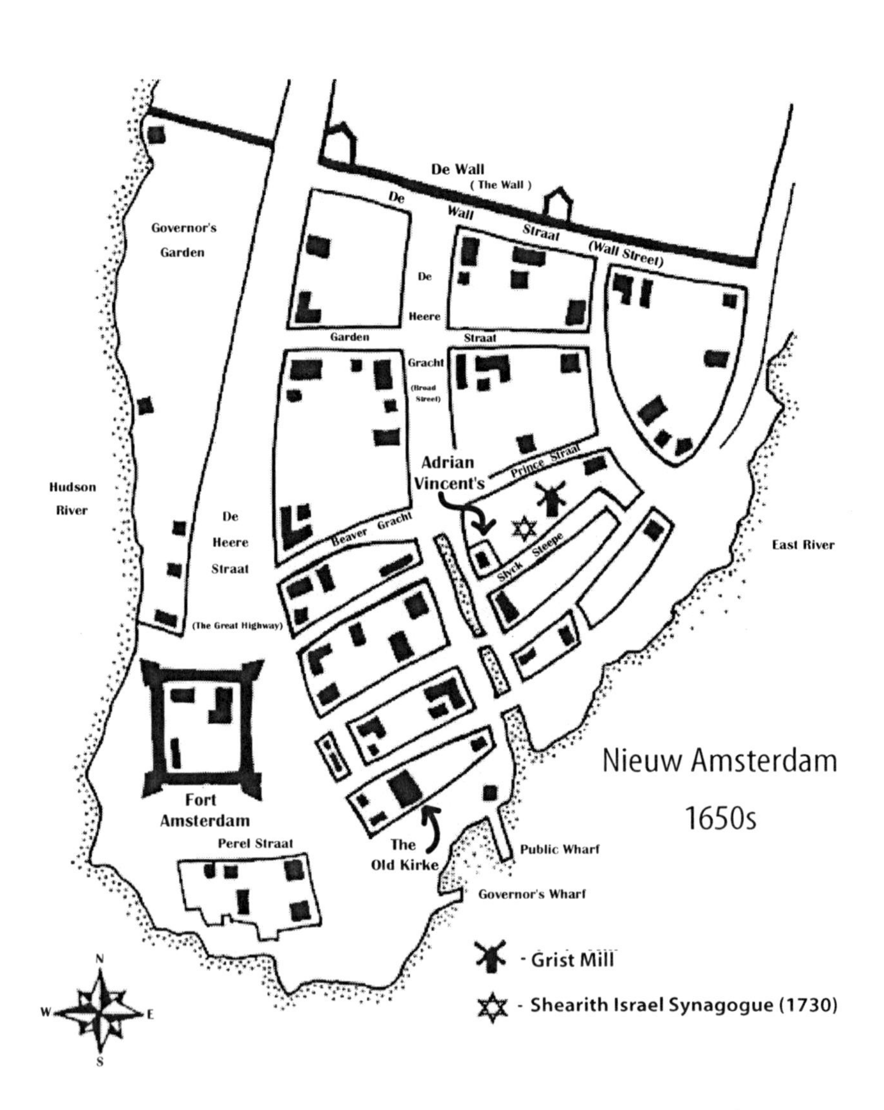
De Wall
(The Wall)
De Wall Straat (Wall Street)
Governor's Garden
De Heere Straat
Garden
Gracht
(Broad Street)
Hudson River
De Heere Straat
(The Great Highway)
Adrian Vincent's
Prince Straat
Beaver Gracht
Slyck Steepe
East River
Fort Amsterdam
Perel Straat
The Old Kirke
Public Wharf
Governor's Wharf
Nieuw Amsterdam
1650s
N
W
E
S
- Grist Mill
- Shearith Israel Synagogue (1730)

2

1630: A Benchmark Year In Nova Belgica and Beyond

The year 1630 became a benchmark year because of significant changes, and certain noteworthy achievements in Nova Belgica, and elsewhere.

Events of the distant past have become woven within the fabric of our pre-colonial and early colonial history. Specific events that occurred in 1630 would eventually have a direct impact on the separation of church and state in America.

This pertinent history is presented, together with one notable accomplishment in Nova Belgica that year, as told from a *first person historical omniscient perspective.*

Pertinent History

The Hudson River is named

Shortly before 1630, the Noordt River had been renamed for Hudson, who discovered it in 1609.

1630: The name Nieuw Amsterdam is coined

The name Nieuw Amsterdam first appeared in an eight-page promotional tract prepared by the Dutch historian Johan de Laet.[1] Reportedly, this was done to protect and enhance the financial investments of his and others in the Amsterdam Chamber of the Dutch West India Company.

Recognizing that people of The Netherlands would need strong inducements to come to the New World, he lauded the opportunities and down-played the risks, the hazards, and the primitive living conditions there. He further promoted the idea of a far more civil and sophisticated place than it was by likening it in name to their cherished city, Amsterdam.

Since they had neither suffered rampant religious persecution, nor been forced from their beloved homeland, the Dutch people had seen little reason to rush toward these "wild lands" as they were called. They were happy and content, "tilling their fertile land and freely worshipping God according to their consciences."[2]

1 Brodhead

2 Brodhead

Whereas the first settlers sailed from a Dutch port, on a Dutch ship to a Dutch territory, and are generally considered to have been Dutch, it would be nearly a decade after de Laet's 1630 promotional tract was written, before many Hollanders arrived. As their numbers increased, the identity of the Walloons and the history of their valiant endeavors to survive and build an enduring community, would soon be lost. It would be further affected by the fact that as many as 18 different languages would be spoken as people arrived from varied ports.

The first fort was built in 1626 and was called Fort Amsterdam from the start. However, the name Nieuw Amsterdam for the settlement was not originated until 1630 and was not commonly used until 1640. The Nieuw Nederlandt territory became a colony the same year.

1630: Two Walloon shipwrights build a 1200-ton ship

Two Walloon shipwrights of Nova Belgica built a 1200-ton ship by hand without a dry dock. This ship was larger than any then afloat. When compared to the 90-ton *Halve Maane* and the 260-ton *Nieuw Nederlandt* that brought the Walloons across the Atlantic, the feat is even more amazing.[3] As impressive as this achievement was in Nova Belgica, it was shocking when this ship they named the *Nieuw Nederlandt* as well, sailed into Amsterdam. The names of these two remarkable shipwrights, has been lost.

This story as told by a first person historical omniscient observer

I did not go into the forests with them that spring, but I wished I had. I could only envision it from what I overheard evenings in the local tavern when they returned in the fall. They told of great stands of pine they eyed in awe. So impressed were these shipwrights to gaze on trees taller than they had ever seen, it caused their minds to swirl. Here were wonderfully erect pine trees especially suited for masts as well as booms and yardarms of sailing vessels. Best of all, the white pine was soft enough to yield to the blows of a primitive, hand-forged ax head. When felled and trimmed, these trees would provide timber of undreamed-of lengths for a ship's hull.

These men spent a whole year selecting and marking those trees that would be just right for each section of the ship, a ship only they could picture in their minds. Much of this timber was found on the east bank of the river that now honored Henry Hudson.

The slender white pine trees with their short, needled branches at the very top pierced the dense canopy of hemlocks, spruce, and cedar. These delighted the Walloon shipwrights who selected from a range of woods those best suited for their ship's various requirements. In addition, there were sturdy oaks and maples on the gentle, virgin slopes.

When these shipbuilders returned to Nova Belgica, they extolled the vivid colors of autumn that interspersed this evergreen carpet. Men in the taverns occasionally questioned their exuberant tales but were to be proven wrong.

3 Wilson

It is presumed that the area where most of these trees came from was about two-thirds of the way up the river on the eastern bank. Nearly a century later, this site would become the location of the towns named Hyde Park, Rhinecliff, and Tivoli. Not only were the trees well-suited to their timbering requirements, of more relevance was the near vertical pitch of the terrain along the river bank. This made it possible to slide slender trunks, trimmed of their bark and branches, down snow-covered hillsides to the river's edge.

In some sections along the river, they could clear a sloping swath and roll these heavy tree trunks onto the river's frozen surface. Back in the taverns, I heard them tell how they had gathered into their rabbit skin pouches precious, hardened droplets of pitch that oozed from the pine trees. Only they could envision the shape and size of the vessel they would build. They knew how many logs they would need for the project of their dream. Lashed together on thick winter ice with rough-hewn hemp, they created a wide platform to float down river in spring, a treacherous task at best.

Two years earlier, the Walloons had erected several wind-driven sawmills at the water's edge north of Fort Amsterdam. Thus, they were able to cut wood to build their own shelters, as well as to export timber back to Holland for houses and ships. But no one could have dreamed what these Walloon shipwrights planned to accomplish.

These tall, muscular men with jet black hair built their ship in only a year. When it was finished, they christened it the *Nieuw Nederlandt*. This achievement was the pride of the Walloons, as well it should have been in this primitive community that now numbered 600 people. By the time it was completed, probably every man and many of the young boys had helped in its construction, caulking, rigging, or launching. Constructed on a series of parallel, smoothed logs, spaced appropriately, it took the stout effort of all the Belgian work horses that had endured a rough Atlantic voyage five years before. Slowly, they rolled this enormous bulk down the slightly sloping shore to splash into the water we know as the East River.

As soon as the ship hit the water, lines of men on shore heaved long, slender tree trunks, freshly felled and trimmed, onto their shoulders. Then, in unison, they waded out to lift them, one by one, to the men on deck who were waiting to receive their precious cargo. These trunks and rough-cut timber from the larger trees were strapped securely to the deck; they would delight shipbuilders in Holland, offering taller masts and longer hulls than anything they had ever seen.

Like all those Walloons cheering from shore, a thrill rippled through my heart too, as I stood there. The pride of Nova Belgica flew the blue, white, and orange colors of the Dutch West India Company high on the masthead. Luckily for these shipwrights, a spare set of sails could be "borrowed" so to speak, from the Dutch West India Company warehouse on Perel Straat.

Unfurled, the sails billowed against the wind to carry this sparkling new rendition of the *Nieuw Nederlandt* through the narrows and out to sea.

In Amsterdam, jaws dropped. Walloons crowded the dock and were aghast at the unbelievable sight. They eagerly booked passage for its return trip, as others would do for those 30 voyages to and from homeport in the years to come. Not only was this achievement further testimony to the courageous inventiveness traditional among the Walloons, but also it was accomplished only seven short years after their arrival in the "wild lands" of the New World. These Walloons were eager to take their place beside shipbuilders of long standing tradition in the Old World.

Pieter Minuet, a Walloon from Wesel, Germany, was then the Director of the Nieuw Nederlandt territory that had been named a Province the same year he arrived, in 1626. He approved the funds for this venture from the small, local treasury of the Dutch West India Company. Whether the funding was done with prior approval of the Amsterdam Chamber of the Dutch West India Company is unclear. Not surprisingly, the final cost was double the original estimate. Was it for this reason, the Walloons' achievement was not met favorably when they arrived?[4]

Was it because they had absconded a spare set of sails from the company warehouse? Or could it have been because, by their achievement, they had inadvertently put to shame the shipwrights in the shipyards of Holland and Zeeland? Perhaps it was jealousy of this establishment, or a combination of these factors. The fact is that a century would pass before another ship of this size would be constructed here.[5]

I was saddened to see that this amazing source of pride was not properly acknowledged, and that these stalwart settlers could not capitalize on their talents. Lost to history are the names of the two remarkable Walloon shipwrights and their scant-numbered crew, those few men in Nova Belgica who had sufficient knowledge of the sea to handle such an enormous and precarious undertaking. We do not know why, but we do know that this chapter of our history has, in fact, remained well hidden.

1630: The Dutch capture the island of Recife

Among the history-making events of 1630, perhaps the most far-reaching was the Dutch capture of the tiny Portuguese island of Recife that lies below the eastern prominence of Brazil. Recife was re-captured by the Portuguese in 1654.[6] Less than ten years later, these seemingly unrelated occurrences in such a remote part of the world would precipitate an event in our country that guaranteed the separation of one's religion and full civic participation. It was through the determined actions of one man, Asser Levy, as will become evident.

Relevant historical background to Recife

During the 1492 Spanish Inquisition, many Jews, who wanted to remain close to their cultural ties, resettled in nearby Portugal that was and had long been a fully tolerant society. They were accepted there as bona fide citizens. They were

4 Wilson
5 Wilson
6 Kamen, 2003

simply required to pay their taxes like everyone else. After 1492, this tolerance continued, but only for a short three years.[7]

That was when Manuel, the son of Portugal's King John sought the hand in marriage of the daughter of Ferdinand and Isabella. She refused unless Portugal, like her home country, had banished its Jewish "infidels."

For decades, even centuries, Portugal had welcomed the services and accomplishments of its Jewish population. Most honored among them was Fernando de Laronha who had led five ships to explore the coast of Brazil in 1500, claiming it for the Portuguese. Like other Jews who had been forced to accept Christianity, Fernando de Laronha was called a "Marrano" because he refused to eat pork.

Early development of Recife

At the time when the Portuguese were forced to mistreat them, many Jews fled to Brazil with Portugal's encouragement to settle those lands. Jews who went there were apparently free to continue their cultural traditions, albeit without the support and formal structure of Judaism.

Over the next 125 years, these Jewish expatriates developed sugar and tobacco plantations, and they were the first to grow coffee and tea. They developed commercial trade to Europe where these products were in great demand.[8] The Jews of Recife established a rousing slave trade, to provide labor for the sugar plantations. The slaves brought the vines of the pernambuco trees from Africa that had traditionally figured in their religious rites.[9]

Many varieties of this tree took root in the verdant rainforest. It can be presumed that on the island of Recife, as well, after a century and a half, there was a rich forest of these tall trees with rough, gray-spotted bark whose heavy canopy shaded the cocoa bean trees beneath, enabling them to thrive.

The wood of the pernambuco tree is known for its unusual strength and flexibility and has been used since the time of Bach for making high performance violin bows.[10] However, two centuries earlier, in the period we are discussing, there were other considerations. As mentioned, the deep red interior of the tree trunks of the pernambuco tree produced a highly desirable extract of red dye that was much in demand for the fabrics of Europe. It is understandable that this land would be fought over to serve the needs of cardinals and kings.

This narrow speck of real estate, only a few miles long, was sought after by both the Portuguese and the Dutch for various reasons. First, it was easily accessible to shipping across the Atlantic, thus crucial to Dutch trade and a distant haven for their ships. Second, the inner harbor at Recife then controlled the trade between inland river routes of the pernambuco and trans-Atlantic ports. Third, this gave those who occupied the island, immediate access to the

7 Kamen, 2003
8 Costobel
9 Rymer
10 Rymer

pernambuco and cocoa trees of the island. By then, the cocoa crop was in great demand by the chocolate industry in The Netherlands.

The Jews of Recife

This tiny island, nestled against the shore, not only controlled navigation up the Rio Capibaribe to the heartland of this vast area, referred to as "the pernambuco," this territory would in time become the State of Pernambuco with Recife, the first capital of Brazil. The Jews who had settled there long ago had prospered unencumbered as growers, merchants, and financiers. However, in 1580, events in the Portuguese homeland changed their lives dramatically.

At that time, there was a vacuum in Portuguese royal lineage that coincided with the death of the powerful Cardinal Henry of Portugal. As an ardent opportunist, Philip II declared he would be the rightful successor, and in order to seize the realm, he brought the aging 73-year-old Duke of Alva out of retirement to lead this three-month campaign. Despite his age, Alva had lost none of his verve for plunder, outrage, and brutality that he had expressed in the lowlands. Quickly, he ordered anyone who was presumed to be guilty of crimes against the Catholic church, to be hanged.

Portuguese possessions overseas subsequently fell under the domination of the people and the events in Portugal, and every manifestation of trial and torture practiced during the Inquisition again prevailed.[11] Those Jews who complied like their earlier counterparts, were called "New Christians." They were also referred to as "Crypto-Jews," as their ancestors in Spain had been.

Under these restrictions, any Jew could be deemed guilty of "heresy" against the Catholic church and taken back to Portugal to face church tribunals. The Jews who remained in South America often continued to practice the traditions of their faith in secret.

Shortly after the Dutch West India Company was chartered in 1623, they had sent an expedition of 2,800 troops to capture the southern coastal plain of Brazil called Bahia. It was seven years later, in that benchmark year of 1630, the Dutch captured the small, elongated island of Recife.[12]

By then, despite the best attempts to maintain Jewish traditions and religious practices, the identity of Jews had diminished; with Philip's nefarious actions in 1580, it had become virtually extinguished over the next 50 years. After the Dutch captured the island and had control over the pernambuco, in 1630, the Jews of Recife were given rights to practice their religion freely and openly as they were entitled to do in The Netherlands.[13]

Five hundred Jews on this tiny island had survived, but it wasn't until the Sephardic Jews arrived from Amsterdam that the practice of Judaism was revived. With this infusion of their culture, their rich religious heritage, and new blood, the Jewish community of Recife regained its identity. Jewish life flourished, and soon the congregation of Israel Tzar established a synagogue,

---

11 Kamen, 1988
12 Pool, 1930
13 Pool, 1955

the first in all of the Americas.[14] Within a few years, the community supported two synagogues, but it is Israel Tzar that stands as the most historic landmark of Recife today.

Among those Jews from Amsterdam who, along with the Walloons and the Dutch, came to settle in Recife after 1630, was Asser Levy whose name would be well recognized much later in a very different place. He was an Askenazi Jew, meaning his family origins were in Eastern Europe; he had come to Recife from Westphalia, Germany. [15]

Long after the Jews had settled the island of Recife in their diaspora of the early 1500s, many Walloons whose families had fled their Belgic homeland in the mid-to-late 1500s also migrated to South America. The Walloons of concern here were those who lived on the island of Recife when it was in Dutch hands. For the next quarter-century, the Dutch, the Walloons, and the Jews lived together peacefully and prospered. Together they put up a fierce fight that followed years of guerilla warfare against the Portuguese on the mainland of the pernambuco.

1654: The Portuguese recapture Recife to oust Jews, Walloons, and Dutch

On January 26, 1654, the Dutch surrendered Recife to the Portuguese commander Francisco Barreto de Menzes after a prolonged struggle and jungle warfare.[16] He gave residents three months to leave this much-treasured trophy of real estate. Since there were too few Dutch ships in the harbor to transport everyone to Holland, Barreto then put at their service as many Portuguese ships as would be needed. In all, 16 ships sailed in convoy on their homeward voyage.

What happened next is found in most references on the subject. However, there may well be more to the story than that. A violent storm erupted. Allegedly, one of these ships veered off course, becoming separated from the convoy. As the story is told, this ship "drifted" into the pirate-infested waters of the Spanish Main where the tortures of the Inquisition held strong sway. This may have been one of those Portuguese vessel that Barreto provided. If so, did a Portuguese crew take advantage of their passengers' misfortune and "guide" it into hazardous waters? It would soon be seized by pirates and most of the captives' money and worldly goods were confiscated.

1654: Refugees from Recife arrive in Nieuw Amsterdam

With five mounted guns, a French vessel, variously called the *St. Charles*, or the *St. Catherine*, but usually the latter, came to their rescue in a Caribbean port. This vessel was on route to Nova Scotia and the captain was willing, for a fee, to detour to Nieuw Amsterdam to drop off the famed group of 23 Jews in Nieuw Amsterdam.

Presumably, there were Dutchmen and Walloons aboard as well, but history of them is virtually void. There is mention by Jewish historians of there being a Dutch Reformed church minister by the name of Polhemus, who arrived with

14 Kaufman
15 Pool, 1955
16 Rymer

them in Nieuw Amsterdam. There could easily have been others, since it is stated that the passage charged the Jews was three times that of Christians.

The Jews were unable to pay the cost that was demanded for their passage. Anxious to get on with his voyage, the captain sought to clear up the matter by auctioning off the passengers' remaining, battered goods. Members of the Walloon and Dutch community of Nieuw Amsterdam responded emphatically by buying these goods and immediately returning them to the rightful owners. This infuriated the sea captain, but later it created even greater problems for the intransigent-minded Governor-General Pieter Stuyvesant.

Laymen and students of early American history are deeply indebted to the detailed accounts of the arrival of these 23 Jewish refugees from Recife. This has been meticulously documented by the pre-eminent scholar and Jewish historian David de Sola Pool (1885–1970) who was the long-time rabbi of the 70th Street Shearith Israel Synagogue. His publication not only documents the emerging Jewish community by the 1650s but also the crucial steps in the religious and civic life in general in Nieuw Amsterdam.[17]

Threads of European history shared between the Jews and the Walloons

Numerous threads of history are shared between the Jews and the Walloons, both in Europe and in America. With surprising frequency, the Jews of Spain and the Walloons of the Spanish-oppressed lowlands shared various experiences. For example, each group faced its own geographical dispersion at the hands of Spanish rulers.

Each diaspora was perpetrated by a Spanish Inquisition. The Spanish Inquisition against the Jews occurred the year America was discovered. The Second Spanish Inquisition, against the Walloon Reformists, from 1567 to 1579 transpired in the Spanish-controlled lowlands. In contrast to the well-known 1492 Inquisition, this 12-year persecution became a silent, poorly-recorded part of the Walloon Reformist history that remains virtually unknown.

During the Spanish Inquisition of 1492, the Jews of Spain were ordered to be baptized in the Catholic church. If they refused, they would be expelled from the country within three months. Although the Spanish Inquisition was administered through the church, it was essentially a political maneuver.[18] No civic laws existed whereby the Jews could be forced to leave, so by requiring them to join the Catholic church, it meant they were governed by church law. As the result, Ferdinand and Isabella could try them in Church Court, and prosecute these converted Jews for "heresy against Catholicism."

The Walloon Reformists had also been accused of heresy. Those who decided to stay in their homeland had to rejoin the Church of Rome; they did so reluctantly, as nominal Catholics, and like the Jews, the Reformists continued to practice their own beliefs in secret.

17 Pool, 1930
18 Kamen, 1997

Many Sephardic Jews, as those whose families originated in Spain are called, sailed to Turkey, Greece, India, and the Orient. Just as the Jews had fled to the adjacent country of Portugal, the Walloons fled to the adjacent provinces of Holland and Zeeland. Both the Sephardic Jews who fled Spain and Portugal, and the Walloons who fled the Belgic Lands, each formed sizeable ethnic communities in The Netherlands.

Much later, people of these two faiths would share an even closer relationship and experience unexpected, historical commonalities in Nieuw Amsterdam.

1654: Early history of the Jews in Nieuw Amsterdam

The population figures vary, but Nieuw Amsterdam was still very small in the mid-1600s. When the Jews arrived from Recife in 1654, they settled on Slyck Steeg, a less desirable location than that around the fort because its swampy terrain lived up to the early name; Nova Belgica, when translated, means "new lowland."

For another ten years after the Jews arrived, Pieter Stuyvesant was the Governor-General of the Nieuw Nederlandt Colony and director of its seat of government, Nieuw Amsterdam. He was called "Old Silver Nails" out of earshot, presumably for the silver bands securing his wooden leg, and perhaps for other reasons as well.

Within a month after their arrival from Recife, Stuyvesant made a plea to Amsterdam to rid his colony of these penniless Jews and take them back to Holland. The answer by "return mail," as it were but certainly by "return ship" was clear.

This was not the answer Mr. Stuyvesant anticipated. It simply reminded him, had it not been for the wealthy Jewish community who invested as stockholders of the ship *Nieuw Nederlandt*, it might not have been built, the Walloon community of the Dutch West India Company might never have existed, and he would not be here as governor. Issue settled![19]

Soon a Torah was sent to the Jewish emigrés from the Synagogue in Amsterdam. By this time there were ten men, as required to form a minion for services. Jews were permitted to hold services in their homes, with the requirement that they "keep it quiet." Lutherans and Quakers in the mid-1600s were not welcomed either and were met by the same constrictions.[20]

Religious history shared between the Jews and Walloons in Nieuw Amsterdam

By 1657, the congregation of the Dutch Reformed Church had moved to larger quarters. Since they were no longer using the second floor of Molemacher's gristmill for services, they offered this space to their Jewish neighbors.

Once again history would be made when the services of the first Jewish congregation in North America, Shearith Israel, were held in Portuguese at the exact same location where the earliest services of the Dutch Reformed Church in North America had been held in French 30 years before. Also of note, Asser Levy,

19 Costobel

20 Costobel

one of the 23 survivors from Recife had also numbered among the congregation of the first synagogue in South America, Israel Tzar.

In time, the Shearith Israel congregation also outgrew the space in Molemacher's mill. Sometime well before 1700, Jan Harpendingh, a cordwainer, built a new frame house adjacent to the gristmill which he rented out as a synagogue.

By 1730, Asser Levy had purchased the land where Molemacher's first gristmill had stood and it was there that the Mill Street Synagogue, the first in North America, was built. It was affectionately referred to as "The Little Synagogue," and with good reason, being only 35 feet square.[21] Mill Street was the name the British gave to Slyck Steeg, which currently is named South William Street.

The congregation moved three times, and each time, the beloved, historic artifacts of the Mill Street Synagogue were carried to the next location. The original Torah, parts of the wooden floor boards, and the lamps can be found today at the Shearith Israel Synagogue on 70th Street and Central Park West in New York City.

In addition, two millwheels were laid at the entrance there. They came not from the 20–22 Mill Street, but at 28, where Molemacher built a second gristmill.

Two of these millwheels can also be found at the Marble Collegiate Church that emerged from the original Walloon "gristmill" congregation.[22] Parallels between these two faiths in this instance seem to be linked in stone.

1540: An unwitting Jewish catalyst helps spark the Protestant Reformation

The unique contribution of Clement Marot, Professor of Hebrew at the Sorbonne needs to be recognized. His translation of 30 psalms from Hebrew to French in 1540 became the spark for the reformed movement to accelerate over the next 25 years, to expand across Europe with lightening speed. Members of the Calvinist denominations have Clement Marot to thank for his role as an unwitting, early catalyst for the Protestant Reformation.

Asser Levy's role in Nieuw Amsterdam

Asser Levy had readily become a well-respected, prominent resident throughout the Jewish and gentile communities. He had established himself in multiple roles: kosher butcher, realtor, financier, and arbitrator. For instance, he helped finance the purchase of land and the construction of the first Lutheran church that was located just beyond the wall. He also acted as judicial referee in disputes among Protestants. The role that he was forbidden to assume, however, was of greater significance.

1657: Asser Levy's role in the separation of church and state

Asser Levy was not permitted to join the army or stand guard at the wall in this "Stuyvesant-dictated" community because he was not a citizen. At the

21 Pool, 1930

22 Pool, 1930

same time, he was required to pay taxes for not doing so. In 1657 he applied for citizenship, but it was denied. Requirement for citizenship at that time was membership in the Dutch Reformed church.[23]

Thanks to Asser Levy's persistence, this requirement had to be dropped. Thus, from that day forward, separation of church and state had a firm legal foundation. In 1730, exactly 100 years after the Dutch acquired Recife and 75 years after the Jews arrived in Nieuw Amsterdam, legislation was enacted in Albany to establish this into law.[24]

23 Costobel

24 Costobel

These three Neo-Dutch Renaissance-style buildings on South William Street today, are opposite the approximate site of the Mill Street Synagogue, the first Synagogue in North America. It was built in 1730 at 20–22 Mill Street by the Shearith Israel Congregation, and affectionately called the "Little Synagogue."

3

A Dutch Heritage: Harmon's Story from Wijhe to Schaghticoke[1]

(1245–1674)

Historical Background

Origins of the "pays bas"

In the 1400s, the Dutch suddenly heard a new language being spoken around them. French troops moved in to the lowlands to occupy it for their King, Philip the Bold. They renamed The Netherlands, the "pays bas," French for lowlands. When the King's daughter, Mary of Burgundy, married the Holy Roman Emperor Maximilian, all this territory became his to rule. Their grandson, Charles V, married Juana, granddaughter of Ferdinand and Isabella. Philip II, who wreaked havoc in the lowlands by his autocratic, Spanish rule in the 16th century, was the great-grandson of Ferdinand and Isabella on his mother's side, and Maximilian on his father's side.[2]

The 13th Century Black Plague

Early shipping to and from foreign ports caused rampant spread of communicable diseases, the Black Plague among them.

The role of windmills in history

Windmills are emblematic of The Netherlands and the struggle of its people. Windmills have been the lifeline for food and security for the Dutch over centuries.

The creaking, grinding windmill arms created power to lift water to higher ground. Early ones were constructed of a wooden grid of poplar perhaps two feet by ten feet in size or larger. The Dutch piled up mounds of soil, or dikes, to hold back the water. The land, called polders, when drained, was a precious commodity in this tiny country. The black soil from beneath the Zuider Zee was as fine as grains of sand, and rich in nutrients.

---

1 The name was originally Harmen van Wyhe, but he had changed it to Harmon van Wye by the time he came to America in 1674. For clarity, Harmon will be used here.

2 In his 1998 book *Philip II* Kamen gives a more balanced view of the king than do most European historians.

In time the Dutch carefully engineered an elaborate system of dikes to control the sea and protect their reclaimed land. Throughout the polders, drainage ditches draw off water that is then pumped up to a higher ditch on top of a dike. That is fed to the next level by meadow mills, or drainage mills, at successively higher levels over miles, until it can be fed back to the sea.[3] Where there is nothing to obstruct the wind, larger windmills called ground-sailers, or monk's mills, operate.[4]

There were many types of windmill construction, often styled in a way unique to a particular part of the country.[5] Over the centuries windmills have filled many functions, some of which are barely known. Besides pumping water and grinding grain for flour, another early function was as neighborhood newscaster. The joyful events of births, marriages, and other celebrations were signaled through the windmill arms. In some areas, attaching bundles of wheat for boys and thatch for girls signaled a new arrival.

Three hundred years after the story of Harmon's ancestors begins, Walloons of the Belgic Lands would be migrating north to escape Spanish oppression. Starting in the 1530s, they came with spindle, spinning wheels, and the knowledge of looms and weaving to spin the flax into warp and weft threads for linen cloth and canvas. Canvas sails powered vessels that crossed the oceans to bring people to our shores. When indigo was available from India and the Orient, and red dyes from the pernambuco trees, they would announce their various celebrations from the sail-arms of the windmills with colored flags.

When facing a windmill, one sees that the sail-arms are always rotated in a counter-clockwise direction. Long ago, when the sail-arms were stopped in the "X" position, 45 degrees from the horizon, they signified an extended rest. When black flags were suspended from the tips of the four sails, they conveyed the irreversible message of the owner's demise. The position of the sail-arms, in the "departing position" just to the right of the base, expressed mortality and sadness in the community, for those departed.[6]

In the 20th Century, windmills throughout The Netherlands would bear another message, one crucial to the safety of Dutch Jews being hidden from the Nazis by the caring Dutch people. To signal the warning of a forthcoming raid, farmers and millers would stop their windmills with the sails set in a pre-arranged position perhaps at twelve, or one, on the clock face.[7]

Of the 7,000 windmills that have dotted the Dutch landscape over the centuries, only 1,000 remain. Unless kept in use, they too will decay.[8]

"New Age" windmills now power turbines for local electrical power. In a long row, they appear like a graceful art form along the countryside or on top of the dikes. Mechanisms control the speed they need to convert wind into electrical

---

3 Kooijman

4 Kooijman

5 Wenkende Wieken in West Vlaanderen

6 Kooijman

7 Kooijman

8 Kooijman

power. By adjusting the position of the sleek propeller-like fins, they can catch the most optimal winds from the Noordt Zee.

The early Walloon settlers on Manhattan Island built wind-powered timber mills.[9] Only four blocks north of that location and four centuries later, low-tech wind power will meet high-tech. At the new World Trade Center, wind will power the utilities that provide for its security, just as wind powered the sails that brought the settlers to the New World for their freedom and security.

The French invasion of North Brabant

Throughout the 1620's to the middle of that century, the French attacked the land they had ruled two centuries before when they called it the "pays bas." The fortified town of Zaltbommel on the River Waal fell to the French after a lasting siege. Much of the Bommelwaardt region and the Province of North Brabant was pillaged and burned. Bommel, the tiny town a few miles to the west of Arnhem was devastated.

Several towns in North Brabant are named Bommel. The hamlet of Bommel west of Arnhem no longer on present-day maps, appears to have been the birthplace of Harmen van Wyhe, as his parents spelled it when he was born in 1648.

The 1672 Battle of Solebay

This was the opening naval battle of the Third Anglo-French War against their rival, the Dutch navy. Under famed Dutch Admiral Michiel de Ruyter, and Cornelis Tromp, next in command, the Dutch assembled 70 ships.[10]

The strategy of Admiral de Ruyter, remarkable at the time, was to send two ships out in full moon, to scout the location of the British and French fleets. A surprise attack at sunrise sent the French scurrying to safety in the English Channel. The British fleet was caught at anchor off Solebay in the River Thames where they were refurbishing their ships for a forthcoming attack on the Dutch to blockade their ports.

According to Kathryn Knickerbacker Viele[11] and others, the Dutch "fought like lions." Both sides lost several ships in the day-long battle. The most significant loss was the British flag ship of Admiral Lord Sandwich, the *HMS Royal James* that was sunk with him aboard.

The annals of Dutch naval history hail this as a brilliant strategy since they were outnumbered by 115 enemy ships to their fleet of 70. Whereas the outcome of the day was a draw, the Dutch were lauded for seriously disrupting a blockade of their ports.

The exact date of the Battle of Solebay differs according to authorities. Kathryn Knickerbacker Viele cites May 28, 1672. David Marley cites June 7, 1672; others claim July 8 of that year to be correct. Each of the latter two occasioned a full moon, so May 28 falls a bit short.

---

9 Wilson

10 Cornelis Tromp, as his first name was spelled then, was the son of the noted Admiral Maarten Tromp who was killed in the final battle of the First Anglo-French War against the Dutch (1652–1654) during the Battle of Scheveningen, outside The Hague, in 1654.

11 This is the spelling of the family name at the time.

Harmon van Wye is said to have fought in the Battle of Solebay and sustained a leg injury. However, other details of this lifelong family story fostered by General Egbert Viele's article suggest disbelief.[12]

The 1673 Battle of Kijkduins

The Battle of the Dunes at Kijkduins took place in 1673 on the island of Texel,[13] the largest and southernmost of the Frisian Islands. Texel forms a sea channel between it and the uppermost tip of the Province of North Holland. This archipelago protects the waters of the Wadden Zee and the Zuider Zee that reached south to the inland port of Amsterdam.

The battle was fought over Dutch shipping access to and from the port of Amsterdam through the hazardous Texel Channel.

The geographical layout offers a clear reason why Texel would be suitable for an enemy blockade.

According to Kathryn Knickerbacker Viele and others, the Dutch were victorious over the English and French forces, thus maintaining free access from Amsterdam to the Noordt Zee and through the English Channel for shipping to and from the Dutch West Indies, as all of Central and North and South America were then called.

Allegedly Harmon fought in this battle as well as the Battle of Solebay, despite the leg wound he had sustained the year before.

Nieuw Amsterdam becomes New York

In 1664 the English Colonel, Richard Nicolls arrived to demand that Pieter Stuyvesant turn over the Dutch colony. He did so without firing a shot. The English then renamed it in honor of the Duke of York.

New York becomes Nieuw Orange

After nine years in English hands (1664–1673), Dutch Commodores Cornelius Evertsen and Jacob Binckes reclaimed this territory, as the Dutch Colony of Nieuw Nederlandt on September 6, 1673. They immediately renamed their settlement Nieuw Orange, for their own House of Orange. The English had changed the name of Fort Amsterdam to Fort James. It was then renamed Fort Willem Hendrick to properly honor their own House of Orange.

Neither of these names, Nieuw Orange nor Fort Willem Hendrick, lasted long enough to appear on a map. Within 14 months, the English would be back.

Nieuw Orange reverts to New York

Under the Treaty of Westminster signed in June of 1674, the English assumed permanent control of this colony. Sir Edmund Andros arrived and peacefully reclaimed it for Charles II on November 9, 1674.

12 Viele, General Egbert. "The Knickerbockers of New York," Vol 54 Harper and Brothers, *New Monthly Magazine #319*, December 1876. New York, Harper & Brothers , Franklin Square. General Viele used the spelling of the family name that Washington Irving had popularized by then.

13 Marley

Harmon's Story from Wyhe/Wijhe to Schaghticoke

(1245–1674)

The wind was gentle that September morning as it came off the River Jssel, as it was spelled then, and the Zuider Zee beyond. The Noordt Zee would kick up harder in a few hours. Bands of wheat and thatch, ready for harvesting, moved in undulating waves of gold as dawn broke over the polders.

From where I stood on the top of the dike, a faint sound caught my attention. Facing the sunrise, I looked to my left, and there, 30 feet below, was a most unusual sight, one for the whole community to celebrate. The glorious news from the "sheath of wheat" tied to each sail-arm of the farmer's windmill announced: "It's a boy!" His name was Jordaen van Wyhe. The year was 1245. Twenty-five generations later, this newborn baby boy would be my own very distant ancestor.[14]

Joy reigned that morning in the half-timbered, thatched farmhouse. Five little girls excitedly welcomed a chubby, blue-eyed, baby brother. They thought it was more fitting for boys than girls to catch seagulls for food on the table, so this was foremost in their minds. Their father was delighted, too, knowing someday he would have help tending the fields, help in harvesting, and help at the gristmill.

When he was old enough, Jordaen, the blonde-haired Dutch boy, could feed the wheat from above to be ground into coarse flour between the millstones below. They were powered by wind in the sail-arms, those same sail-arms that announced his birth this day at dawn. Someday he would become its miller.

From where I stood on top of the dike that morning, I could see windmills with sides of thatch silhouetted against the skyline for miles. In addition to the grist-grinding windmill at his farm, Jordaen's father had built one nearby, on top of the dike. Ever vigilant of the peril that the Noordt Zee could impose at any time, the Dutch kept them working almost without stopping. Jordaen's father was ever mindful of the alarming reality that their home and land were far below the level of the sea, and could be wiped out in an instant should a dike break.

From my unseen role, in the 13th century, I looked ahead to the 21st century, where the hamlet of Wyhe has become a charming, flourishing present day community spelled Wijhe. It was located in the Oberyssel region that is now the Oberijssel Province between Zwolle to the north and Deventer along the river to the south. This town is on the east bank of the River Jssel was now spelled IJssel. Standing there on the top of the dike as I did, 759 years after Jordaen's birth, I could still see a row of ground-sailers in the distance.

---

14 See Appendix A. This penned document was discovered in the New York State Library Archives by Paul Knickerbocker in 1960 among the papers of Kathryn Knickerbacker Viele. It is unknown whether this was her own genealogical work. It is known that she made a trip to The Netherlands in 1913 in search of family history. However, her 1916 writing cited in the bibliography, comprehensive as it is, does not include data from this document. This suggests it was located in The Netherlands by someone else, and filed with her papers.

Soon my mind was drawn back to the 13th century, to watch ships plying the River Jssel in view before me. Ships of the Hanseatic League were transporting goods from their homeports on the Rhine in Germany to ports along the River Jssel as it flowed north past Deventer and farther north, beyond the hamlet of Jordaen's birth, to Zwolle.

In Jordaen's time, this important commercial river course emptied into the Zuider Zee at Kampen and out to the Noordt Zee at Texel, to enable ships to carry goods to the docks in London and as far north as Bergen. Only shallops, or small river boats, might stop in Wyhe. Rivers were the routes of trade, travel, news, and disease. So it was with the plague.

When it hit the countryside as it did here, bodies could be buried in the fertile soil, along the edge of farmland defined by a shallow ditch. Day after day loved ones were buried, until more had died than were left to bury them. Mothers and the infants who died in their arms were buried together. Families of Jordaen's five sisters and those of his three sons, numbered around 60, but few would survive. Only Jordaen, his grandson Johannes and his family, to include his wife and four of their six children, remained.

Back in 1271 Jordaen, in his youth, had met the daughter of the First Lord of Echteld, hence an heiress in her own right. Jordean was not expected to marry her until it was proven she could bear him offspring for this title to be passed down to succeeding generations. This welcome news was spread along the dikes from windmill to windmill in the morning breeze. Hence, Hendrick, the oldest son of the next generation, carried this minor title, as did Jordaen's grandson, Johannes.[15]

Johannes, now Third Lord of Echteld, married Hille van-Rivierre. They lived with their six children over the dike in an adjacent polder. On hearing of this rampant disease, she relied on a mother's intuition and refused to let her young children climb the dike to play with their cousins at the farm on the other side. They survived, but the two oldest boys who worked at the gristmill were in contact with people who came for flour. Both died.

A few months later, Jordean gathered his grandson Johannes and his family at the old farmhouse for a final meal of rough-grain bread and roasted seagulls. Then they filed past the gristmill for the last time. At the top of the dike the sunrise cast their long shadows toward the River Jssel. This blond-haired, blue-eyed family walked until they came to a dike at right angles that took them to another, near the river bank. They went down the other side of the dike to the dock and the waiting shallop.

Besides the dreadful plague, there was another fear, more imminent and everlasting. Over the past months, Jordaen had urged them to leave since they constituted the last hope of the family's survival. "Leave now, and be safe on higher ground. We can never know when the sea will be 'king' and take back the land that is his." A few minutes later, he reiterated his plea: "Just remember wherever you go, seek higher ground and stay out of the cities."

15 Appendix A

As the shallop left the dock, Jordaen waved goodbye and turned to climb up the dike, dressed in age-old, dirt-colored stiff pants of wild boar skin, re-contoured from past generations to fit his own short, stocky frame. He pulled his dark, skin cap forward to shield his eyes from view, and continued to bite hard on the stem of his clay pipe. He sauntered back to the gristmill that he would continue to operate, until the sail-arms were stilled to signify he had "departed."

As was customary at the time, my early family assumed the name of the town of Wyhe, now spelled Wijhe, from whence they came. "Van," meaning "from" became part of the surname, later shortened from "van Wyhe" to "van Wye." It is astonishing how this family name has been preserved throughout 12 generations in The Netherlands.[16]

As an important sidebar to history, genealogists in this country who try to trace their ancestry back to The Netherlands often proceed with the assumption that all their Dutch ancestors migrated to America from Holland. This is because any ship that brought them had to sail from Amsterdam or Rotterdam, both ports being in that province. If the family traveled from another home province to catch the ship, any record of it may well have been lost.

Sailing south, in that rocking river shallop, Johannes van Wyhe and his family, were awed to see a marked increase of greenery along the banks. There were more trees than they had ever seen, and a different kind, too. This came as a curious surprise, for they were accustomed to only the erect, slender, and shimmering-leafed poplars that had sprung up around the old farmhouse and stood like sentinels in a line on top of the age-old dikes. Johannes asked the captain what these unusual trees with such an alluring scent, were called: "Evergreens," was the proud answer of this Rhine river captain whose home port was faraway Cologne.

I could see how sad, how troubled they all were, how anxious the children seemed, going to a strange place without friends or family. They especially missed their beloved great-grandfather whom they affectionately called "Gramp." He was their link to safety, but not even he could assure them anymore. Now they would have to adjust to new surroundings, new experiences, and make new friends.

Johannes stood up in the prow of the riverboat with his sons, Herman, age ten, and his brother, eight. By the sudden, untimely deaths of their brothers, they had become the two oldest boys in the family. Little Katrina, now six, ran from her mother's side to join them. Cuddling close to her father to keep warm, she said, "Where we're going, will there be honey bees like those are at Gramp's farm?" The honey he made had been the most direct and most pleasurable link to him that three generations of children had ever had. Little Katrina would never forget the honey nor its endearing association with her Gramp.

Soon she ran back to her mother, with arms wrapped together, and shivering. I was curious to watch what happened next, as I, too, was shivering from the river breeze. Little Katrina put her head in her mother's lap so she could pull

16 Appendix A

the garment up from the bottom and over the little girl's head to turn it inside out. Now the grey and white rabbit fur was close to her skin for cozy warmth. Katrina was the proud, but temporary, owner of this much-valued childhood garb handed down from her maternal grandmother, and when she grew too big, it would be handed down to the baby boy on her mother's lap.

Despite the chancy rocking of the boat, little Katrina chose to keep her arms inside, close to her body for warmth. On occasion, she was tossed harmlessly against the rolling deck.

After a few days of sailing on the Jssel River, past Deventer, and south to the branch of the Rhine called the Neder Rijn, for "lower Rhine," the boat headed west and the family disembarked soon at a dock near Arnhem. When they left the shallop, the little boys and their parents, too, were awed to see the stony river bank, so different from what they knew at home. Leaving the dock to walk along the bank toward the town where they would live for a while, they were most intrigued by boys skipping stones into the water. Soon the father and his sons mastered the technique for themselves and learned to select thin, flat stones that skipped best.

The boys collected these stones in the pockets of their deerskin pants, until they became so heavy, their pants began to slide. Katrina, the imp, took this opportunity to reach around and give a firm tug on Herman's pants, making it appear as if his brother on the other side had done so. Screams and a chase ensued over the stony river bank until the true culprit was caught. She was given her just due amid giggles normal to siblings throughout the ages; more than that, they knew how very ticklish she was.

Stones of the Neder Rijn had been washed over the centuries. Boulders the size of Hannibal's elephants presumably rained down mountainsides in the Alps and into the River Rhine, carried toward the sea by spring ice flows. Stones carved from these boulders had lined the river banks of the Neder Rijn and the River Waal, before the birth of Christ, when the Walloons were already fighting Caesar's legions.[17]

Looking ahead, in my timeless role, I could envision the change that was bound to come. By the 21st century, these stone-strewn banks would be covered by rising waters due to modern-day construction for water control and navigation, in the natural rivers and network of canals.

I watched the boys on the river bank near Arnhem search for special stones, they selected with the dedication of a gem polisher. These had blade-like edges with which to carve the local poplar into wooden shoes. They began to devise new ideas for gliding across the ice when winter returned. All summer, these boys worked in high competition along the Neder Rijn, to shape and refine their winter shoes. They discovered that a carved wooden projection extending the length of their shoe enabled them to glide like the wind, across the frozen surface. Some lined their shoes with rabbit fur for warmth. As soon as the ice was safe, they anxiously tried out their latest summer creations designed to carry them with speed and skill.

17 Lamb

Soon they created a game of their own, using a round stone and a stick, making up rules as they went along. Rivalry burst forth, groups formed, and teams developed to play their game up and down the frozen river, and into the adjacent canals. People started to travel over these winter waterways from hamlet to hamlet on primitive skates. News spread, ideas were exchanged, and a broader and deeper sense of community evolved. Whereas travel by boat had been limited to those few who had the means, or a need to do so, now with these new-styled wooden shoes and their crude blades, people could become friends with those who had previously been inaccessible.

Other stones were also curious to these newcomers. Palm-sized, like an oval biscuit ready for the oven, these stones had been rounded smooth by rushing water buffeting them against the rocks for centuries. Katrina's mother borrowed one of the boy's sharp-edged stones to scratch a smiling face on the broad, flat surface. To create a doll, she wrapped pliable green bulrushes, or cattails, around the head, and made the stalks into arms and legs that extended from the long, brown fuzzy body. As these cattails dried, the doll's body barely survived until it could be replaced by the next season's crop. However, the treasured stone face was carried from Arnhem to Bommel, and lasted as a family heirloom for generations of dolls that followed.

Katrina was thrilled to find honey in Arnhem almost as tasty as that which her great-grandfather had given her, for as long as she could remember. She noticed the windmills were different here. Ground-sailers needed for water control near the Zuider Zee were seldom seen, but elevated box-like structures to support the sails, called "post" windmills were used to grind local grains.

The heavy, brown dirt, so unlike the fine-grained soil of the polders, was just right to devise a game where the children drew out ahead of them five, two-foot squares in a straight line. Then the player threw one of the flat skipping stones into the first square. They hopped on one leg to pick it up, trying to do the same to the end and return without losing his, or her, balance. This game, like hop-scotch, had a more challenging version that used one of the rounded stones, like the head of Katrina's doll, likely to roll unpredictably.

According to the best records available, plus intense study of maps of that time, and on-site research in 2004, it would appear that the early van Wyhe family had lived in the Oberyssel region on the River Jssel, in the hamlet of Wyhe, now spelled Wijhe. This was long before the French invasion of the 1400s. The third generation, headed by Johannes van Wyhe, can be traced to the area north of the Neder-Rijn and west of Arnhem, to the hamlet of Bommel. In 1392, Herman van Wyhe, of the fourth generation, was made governor of Neder-Betue, a district of North Brabant Province.[18]

Throughout the next nine generations, the family continued to live in North Brabant. Some resided in Arnhem, others in Wageningen; in each of these towns, some among them served as magistrates and judges.

Seventy years after the 1579 Union of Utrecht that freed the northern Dutch provinces from Spanish rule, Harmen Jansen van Wyhe was born in the hamlet

18 Appendix A

of Bommel. The year was 1648, famous for the Treaty of Westphalia that ended the Thirty Years War. Westphalia, Germany, is located 75 miles to the east.

Harmon, the name by which we know him, quickly became the family prankster. When he left his home as a young man to join the Dutch navy, he took his lively sense of humor with him. Perhaps it was due to his sense of humor that he changed the spelling of his name from "van Wyhe" to "van Wye," before he came to America, and morphed the "Harmen" into "Harmon." His tongue-in-cheek attitude may also have contributed directly to his surname becoming "Knickkerbak," explained later in this story.

The French returned to North Brabant in the mid 1600s and devastated the Bommelwardt region and his home in Bommel. With neither family nor home to return to, Harmon had to make other plans when the time came. Meanwhile, we will return to the events that shaped Harmon's naval career and our family legend.

I watched Harmon on board as the ships of the Dutch navy assembled in the weeks before the Battle of Solebay. Across the horizon 70 Dutch ships gathered under the command of Admirals Michiel de Ruyter and Cornelis Tromp. Harmon was aboard a ship that I had always understood during my childhood was commanded by his father, Johannes van Barghen Knickerbakker. However, throughout this day-long battle, the wheelhouse was shrouded in mist. I thought this was strange; it was the very first occasion in my timeless role as historical observer that I was unable to have a direct view of any action or event. Indeed it was puzzling, and I wondered about this unusual situation for a long time.

Could it be, in the heavy fog of battle, the captain failed to place his ship in the designated position for attack? Did he, by some grave error, mistakenly fire on a ship of his own nation, causing death and mayhem to his compatriots? Why, when Harmon was injured and lying among the other wounded and dead on deck, did his father not come to the side of his pain-ridden son? I never saw the captain, nor heard his voice, but I witnessed the courage it took for him to put two enemy vessels out of action as his own ship limped back to port with rigging draped in imprecise lines and angles.

While Harmon was in Delft, recovering from a serious injury to his left leg, he hobbled along on crude poplar crutches to a nearby tavern to amuse himself by playing the newly popular game of table shuffleboard. With his left leg propped up on a chair, he could get himself into position to shoot the round, wooden disk called a "knikker." Over the many months of his recuperation, he became an awesome competitor, challenging his battle-weary buddies, as well as the old-timers who stepped back to watch his daunting performance. This was all the more impressive given his awkward sitting position and enduring pain.

Despite this handicap, he fought the following year at the Battle of the Dunes at Kijkduin, on the island of Texel. Again he was wounded, but with a less severe injury to his arm. Throughout the summer, he and other wounded seamen tried to recover from their battle scars. Cleansed by the tides, the blood of battle no longer stained the beaches, but their unmitigated emotional scars, in service to their homeland, were evident.

The seamen watched children play on the white sand, now cleansed of the bloody battle. I overheard them wonder with a distinct tone of despair, when they would ever begin a family and have children of their own to bring to the beach. Often they sat with vacant stares as ships of the Dutch West India Company passed through the dangerous channel with the help of a pilot on board. Ships entering the Noordt Zee headed south for the English Channel. Some would be going to the islands of the Carribees in the West Indies for salt, cocoa beans, and cinnamon, others to Brazil for coffee and dyewoods.

Suddenly one day a channel pilot brought news that impacted many of them. Word off the docks in Amsterdam was that the English had been routed out of the Dutch colony. Eight years earlier in 1664, Colonel Richard Nicolls had arrived to take possession, and named it for his Duke of York. Now that it was once again in Dutch hands, many of these blond-haired sailors decided that as soon as they had recovered from their battle wounds, they would board a ship for America. So did Harmon.

Meanwhile, they watched the innocence and the irony of boys playing "war" along the now-peaceful dunes. Hopefully, the wounds and fatalities of the children's imaginary world would never become reality when the young boys became adults. There, amid the tall dune grasses, gleeful children played hide and seek amid shrieks of laughter. Little ones made castles and moats, or shaped their miniature polders and dikes. I chuckled along with the youngsters as the summer waters rippled up, coming closer with each returning wave, to wash their treasured constructions into oblivion.

Here amid the sandy dunes, the ultimate paradox between pain and play unfolded. Blood lost by buddies together in battle created a bond between them often deeper than that which flowed in family veins. Their anguished memories of battle would take far longer to quell and be in stark contrast to those structures of sand being gently eroded by incoming tides.

The incessant rolling had stopped. I crawled out of my bunk, green as usual, but something was very different. Up on deck the calm water and a soft breeze made me feel alive once more, even as a recovering seasick observer.

Then I saw Harmon come up from his bunk below to gaze out in utter dismay. In the navy, he had often heard about this enormous, natural harbor, but its reality far exceeded his expectations. As he stood on the bow that morning in the late summer of 1674, his left leg ached, as it would every morning for the rest of his life. For now, he tried to put it out of his mind to concentrate on more timely matters.

Immediately I recognized the vast changes of this fast-growing colony on Manhattan Island. Many changes had taken place in the 40 years since I had stood beside Adrian when he arrived in 1634, and a decade before that when those first, courageous Walloons came ashore in 1623 to meet the natives whose land it was. The population had greatly increased since Adrian's arrival. By now, there were many languages besides the French of the Walloons, the Dutch of Harmon's native land, and the English that Adrian had learned. In all, 18 languages could be heard in the various enclaves concentrated in this small geographical space. [19]

Suddenly, I was struck by the parallels between that tiny sliver of real estate, the island of Recife—so distant to us in calendar time, always distant in geography—and the island of Manhattan. Many times the size of Recife, but similar in its outline, the island of Manhattan, too, is nestled against nearby shores, has a protected harbor, and is the gateway between an adjacent navigable river and international ports.

From the early 1500s, the island of Recife held by the Portuguese and populated by their Jewish emigrés, developed a viable financial center there that was a hub of international trade of the times. While Manhattan sports no pernambuco trees, nor cocoa beans, it became the springboard of the world investment community. The New York Stock Exchange is located close to the location of money changers of wampum at Exchange Place, and two blocks north of Adrian Vincent's original six plots on Broad Street.

In addition to the wide diversity of language and a booming commercial center in this Dutch colony, following the nine-year English rule, Harmon also found a diversity of religion and a newly elected representative community council. These changes do not account for those often wrenching adjustments of governance that were required over a decade when possession shifted back and forth at a lively pace between the Dutch and the English from 1664 to 1674.

Now, in 1674, the same cool breezes blew upon Harmon that had greeted Adrian forty years before and had wafted across those shivering Walloons the day they reached the shore of the New World fifty years ago. Those harbor breezes rippled over the waters now called the "Hudson."

Adrian's view of the island in 1634 would have been much different. Then, the tip of the island was dominated by the director-general's house and occupied by Wouter van Twiller, who proved to be only a marginal leader. His job was acquired more by family ties than job suitability. Besides this, the barracks where the soldiers and sailors of the Dutch West India Company bunked, then stood within the primitive sod confines of Fort Amsterdam. A few wooden houses dotted the waterfront on either side of the company warehouse on Perel Straat.

Harmon's view from the harbor included the sturdy stone walls outlining the new fort that had been completed in 1640. When the English took possession of the Dutch colony and renamed Nieuw Amsterdam for their Duke of York, this offended the Dutch to the core; many returned to their homeland, but the Walloons had no place to go.

Thus, when Harmon arrived, this was neither Nova Belgica, nor Nieuw Amsterdam, nor New York. It was Nieuw Orange. From the deck, he could see the Dutch flag of orange, white and soft blue bands flutter from the flagpole above the earlier residence of "Old Silver Nails," the peg-legged Governor Stuyvesant.

Paradoxically, unintended consequences were perpetrated by the actions of this staunch, arbitrary leader—consequences that he would not have expected, let alone condone. It was indeed the "unplanned legacy" of this unpopular leader

19 Lamb

that helped to establish the foremost milestones of our society. His forthright, adamant intolerance of Jews led to steps that not only granted them the right to remain in Nieuw Amsterdam (1655), but (1) laid the groundwork for a rich ethnic diversity of our country; (2) established citizenship regardless of faith; and (3) created the legal foundation for subsequent separation of church and state.

How truly ironic it was that these fledgling liberties happened on his "watch," and within such a brief span of time, those ten years between 1654 when the arrival of Sephardic Jews from Recife and 1664 when dismissal from his post was suddenly thrust upon him. That was when Richard Nicolls arrived to claim the Dutch territory for the English in a bloodless take-over.[20]

In addition to the governor's residence and the soldiers' and sailors' barracks, a new image was now visible from the ships. Inside the reconstructed walls of the fort stood the Dutch Reformed Church of St. Nicholas, built of stone in 1642.[21] When Harmon saw it from shipboard, he wondered if services were still conducted in the Walloons' native tongue; indeed they were.

Standing beside Harmon on the deck, I, too, felt the mild jolt as the captain responded to the signal he was waiting for. The anchor was raised. Without turning to glance back at the fo'c'sle, Harmon sensed the wind gripping the sails. The sailors had made them slightly taut, ready to be loosened at the captain's command as he eased this bulky vessel safely against the pier. Lines were cast around the chocks.

Passengers and crew faced the imposing waterfront warehouses. The four-story one in the middle was built by the Dutch West India Company and housed the company store on the first floor. Furs and tobacco were stored on the floor above, to be loaded on the ship for their return voyage. To be sure, there were now ample sets of sails in the company warehouse, the same place where the ambitious Walloon shipwrights had borrowed a set for their ship's maiden voyage. The three-story buildings on either side were owned by Mr. Augustine Herman, the surveyor, and by Mr. van der Grift, a merchant and importer. These high warehouses along Perel Straat, or Pearl Street as the English had "respelled" it, obscured the newcomers' view of the fort and of the new stone church a block or two to the west.

After six weeks on the rough and rolling Atlantic, Harmon's legs swayed as he stepped onto the pier. He started walking, but his knees insisted he was still at sea. I felt the imprint of that rhythmic shift on my joints as well, and groped for a railing to steady myself.

Sailing directly across the Atlantic from the Azores was the preferable route until tricky hurricanes loomed in September. It was shorter by two weeks from that which Adrian Vincent had experienced. Nevertheless, passengers and crew on each of the voyages were fraught with seasickness, as much from the food as from the sea. I could fully appreciate how most arrivals never wanted to face a return trip. Neither did my ancestors.

Harmon was glad to be free of the cramped quarters on shipboard, and able to stretch his legs. Walking east along Perel Straat past the warehouses, he noticed

20 Brodhead
21 van Rensselaer, Mrs. Schuyler

a hatter's shop owned by Samuel Edsel. He made plans to return and buy a well-styled beaver hat for the hard winters he would face up north.

He proceeded past the hatter's shop to the corner of Perel Straat and the Herre Gracht Canal; Perel Straat resumed on the other side. The canal was the pride of the settlement. Everyone was grateful that this trickling brook and broad, smelly ditch for garbage and waste disposal had been dug deep enough now for a respectable canal. It was built with sturdy planks cut from bountiful trees, to line the sides and secure them against the tides.

Harmon ambled past the tavern on the corner owned by Hans Dreper and turned a sharp left to walk along the canal, so new, so advanced, so promising. As progressive as it was in Harmon's time, it would someday be paved over and renamed Broad Street. Thus the world financial center sprouted roots near Exchange Place, where guilders, stivers, and wampum were being traded. Harmon would go there to exchange his guilders before continuing his journey northward.

Ambling along the canal, Harmon first came to Bruge Straat. The English had converted the cherished name to Bridge Street, but the Dutch quickly corrected this insult. The next street had originally been Brouwer Straat but the English renamed it Stone for the stone crossing of the canal they built, a name that seemed totally unimaginative to Harmon.

The next street was Beaver Straat where a new bridge crossed the Herre Gracht Canal. Harmon gazed toward the row of step-gabled and mortared brick houses on the east side of the Herre Gracht. On the corner of the Herre Gracht and Slyck Steeg, recently renamed Mill Street by the English, stood the tavern of the now elderly Adrian Vincent.

There were numerous taverns cropping up throughout this burgeoning community, and Harmon was sizing them up. He lingered. This was an electrifying moment for me, the historical observer of my family's past. I suspected he would cross the bridge and enter Adrian's tavern, but he did not. Closer than the bridge that could have brought these strangers together would be the genes that each of them carried, which would be merged in my own many generations later.

I felt somewhat disappointed to see that these two men never met. Each brought such a colorful background: Harmon's patriotic battles for his country, and Adrian's family legacy of fighting for religious reform and political freedom. Whereas in the lowlands of Europe, the stately poplar trees and gnarly pollard willows could put down only shallow roots beside the canals, these two men and their ancestors had laid down inspirational foundations that became important underpinnings of our society on this side of the Atlantic. I felt enriched by the legacy these families provided. Together with fellow countrymen of pre-colonial America, they established a rich legacy for us all.

I hurried to catch up to Harmon as he paused before turning west from the Herre Gracht Canal onto Beaver Straat to stroll through town. It did not take long. He could see ahead what had originally been named Fort Amsterdam, a name that would endure despite the brief, intermediary changes. He was not accustomed to the terms "Nieuw Orange," nor "Fort Willem Hendrick," but he would not need to be. These names would soon disappear from Harmon's mind and history's record. Crucial to him right now was the fact that the Dutch were in control. He would never have come if the land was still in the hands of the English, those people who had inflicted pain upon him for life.

Before I turned to follow Harmon onto Beaver Straat, I looked straight north to see the high wall two blocks away. I was struck by the parallels. The Walloons were so named for living below the Waal, the river that ran east to west from the Rhine toward the Noordt Zee. Here the Walloons lived below the wall that also ran east to west, from the East River to what was earlier named the Noordt River. What a striking coincidence to have these parallels spaced sixteen centuries apart, when the Walloons of the early Belgic tribes, first came into existence.

There was another parallel in the ancestral backgrounds of Adrian and Harmon. The River Waal, that defined the early Walloon tribes, joined the Neder-Rijn, or lower Rhine, of Harmon's ancestral roots, and together they flowed into the Noordt Zee at Rotterdam—hauntingly symbolic of the convergence of two ancestral families that would unite in my generation.

Now my gaze turned, from the wall and the recollections of historical evolution, to follow Harmon's trail. He looked at the new fort's sturdy construction for a while then turned back to walk east along Perel Straat toward the pier. In the middle of the block, he stopped at a tavern owned by Michiel Tadens. Beer was plentiful. Michiel exchanged a cordial greeting with Harmon in the language native to both of them. It was not easy to find someone to converse with since French, German, Swedish, English, and Polish were popular in most taverns.

In due course, the bartender, happy to have a countryman to chat with over the din a few hours of drinking brought, ventured: "See you got yourself a gimpy leg there." Harmon gave a nod, in response to a reminder he scarcely needed.

"Wha' happen'd?"

"At sea," came the dismissive reply.

"Ah, hurt on the trip over.... Storms come up fast in the Atlantic.... Easy to get hurt."

Harmon hoped the bartender had answered his own question and it seemed that he had. As solicitous as this fellow countryman meant to be, his efforts only served to remind Harmon how much he missed his close buddies who had recovered together after the Battle of the Dunes at Kijkduin. He rested his long-stemmed clay pipe on the bar. His head drooped in silence above his hands that curved around a tankard of beer.

Harmon's question about available lodging was met with a shake of the head and a scornful face. "Not with 100 passengers coming in on your ship. This ain't Amsterdam yo' know." It was what he had expected. He and others had left their belongings on board until they knew their next plans.

After a few hours, he left Michiel Taden's crowded tavern. With nothing better to do that afternoon, he ambled back to the fort then turned toward the water's edge. Harmon looked out over the embankment toward a distant island in the harbor originally called "Nut Island," for its plentiful crops. In part, at least, those rich nuts had helped stave off starvation of the eight brave families that first winter at Nova Belgica. This island had been purchased from the Indians by an early settler, Willem Kieft, when he was the Governor-General. For a fleeting moment Harmon wondered if his chances for lodging would be any better over there, but he dismissed the thought. It appeared that there were only trees.

Watching the waves roll in, he was suddenly caught off guard. As accustomed as he was as a seaman to being at sea, he certainly did not expect to experience "land sickness." This abrupt visceral sensation was often felt by passengers, unaccustomed to being on the rough water, when they stepped ashore. Quickly diverting his eyes back to his land-based surroundings, the unpleasant nausea subsided. Some passengers, and even an embarrassed sailor, would admit this disturbing sensation might recur for as long as a week. Just knowing it could happen caused me to turn green.

He had asked at the tavern when the next ship might be coming down from Fort Orange. That possibility was even less certain than finding lodging.

"Once in a blue moon" flashed through his mind, but the blue moon, the second full moon in a month, was a certainty in August that year; the ship's arrival was not.

Back at his ship he checked with the first officer to see if he could arrange to stay on board, willing to work in exchange for a bunk or a hammock.

"What can you do?" was the predictable reply.

"I've mended a ton of sails in my career."

"Can't use you, have all the sailmakers we need.... Ever been a cooper?"

The answer was forming in Harmon's mind: "No, and I'd rather not start." It was not that he objected to learning new skills, but he knew it required lots of standing, whereas he could mend sails sitting down. In his soft, deliberate voice, he replied: "Mending sails would suit me best."

"Sorry, cooper or nothing." Thrusting his head toward the warehouse on Perel Straat he added, "Going to need lots of barrels to load this ship. Need coopers."

Harmon was measured in his acceptance, pondering the possibility he could find a place to stay in town before too long, or better yet, a ship would appear on the Hudson River some day soon. However, another month would have passed after the blue moon before the riverboat with tobacco and beaver skins showed up.

In the evenings, to relieve the pain of standing all day and turning out barrels with marginal results, he would head back to the tavern on Perel Straat in hopes of dulling the hot spikes that seemed driven into his thigh.

"Not walking too well there, buddy.... Have to fix you up with a stiff one."

When Harmon had arrived on this side of the world, he was both surprised, and saddened, to find so few people speaking his language on the street. He hoped he would find more Dutch spoken where he was going, unless of course, it had been banned during the painful days of English possession of Fort Orange, which they renamed Albany. Here at the tavern and throughout town he was in the midst of so many languages and people from faraway lands he had never encountered before, it made him very uncomfortable and he disparaged the thought of a lengthy delay.

One evening in particular, after a grueling day juggling barrel staves, the bartender's hyped-up hops helped him get a tolerable grip on the pain. At the same time, it loosened his tongue more than he had ever planned.

"You say you were in the navy?" the bartender probed, delighted his Dutch customer could feel more at ease. Harmon timidly acknowledged he had fought under de Ruyter, the most "haloed" of Dutch admirals, respected for his adept, historic strategy. On hearing this, Michiel Tadens pounded his fist on the bar for all to be silenced as he announced this news in a booming voice. Harmon was utterly embarrassed. He had never wanted accolades for the service he fully expected to give his country, and in his depressed mood he felt almost accosted through this bald exposure and the immediate response.

The small smoky room was suddenly transformed, cloaking this stranger like a harbor mist, with awe and respect. It mattered little whether he had been the galley cook, the one who polished the captain's shoes, or pulled the cord of the cannon's fuse. He had served under the best, which in their eyes automatically gave him the same status. Here was a "hero" in their midst! Uncommon hospitality was vested upon him from all directions. He never stayed another night on the ship and gratefully his days of coopering were behind him, too. From beneath his somber demeanor, his depression lifted as well.

He had been disappointed originally over the long delay for his trip north, but by the time the next ship arrived, he was even more anguished to leave. He would have to say "good-bye" to the gregarious ruffians so foreign to him, who had taken him in as one of their own. They were tough souls who had endured much, had much to tell, and were without much to sustain them. Here, however, in this now-emerging center of commerce, differences among them disappeared. Men of all stripes and many languages would quickly become Americans!

No matter how loose his tongue might have become in the wee hours of tavern revelry, one thing is absolutely certain. Never did he mention the name of Captain Johannes van Barghen Knickerbakker, the legendary name of my childhood.[22] Why, I wondered? Was there some shame this captain had brought upon his ship and crew that kept his name secured? Had his captain been admonished by the renown admirals for some misdeed or miscalculation?

It is apparently true that Harmon had fought under Admiral de Ruyter, but why did the name of my ancestor, as prestigious as it always seemed in the memory of Grandma Knickerbocker, never pass his lips? This mystery loomed even greater for me, as an unseen historical observer, having been right there on shipboard, yet I was unable to shed any clear light on the facts. And now, I was to witness by his silence, that Harmon virtually denied the existence of this man, supposedly his own father.

From the time Harmon was a youngster growing up in the farmlands of Bommel, he had heard stories about America, and in particular, the Province of Nieuw Nederlandt. His family had talked about the rich farmland the sailors

22 General Egbert Viele

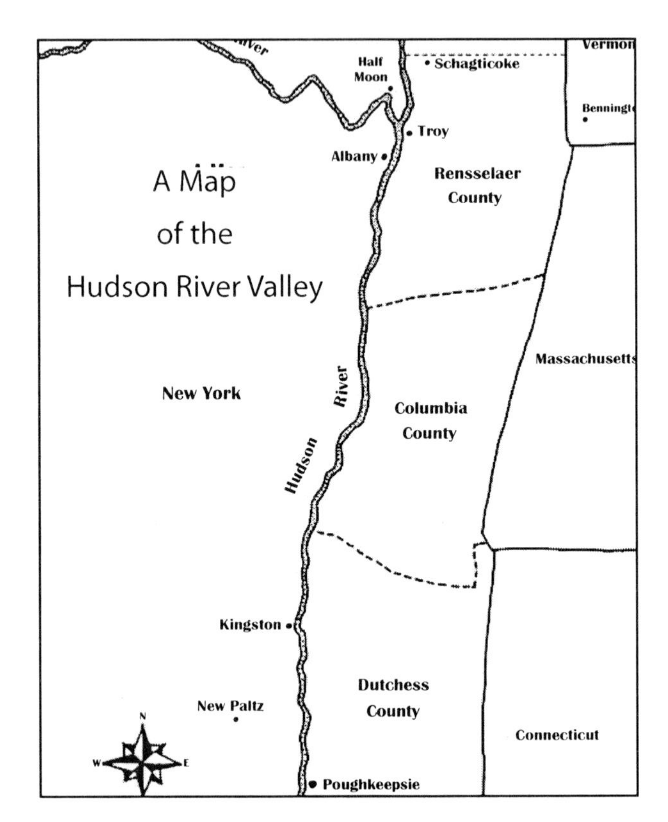

of the *Halve Maane* had found when they paddled up toward the headwaters of this mighty river. Some of the sailors had talked about returning to these rich lands they had found nearly 40 years before Harmon's birth. The stories he had heard in childhood lingered with him well into adulthood. At the age of 26, they became the commanding attraction for his coming to America.

For several days, the riverboat from the northernmost settlement on the Hudson, now called Albany, tied up at the Manhattan Island wharf in Nieuw Orange. It unloaded its cargo of tobacco and furs into the Dutch West India Company warehouse on Perel Straat. It would sail early the next morning and one of the passengers ready to head up-river was Harmon Jansen van Wye.

The greatest surprise he found was the transformation that had occurred in himself. From the somber, lonely, and withdrawn Dutch sailor who arrived in August he had, by October, become a spirited young man, and part of the human amalgam that was America.

Just as he was about to climb down the ladder to the riverboat below, he heard shouts approaching him. Michiel Tadens and Harmon's newfound buddies from the tavern were anxious to bid him a hearty farewell. Michiel carried the tankard from which Harmon had drunk his beer, and thrust it into his hand amid a rousing round of cheers.

The lines were released from the chocks and the riverboat eased out into deeper waters, to sail around the tip of the island, past the fort and the Church of St.

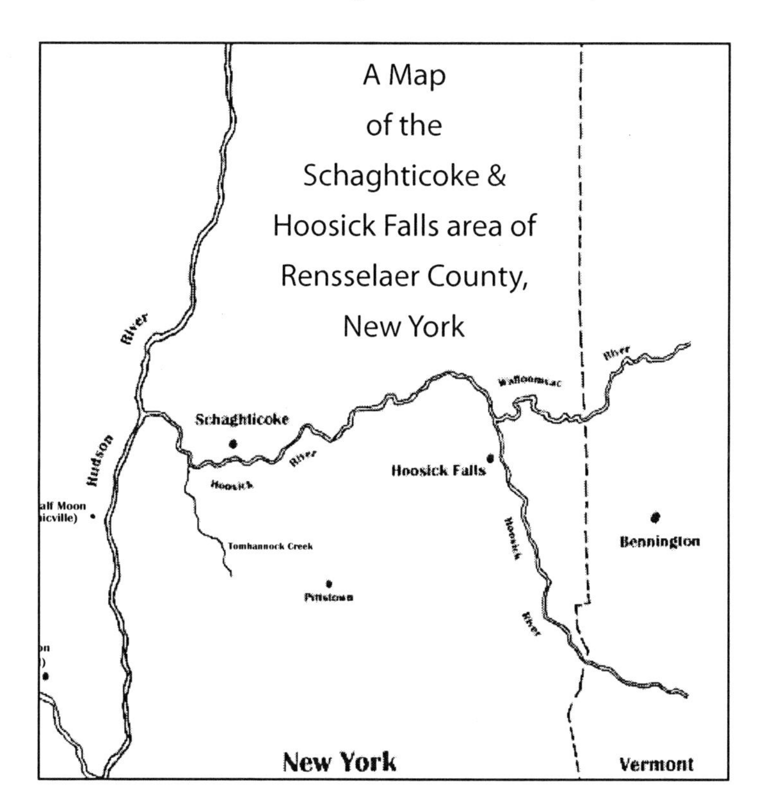

Nicholas. Just beyond, the timber-cutting windmills near the river's edge came into view. They caused him to have a sudden flashback to those windmills of home and the blood-stained sands of Kijkduin. It was nearly impossible for Harmon to believe that friendships made in lighthearted revelry could become as close as those developed in battle. Here, he discovered, friendships borne of fun and joined by laughter signified the promising new life they all sought as "Americans."

I was standing but a few feet away from Harmon, as the boat edged up the river, I noticed how his eyes virtually bulged when he saw the mile-wide span at the Tappan Zee. His head swiveled side-to-side and shook in disbelief to see the beauty of this pristine river course wind around, straighten out, then follow a wide curve once more. Never had he seen trees like those on the steep shoreline that often touched the water's edge. For someone accustomed to hills no higher than sand dunes, the 150-mile trip up the Hudson was enough to make Harmon think he was dreaming. In fact, it captured so much of his attention he could briefly ignore the pain in his thigh.

As the riverboat reached the point about two-thirds of the way upriver, it was I who was awestruck, not only by the beauty, but because of earlier history that had been written along the eastern shoreline. It was there where those enterprising Walloon shipwrights had presumably felled the masts and timber for the hull of their ship, the *Nieuw Nederlandt*, which made such a splash as it rolled into the East River, but scarcely a ripple had been heard about it since. This epoch in history was unknown except for those few settlers directly involved in its creation nearly 50 years before Harmon arrived. I knew few, if any, were still alive to recount the story of this remarkable feat.[23]

Above those same rising hillsides of the shipwrights' history, there would be history of a much different kind, yet to be written. A man, whose ancestors also came from The Netherlands, would live there in a classic brick home, a home I would visit in my youth, high above the river on a flat prominence. The Dutch spelling of his family name was "Rooseveldt."

From the deck, I looked across the river to the western shore. Below the rounded hills and mountains that would be silhouetted against evening sunsets, was the location where the Huguenots from the Rhinephaltz would come to settle more than a decade later, and name their village New Paltz.

Most spectacular that warm, October day was the panoply of color in every direction. Reds, orange, and yellows against darker bronze, all mingled amid evergreens, to take on a purple hue as the sun began to set. What an introduction to the country that Harmon chose to call his own.

Early the next morning the riverboat passed Castle Island where the crew of the *Mackerel* had wintered in the "year of dispute," presumably 1622. The riverboat docked at what had been Fort Orange. I noticed that the Dutch were reluctant to utter the name "Albany," instituted during the English stay there. Harmon and other new arrivals signed in at the desk of the town clerk. I watched Harmon Jansen van Wye sign his name in a flourish of strokes with the fresh quill pen provided. He hesitated for a moment as he finished. Then, a smile rippled across his face as he summed up whether the clerk spoke his native language. The smile widened as he added the Dutch word "knickkerbak" on the line below, just as a carpenter, miller, lawyer, or pastor might distinguish himself by his life-work.

"Knickkerbak" it was, and so it became his American name and the Dutch moniker of New York in time to come.

Playing games, as he did with the town clerk, by creating his signature of jest, as one whose life constituted playing table shuffleboard, showed that he had regained the playful frame of mind of his youth. This lightheartedness would be short-lived. Only three weeks after he had left with such warm memories, Nieuw Orange fell into English hands to become New York once more.[24]

There was an abundance of color that autumn day, across the low, rolling hillsides that bordered these narrowing waters of the Hudson. Harmon took out his long-stemmed, clay pipe to wait for the next boat. Soon a rowboat and its oarsman approached to take passengers north along the Hudson, to the fertile soil of Half Moon, the Anglicized version of the spot named by Hudson's crew. Across the river and three miles to the east at Schaghticoke, the Knickerbocker family homestead would be built and in centuries to follow, become an historic landmark. I smiled to myself, for as an unseen, historical observer I knew that not all the legends of this family were true.

---

23 Wilson

24 Sir Edmund Andros reclaimed the Nieuw Nederlandt Colony for Charles II on November 9, 1674, as authorized by the Treaty of Westminster.

4

Historical Housekeeping

The timeless, unseen historical observer of the previous chapters in Part III has been laid to rest. This summary chapter provides certain insights about the "Knickerbockers of New York" as presented by Washington Irving. It then attempts *first* to unravel family legends of my childhood, *second* to provide a new version of the origin of the family name and *third* to offer a possible resolution to the mystery surrounding an esteemed family ancestor, Johannes van Barghen Knickerbakker

Unintended Consequences: Washington Irving

Arising from Irving's popular parody, *The Knickerbocker History of New York*, the name and the image of "Father Knickerbocker" quickly became the patronym for New York. Associations in the public mind are many, to include: the pseudonym of journalist, Cholly Knickerbocker; the Knickerbocker Hotel in New York, among others by that name in various locations; the Jacob Rupert Knickerbocker Beer Company; and currently of course, the New York "Knicks" basketball team. None of the above has any ancestral connection to the Knickerbocker family that anyone knows of; neither did Washington Irving. He was, however, a friend of Herman Knickerbacker when Herman was a representative for the State of New York in the 11th U.S. Congress.

Irving's youthful fantasy was first published in 1809 by Inskeep and Bradford of Philadelphia and later by Putnam, Company. By the twist of his pen, he changed forever the spelling from "Knickerbacker" then in use, to the present form. This story depicted a whimsical life of the Dutch as the burlesque of New York.

In part, Irving may have found the germ of his idea during a visit to his friend Herman's at the Knickerbocker Mansion in Schaghticoke, New York.

Herman's 15-year-old nephew, Diedrick, came in from his home nearby, all dressed up in knee-breeches and a cocked hat. Perhaps, this furthered the author's fanciful ideas and led him to adopt the name of young Diedrick Knickerbocker as his "nom de plume." Part of the parody, it is reported, was written at the mansion, supposedly in the room to the right of the large front hall. A vivid recollection of that room, when I visited there as a young child, was the brick-lined chamber of the fireplace that seemed high enough for me to stand in.

From my point of view, Washington Irving's fantasy-ladened writing, more than anything else, did a disservice to early settlers. He was dismissive of rudimentary historical accuracy, and his attitude precluded offering any factual

Old fireplace at Knickerbocker Mansion at Schaghticoke, New York. It is in this room that Washington Irving supposedly composed part of his parody: ***The Knickerbocker History of New York.***

account in balance. Apparently, other writers of the day were also dissuaded from doing so by Irving's flamboyant, authoritative stance in the literary community. Although he presented this work as a parody, and not as a legitimate account of Dutch colonial days, the title suggests the contrary.

The unintended consequence of Irving's tongue-in-cheek satire was so subtle and was written in such a detailed, convoluted style, the reader's ongoing awareness that it was the author's fantasy could easily have been overlooked.

He needlessly and unabashedly transposed people and their times in ways that not only distorted history but maligned the people he claimed to exalt. He refers to the "Knickerbockers from Schaghticoke," with utter disregard for fact, telling of their convening with others at Bowling Green to support Stuyvesant in his bid to overtake the Swedish colony along the Delaware.

This juxtaposition of facts is ridiculous. Stuyvesant was displaced by the English in 1664, ten years before Harmon's ship arrived. It would be another half-century before the first Knickerbocker lived in Schaghticoke.

Furthermore, it is doubtful they would have supported the rancorous Stuyvesant had they been at his side. Thus, Irving glibly portrays with a sampling of fact, the lives of the Dutch that can unwittingly be accepted as history by the uninformed, casual reader.

In addition to clouding the early legacies of a proud Dutch people, an even greater travesty was visited on the fast-vanishing Walloons. Their courageous will, their innovative contributions, and the foundations they brought to our Constitution and representative form of government vanished into an unspoken, unwritten, unrecognized past. Unmitigated belief in this popular parody left the colorful, dedicated, early period of legitimate New York history without validation.

Ancestors of Nieuw Orange

It seems feasible that for a brief time in the summer and early fall of 1674 Adrian Vincent and Harmon van Wye were possibly living at the tip of Manhattan Island, where the settlement was then called Nieuw Orange. Given that there were an intervening 40 years between the dates of their arrival Adrian would presumably have been quite elderly. He may not have been alive, but his immediate descendants would have been.

There would have been no reason for any connection between these families then. However, a lasting bond was created in my own blood, through their combined DNA, ten generations after Adrian, and 13 generations after Harmon, arrived.

The English return; Harmon adjusts

Since the English had returned unexpectedly to Manhattan Island within weeks of the day Harmon had arrived as an early settler in Half Moon, this 26-year-old Dutchman had to adjust his thinking quickly. Perhaps keeping a sense of humor helped. Harmon concluded that his decision to come to America had been the right one, whether under Dutch, or English, rule. It meant he would have to set aside his feelings against those whose fellow countrymen had inflicted on him severe daily pain.

He was determined to give it his best. Just as he had fought hard under the Dutch Admirals, he was now willing to support the current leadership, to do his best to make this new-found land a viable, secure place in which to live. Just how this unfolded has become the meat of legends in oral history, as well as literature.

Family myths, legends and truths

First, I will address the family legends of our house that differed profoundly from the fantasy world of Washington Irving. The bible of family fables was the Harper Brother's magazine article of 1876 by General Egbert Viele. My grandmother believed it like the New Testament Scriptures, and often brought out her original copy as noble proof. She would have been greatly offended and maintained staunch disbelief to have learned the General's daughter, Kathryn Knickerbacker Viele put much of this legend to rest in her little-known document *Sketches of Allied Families, Knickerbacker-Viele, Historical and Genealogical*, published in 1916. With only 75 copies printed, it was hardly a best seller.

According to Viele's account, and that of others, it was the English governor in Albany, Edmund Andros, who, in 1676, invited the Pequot Indians to make their home in the Hoosack Valley. This was after they had been run out of the Massachusetts Colony by the English as a result of the King Philip Wars. It was at that time Governor Andros invited 1,000 Indians to convene the Onandoga Council at Schaghticoke. They included those from the Eastern branch of the Iriquois of Canada, together with the Pequots who now called themselves "The Schaghticokes," a name that signified "mingling waters" for the land between the Hoosack River and the Tomhannock Creek.

Clearly, Kathryn's research has dispelled the family myth that Harmon had been directed by Governor Andros to lead 12 families to Schaghticoke to make peace with the Indians around the Onandoga Council.[1] And, it was not Harmon, but Governor Andros himself who, together with the 1,000 Indians just cited, planted the sapling of the Witenagemot Oak in 1676, which was then called the "Tree of Peace." This is the first known monument to peace on this continent between the Indians and either Dutch, or English, settlers. It was still standing nearly 275 years later when, in 1948, it was felled by a heavy spring flood. That year also signaled the 300th anniversary of Harmon's birth in that faraway town of Bommel.

It was during 1609 that Henry Hudson's ship, the *Haave Maane*, reached the upper waters of the river that would carry his name. On the shore west of where Hudson apparently anchored, that would later become Albany, Hudson sent his sailors upstream in a skiff to search for navigable waters. About 15 miles north, they allegedly stepped ashore and named this site Haave Maane, too. It was not for the name of Hudson's ship, but for the crescent-shaped hills they saw. My

1 Onandoga was the correct spelling of the time.

The Witenagemot Oak, the first monument to peace in this country, was planted in 1676 by the Indians and settlers of the Onandoga Council location that became Schaghticoke, New York. This tree stood for 275 years.

recent observation of this area, however, fails to discern what they may have seen to warrant this name.

The original site of Half Moon, the Anglicized version, is on the west bank, where the river narrows to approximately 500 feet; this community is currently called Mechanicville, New York. On his arrival, Harmon could have gazed directly across the river to see the large Witenagemot Tract; three miles beyond the riverbank is where the "Tree of Peace" or the Witenagomot Oak was planted in 1676.

Historians of the Knickerbocker family at Schaghticoke verify that Governor Andros did request the services of Harmon early on, to maintain claim to this vulnerable riverfront location north of Albany, at Half Moon.

There is, however, good reason to believe that, at some later time, Governor Andros asked Harmon to recruit 12 men to help him build Fort Schaghticoke, a defense located a half-mile from the Tree of Peace. This fortification, intended as protection from the French and the Indians, was on the tract of land six miles wide, on either side of the Hoosack River, that had been purchased from the Indians by the government in Albany.

General Viele's 1876 article lends credibility to the latter event, for it cites the names of the 12 men whom Harmon supposedly recruited. The legend at our house, about those 12 families from Albany being recruited by Governor Andros to go to Schaghticoke to build a settlement, may have resulted as a convergence of related numbers, places, and events. It is very possible that Harmon also had been asked earlier by Governor Andros to lead 12 families from Albany to go to Half Moon, but this is not proven.

One has to wonder whether these two incidents may have become melded in Grandma's mind as the result of being misinformed about local geography.

Whether the details of history have been distorted in family legend, or by the distance of my childhood memory, they served me well at the time as a dramatic foundation on which to paint colorful fantasies. These Indians of Schaghticoke and their vivid headdresses danced around the campfires of my mind amid the "whoops and hollers" I provided whenever my father could tell me these tales. Historical fact never interfered with these imaginary playmates, who were so important to me.

According to Kathryn Viele's account, Harmon Jansen Knickerbakker, as an early version is spelled, bought the land at Half Moon in 1689, 15 years after he first settled there. According to Grandma, this was the land that he purchased from Pieter Schuyler and Goosen Garretsen, that name I found intriguing as a child. In actuality it may have been deeded from Schuyler's son-in-law, Anthony Schiack. I found that the original tract had been purchased to keep the "people from Connecticut" from doing so, just as Grandma said.

What was more crucial to this situation, than just keeping the people from Connecticut at bay was Harmon's settling there to provide an outpost of protection for Albany. Apparently Governor Andros further recognized Harmon's leadership talents when he directed him to gather together the men to build Fort Schaghticoke. Had the French, and the Indians they had armed, proceeded south along the shores on either side of the Hudson this early, the unity of the emerging colonies could easily have been compromised. Helping to stabilize this region even with such primitive resources is worthy of more recognition than anything Washington Irving perpetrated to exalt the Knickerbockers of New York.

Between 1701 and 1703, Harmon purchased land of the family homestead in Schaghticoke that had been part of the Witenagemot Tract. Just as Grandma had told, I found Harmon was the first white man to own this land. It is not clear if he ever lived there, but his oldest son, Johannes, resided there and rented an adjacent 1,200 acres from the Albany government. It was not until the early 1800s that this property, or parts of it, may have come into the hands of Harmon's descendants.

Leaving his oldest son, Johannes, behind in Schaghticoke, Harmon moved with the rest of the family from Half Moon in 1704. Moving with him were his wife, Lysbeth Jansen Bogaart, their two daughters, Cornelia and Jannetie, and

The Knickerbocker Mansion shown here with flags from four nations American, French, British and The Netherlands.

the three younger sons, Lourens, Evert, and Pieter.[2] They settled on property Harmon had bought along the east bank of the Hudson at Tivoli. The hamlet of Tivoli is located just north of Red Hook and about 20 miles north of Hyde Park. Later, all this land became part of Dutchess County. It was in Dutchess County that the branch of the family headed by the second son, Lourens, developed. It is from Lourens' branch of Knickerbockers that my family is descended.

According to the Knickerbocker Historical Society, the handsome, classic structure at Schaghticoke, called the Knickerbocker Mansion, was erected on the site of the original cabin built in the early 1700s by Johannes Knickerbacker. In the late 1700s, the mansion was completed by Harmon's great-grandson, Johannes III. It was built of red bricks from clay obtained in the surrounding hillsides. Family occupants of this mansion were witness not only to Washington Irving's visits but also to General Lafayette, who stayed there during his 1825 visit to America. The Knickerbocker Mansion is listed on the National Historical Register. It is being restored and is open to the public during the summer; descendants currently gather for July reunions during odd-numbered years.

Even before Washington Irving's publicized change in the spelling of the family name, there were many variations. I have tried to use whichever spelling correlated with the time frame of its use; hence many versions are seen in this writing.

And now we come to the ongoing family discussion of the origin of the name "Knickerbakker" in an attempt to discern which version among many may be

2 *Genealogies of the First Settlers of Albany 1630-1800*, with contributions by Jonathan Pearson, published in Albany, New York, 1872.

most accurate. While several of these versions seem legitimate, I offer another, one which has not previously been put forth. Apparently, it is true that the local clerk in Albany who met Harmon that first day mistook the foreign word "knickkerbak" he wrote on the line beneath his signature to be his surname. Thus, the name van Wye which had survived for a remarkable 12 generations in Europe vanished instantly and Harmon became Mr. "Knickkerbak." Here is a new twist to the story that I have only now learned.

During my trip to Europe in 2004, I was discussing the origins of our "Dutch" name with Jeremy Bangs, Ph.D., historian and curator of the Pilgrim Museum in Leiden, as the name of that city is currently spelled. When I offered the customary translation of our family name most frequently cited during my childhood, as a "baker of clay marbles," he smiled and then shed an entirely different light on it. He told me a story about table shuffleboard. This was a frequent pastime the Jews played, one very possibly brought with them from Spain in the 1490s. Later this game came into general use throughout The Netherlands.

He told me that the word "knickker" in Dutch meant the round wooden disk used to play this game, which comprised a six-foot long board perhaps 15 inches wide, with a row of five archways positioned a short way from the far end. The player's challenge is to direct his disk through the center arch for the highest points, while attempting to knock an opponent's "knickker" out of position in the process. He also told me the one who played the game was called a "bak."

Upon hearing this I smiled for I could see how easily these two words could be combined. To what extent Harmon may have played this game in his homeland, as is suggested he did as he recovered from battle wounds sustained of the Battle of Solebay in 1672, is speculation. But for sure, he played a "game" with the unsuspecting town clerk. To suggest "tongue-in-cheek" that playing shuffleboard was his "life-time work" is, in itself, worth a laugh. The family prankster from Bommel had quickly become one right here in his new home in America.

So, is it any surprise no one can find relatives by the surname of Knickerbocker in Holland or elsewhere in The Netherlands? Unaware of the fictitious nature of the family name, descendants have tried to locate long-dead Knickerbockers in the homeland. Individuals of many generations who have tried have met with difficulty. My own curiosity and frustration was limited to phone books that yielded nothing when I visited there during various leaves from my post in Germany.

Hero of Breda, false ancestor

One Knickerbocker descendant was so frustrated in his search that he sought local assistance. The enterprising genealogist whom John Hale Knickerbocker engaged during his 1855 trip may have sought to mitigate the disappointment of this visitor who had come from faraway America with such avid hopes. For whatever reason, this "genealogist-for-hire" informed him that our family was related to the "van Barghen" family, a very famous name in The Netherlands. Varied spellings were common then and throughout history, and perhaps this name may also have undergone minor changes. This "discovery" of Johannes van Barghen Knickerbakker, who allegedly captained the ship on which Harmon served under Admirals de Ruyter and Tromp, was provided a place of haloed prominence in our "Knickerbocker" family tree. In Grandma's household, it was viewed with the same reverence and "gospel status" as other facts which have now become illusory legends.

Upon reading Russell Shorto's recent book, *Island at the Center of the World*, I was immediately struck when I read the account of Adriaen van Bergen, hero of Breda.[3] The spelling was close; the dates and locations, too, might well have coincided sufficiently between the backgrounds of each family for our inventive family "researcher" of the mid-1800s.

To understand this better, it should be noted that Breda is located directly south of Amsterdam in an equilateral triangle with these two cities and Arnhem to the east; the distance of each is estimated to be 50 to 60 miles. Thus, Harmon's home of Bommel, adjacent to Arnhem, is not that far from Breda. Shorto's comments about the siege of Breda has shed new light on our most mysterious ancestor, Johannes van Barghen Knickerbakker.

When John Hale Knickerbocker went to Amsterdam in search of family history, his creative assistant may well have had the hero of Breda in mind. Presumably, this genealogist would have had no knowledge of the family history that was found a century later in the New York State Library Archives in Albany.[4] It would appear, that he nefariously created a fictitious connection in our family, that is totally without merit. However, I found this hero's actions were fascinating and I feel they warrant mention here.

There was a ten-month struggle by the Dutch in 1624 to take back the starving city of Breda from the Spanish. This clever Dutchman, Adriaen van Bergen, led 70 Dutch soldiers who hid themselves under mounds of peat, carried by boats into the waterways of Breda. Like the Trojan Horse of Troy, these boats smuggled avengers into the enemy's midst. Adriaen van Bergen is credited in Dutch history as a hero for devising and leading the recapture of Breda.

Was it really the name of Adriaen van Bergen's family that was absconded, to falsely head the lineage in my own family? Who can say for sure? What is certain, however, is that the captain of Harmon's ship in the Battle of Solebay in 1672 was not the Johannes van Barghen Knickerbakker held in uncanny esteem in the Knickerbocker household of Bangall, New York. It surely would have been under another captain that Harmon served, father perhaps to someone else, but not he.

Coming full circle

The unwitting effect of my grandmother and her interminable memory of family history played a significant role through which I created rich fantasies and imaginary playmates in childhood. Undoubtedly, it was this experience that enabled me to become the unseen historical observer of Adrian Vincent and Harmon van Wye, by which I could attempt to portray their feelings, their dialogue, and their settings in history.

3 Siege of Breda
4 Appendix A

Added to this, my mother instilled a Walloon heritage in me that led to my own investigation. In *Powder Keg,* I have presented the effect of history (1) on my own life, (2) then the effect on individuals within our family whose lot was cast by world events; and (3) ancestors whose lives impacted pre-colonial and early American history.

Before I started school my father spelled out the name for me in rhythm, "SCH AGH TI COKE," just as his father had taught him: same age, same rhythm, same table.

My mother's words, too, were clear in my ear. From the time I was four, I heard her say: "Don't ever forget you are a Walloon!"

I never have.

The End

Appendix A

Excerpts of Knickerbocker Genealogy

The following is comprised of excerpts from research uncovered in the New York State Library Archives, Albany, New York, in 1960 by Paul Knickerbocker. This version has been adapted from the original provided me, by repositioning material within generations for consistency and readability.

Brackets include details of my research, in attempt to define locations, and cite relevant cultural practices of the times.

1st Generation: Jordaen was probably born around 1245. (It was then the practice to take the name of one's town as a surname, preceded by "van" meaning "from." Thus I researched the name **Wyhe**, and located it on maps of the time, on the eastern bank of the River Yssel. The current spelling of this town is **Wijhe**, located in what was originally the Oberyessl region, now called the Province of Oberyessl. The spelling of the River Yssel, was changed to Jessl; the current spelling is IJssel.)

It is stated that in 1271, he married Miss Echteld. She was apparently an heiress in her own right, as ***Jordaen*** became the First Lord of Echteld, a minor title of Dutch nobility passed through the eldest son or son-in-law if there were no sons. This was the beginning of the branch of the family known as "van Wyhe–Tot Echteld," which became extinct in 1753. ***Jordaen van Wyhe*** had three sons. We are descended from the eldest, ***Hendrick***.

2nd Generation: *Hendrick van Wyhe* had one son, ***Johannes***, and a daughter, Hermana. Little is known about ***Hendrick*** other than the fact he died before his father, ***Jordaen***. We are descended from ***Johannes***.

3rd Generation: *Johannes van Wyhe*, Third Lord of Echteld, married Hille van-Rivierre. They had five sons and one daughter; he died in 1371. We are descended from his third son, ***Herman van Wyhe***.

4th Generation: *Herman van Wyhe* married and had four children. We are descended from his son, ***Willem***. In 1392, he was made Governor of Neder-Betue, (meaning "lower Betue") a district in the Province of North Brabant that includes the town of ***Bommel***. From this time, our branch of the family seems to have been located in, or near, ***Bommel*** in ***North Brabant***.

5th Generation: *Willem van Wyhe* had three children, among them ***Herman*** from whom we are descended. Little more is known about ***Willem***, other than that he was alive in 1434.

6th Generation: ***Herman van Wyhe***, married Miss van Heerdt. He was magistrate of the town of **Arnhem** in 1459 and was alive in 1490. He had two children, one being ***Harmon Harmansz van Wyhe***, from whom we are descended.

7th Generation: ***Harmon Harmansz van Wyhe*** married Aleid van Bommel. He became "Lord of Ressenerbroek," near **Bommel**. He had a son, ***Gybert***, from whom we are descended. ***Harmon Harmansz van Wyhe*** died in 1531.

8th Generation: ***Gybert van Wyhe*** married and had a son, ***Cornelis***. He, ***Gybert van Wyhe***, was a judge at **Arnhem**, and died in 1548. He belonged to the nobility of the Upper Betue.

9th Generation: ***Cornelis Gybert van Wyhe*** (may have been spelled Cornelius Gilbert van Wyhe, later) was a judge at ***Wageningen*** in 1563. He married Wilhelmina van Haeften and had a son, ***Roelof***.

10th Generation: ***Roelof van Wyhe*** was a captain in the army and married Johanna Splythoff. It appears that he died in 1600. They had a son, ***Johannes***.

11th Generation: ***Johannes van Wyhe*** of ***Bommel*** married Jennetje Jansen of Masterlandt. Their son was ***Harmen Jansen van Wyhe***.

12th Generation: ***Harmen Jansen van Wye*** was the way he chose to spell it. He was born in 1648 in **Bommel** of North Brabant, and it was from here that ***Harmen Jansen van Wye*** (***Knickerbakker***) left in early adulthood.

(The date when he left to join the Dutch navy, is presumed to be on, or about, 1670. He could not return home after his tour of naval duty because his town had been decimated by a French invasion. After recovery from battle wounds incurred in the 1672 Battle of Solebay, and another at the Kijkdunes in 1673, he sailed for America. This is calculated to have been in the late summer, or early autumn, of 1674. He would then have been 26 years old, and single. At that time men did not marry until after they became adults, at age 25.)

In America, he used the name "van Wyebacke" to sign a land contract in 1682. He is the ancestor of all Knickerbockers in North America.

(One of the family legends has it, that he signed his last name van Wye for the town clerk in Albany when he arrived, and below it, the word "Knickerbakk"—perhaps to indicate a trade or profession—and the clerk misconstrued it, entering this as his family name.) The name ***Harmen*** was changed to ***Harmon*** in America.

The fortified city of Zaltbommel on the River Waal and the city of Maasbommel to the south, both lie within the region of Bommelwaardt in the province of North Brabant. People refer to being from "Bommel," when they come from either of these towns, or the region. However, the town of Bommel in the Neder Betue district of North Brabant, west of Arnhem is the specific location with which we are concerned here. (Bommel is not shown on current maps.)

Appendix B

1530–1730

A summary chronology is presented here, citing the identity of individuals, groups, and the relevant history depicted in *Powder Keg.*

Many of these people and their noteworthy actions have failed to fall within the mainstream of historical records.

The temporal sequence of these early events appears in capsule form to provide a concisely interrelated picture. Here are the specific features of hidden history that took place prior to, and within, this two-century span of time:

§ The technological expertise of the Walloons, their notable scientific advances of the time, and the rich literary culture of peoples of the Belgic Lands, as this area was referred to then, were well recognized in Europe, long before the Reformation.

§ The unwitting contributions of Clement Marot, Professor of Hebrew at the Sorbonne, who translated 30 psalms into French in 1540 and put them to music, sparked a Calvinistic fire storm across France and the lowlands.

§ The courage, and the resolve, of the Walloons to stand up to the power of the Catholic church, and the vengeance of their Spanish oppressors, was extraordinary.

§ The tragic devastation of symbols and property of the Church of Rome in 1566 by the reform-minded Walloon iconoclasts called "protestors," precipitated the two-year war for religious and political freedoms (1567–1569). Walloon Reformists, not Huguenot Walloons, as they are incorrectly called, fled to Holland, England, and elsewhere, spreading the idea of representational governance and the Protestant religion.

§ The Second Spanish Inquisition that lasted 12 years, was perpetrated by the Duke of Alva against reform-minded Walloons and some Flemish. (1567–1579)

§ The author of the 1561 *Belgic Confession of Faith,* was Walloon Calvinist leader Guido de Bray.

§ When the Walloon Reformists fled to Holland, they carried with them the *Belgic Confession of Faith.* Circa 1612, the Dutch Reformed Church fiercely debated the founding articles of faith they would follow. They eventually rejected the *Heidelberg Catechism* that pastors had endorsed in 1574, and the *Calvinist Confession of Faith* created several years earlier than de Bray's. It was the latter's *Belgic Confession of Faith* that was adopted, and this document of 25 typed pages continues in use throughout the Reformed Churches today.

§ The United States Constitution has roots in the *Belgic Confession of Faith,* brought by the early Walloon settlers. Our civic government stems from the representative church government adopted by the early Walloon synods in the Belgic Lands. (1563–1566)

§ The date of the arrival of the first eight Walloon families to settle Manhattan Island, according to the Dutch West India Company records in Amsterdam, researched by John Romeyn Brodhead, was 1623, not 1624 as is commonly thought.

§ It was the Walloons, not the Dutch, who were the first to come as settlers, with families, flax, and farming tools.

§ The extraordinary range and depth of survival skills of the early Walloon settlers has not been recognized.

§ The names of the first 100 people aboard the *Nieuw Nederlandt,* and those Walloons who followed them, were lost.

§ The Sephardic Jews of Amsterdam were among the principal stockholders to finance the construction of the *Nieuw Nederlandt* and its maiden voyage that brought the first 100 settlers, all Walloons but two reformed-minded Flemish, to the New World. (1623)

§ The remarkably inventive shipbuilding achievements in the wild—without a dry dock—and the names, of the two Walloons of fortitude who mastered the task, did not survive. (1630)

§ The name "Nova Belgica," the formal Latin for "new lowland," is found on maps to signify the territory of Nieuw Nederlandt for many decades following the 1623 landing on Manhattan Island. The name "Nova Belgica" is presumed to have also been the name the Walloon settlers gave to their tiny, partly swampy settlement at the tip of the island. (This is supported by the following statement.)

§ The name Nieuw Amsterdam was first coined in 1630 by Johaan de Laet, Dutch historian and investor in the Dutch West India Company. In an eight-page promotional tract, he urged the Dutch to settle there by falsely likening it to the charm of their beloved city. The new name did not come into general use until 1640.

§ This territory was granted the title of Province of Nieuw Nederlandt in 1626, but was not a colony until 1640.

§ Walloons whose families had fled the Province of Hainaut constituted the predominant group of settlers throughout the Hudson Valley for the first 40 years. They were followed by the Dutch and in the 1670's by the Huguenots.

§ The role of Asser Levy to seek citizenship in 1657, without adhering to the faith of the Dutch Reformed Church, created the foundation for a separation of church and state that year, and was written into law in Albany in 1730.

§ Francois Molemacher's horse-driven gristmill provided meeting space for 50 people on the second floor, at 20–22 Slyck Steeg and was the location of the following history:

(1) the first services of the Dutch Reformed Church in America, held in 1626 and conducted in the Walloon's native language, French;

(2) the first celebration in the Province of Nieuw Nederlandt of The Lord's Supper, August 11, 1628; and

(3) services of the first Jewish congregation in North America, that of Shearith Israel. (1655)

§ The first congregation of the Dutch Reformed Church that met in Molemacher's mill evolved into the Marble Collegiate Church of New York, with continuous records of births, deaths, marriages, baptisms, and church membership since 1638.

§ The first synagogue in North America was located at 20–22 Slyck Steeg, renamed Mill Street, and is currently called South William Street. This tiny Mill Street Synagogue built in 1730, was the first home of the Shearith Israel congregation, built in 1730.

§ Asser Levy and other members who had been among those who arrived in 1654 from the island of Recife, off Brazil, had also helped to organize the first synagogue in South America, at that location.

§ Millstones from Francois Molemacher's adjacent gristmill at 28 Slyck Steeg grace the entrance to the present Shearith Israel Synagogue, located at 70th Street and Central Park West. Other millstones from that location can be found at the Marble Collegiate Church in New York.

§ The Tree of Peace planted at Schaghticoke, New York, was the first monument to peace on this continent, between either the Dutch, or English settlers, and the native Indian tribes. (1676)

§ Early settlers of the Albany region that included the first Knickerbocker in North America, helped to stabilize the region from invasion by the French in Canada, and the Indians they armed, and to preserve the unity of the early pre-colonial structure of the Hudson Valley (starting in 1674).

§ The Belgic tribe—which existed before the birth of Christ—became Walloon Reformists in large part. They contributed significantly to advancing the Protestant Reformation and additionally to the development of a lawful, civilized world. Much of this information has disappeared from the pages of history.

Bibliography

Bainton, Roland H., *The Reformation of the 16th Century*. Boston: Beacon Press, 1985.

Baird, Charles Washington, *History of the Huguenot Emigration to America, Vol. I*. New York: Dodd, Mead and Co., 1885.

Bayer, Henry, *The Belgians—First Settlers in New York and the Middle States*. New York: The Devin–Adair Co., 1925.

Blok, Petrus, Johannes, *History of People of the Netherlands, Vol. II*. New York and London: G. P. Putnam and Sons, 1898. (Petrus Johannes Blok was Professor of History, University of Leyden at the time. Translation by Ruth Putnam)

Blok, Petrus Johannes, *History of People of the Netherlands, Vol. IV*. New York, and London: G. P. Putnam Sons, The Knickerbocker Press, 1902. (Petrus Johannes Blok was Professor of History, University of Leyden at the time. Translation by Oscar A. Bierstadt.)

Brodhead, John Romeyn, Ph.D., *History of the State of New York Vol. I*. New York: Harper Bros., 1853.

Condon, Thomas J., *New York Beginnings, The Commercial Origins of New Nederland*. New York: New York University Press, 1968.

Costobel, Eva Deutsch, *The Jews of Nieuw Amsterdam*. New York: Atheneum, 1988.

Cotton, Julia, *Annals of Old Manhattan*. New York: Brentano, 1902.

de Forrest, Major John, *The Walloons of Avesnes and of New Netherland: a Huguenot Thread in American Colonial History, 1494–to the Present Time*. New Haven: Tuttle, Morehouse and Taylor, 1900.

de Forrest, Mrs. Robert, *A Walloon Family in America. Vol. I*. New York: Houghton & Mifflin, 1914.

de Forrest, Mrs. Robert, *Jesse de Forrest's Journal—in Guiana Vol. II* (in French and English). New York: Houghton & Mifflin, 1914.

Dunshee, Kenneth Holcomb, *As You Pass By*. New York: Hastings House Publisher, 1952.

Edwards, Harrington, *A Condensed Genealogy (of one branch) of the Edwards Family and Allied Families of Concord and Acton, Mass, and of Allied Families*. (Knickerbockers included) Brooklyn, 1907.

Encyclopedia of North American Colonies, Vol. I. New York: Schribner, 1983.

Fabend, Firth Haring, *A Dutch Family in the Middle Colonies, 1660–1800*. New Brunswick: Rutgers University Press, 1991.

Gallagher, Hugh Gregory, *F.D.R.'s Splendid Deception*. New York: Dodd, Mead, 1995.

Gazatteer No. 73rd Belgium, Office of Geography, Dept. of the Interior, Washington 25, D. C., March, 1963.

Gehring, Charles T. and Starns, William, Translated and Edited, *A Journey into Mohawk Country and Oneida Country 1634–1635.* Syracuse: Syracuse University Press, 1988

Griffis, William Elliot, *The Story of the Walloons, At Home, In Lands of Exile and in America.* New York: Houghton & Mifflin, 1923.

Grun, Bernard, *The Timetables of History, 3rd Revised Edition.* New York: Simon & Schuster, 1991.

Hall, Edward Hageman, L.H.D., *Philipse Manor Hall at Yonkers, New York.* New York: American Scenic and Historic Preservation Society, 1912.

Historical Atlas of the World, Edited by R. R. Palmer. New York: Rand McNally, 1965.

Homberger, Eric, *The Historical Atlas of New York City.* New York: Henry Holt and Company, Inc., 1994.

Irving, Washington, *Knickerbocker's History of New York by Diedrick Knickerbocker.* Philadelphia: Inskeep and Bradford, 1809.

Irving, Washington, *Knickerbocker's History of New York,* Edited by Anne Carroll Moore. New York: Doubleday Doran, 1928.

Jamieson, John Franklin, Ph.D. (papers from the American Historical Association) *Vol. II, #3, "William Usselinx."* New York: G. P. Putnam Co. 1887.

Jamieson, John Franklin, Ph.D. Editor, *Narratives of New Netherland, 1609–1664.* New York: Charles Scribner, 1909.

Journal of Jasper Danckaerts 1679–1680, Edited by Artlett Burleigh James, Ph.D. and John Franklin Jamieson, Ph.D. New York: Charles Scribner's Sons, 1913.

Kamen, Henry, *Philip II.* New Haven: Yale Press, 1997.

Kamen, Henry, *The Spanish Inquisition.* New Haven: Yale Press, 1998.

Kamen, Henry, *EMPIRE, How Spain Became A World Power, 1492–1763.* New York: Harper Collins, 2003.

Kaufman, Tania Neumann. "Pernambuco." A Presenca Judaica em Permambuco: Passos Perdidos, Historia Recuperada. Ph.D. Thesis. Recife: Universidade Federal de Pernambuco, 1998.

Kouevenhoven, John A., "The Columbian Historical Portrait of New York," An Essay in Graphic History. New York: Harper & Row, 1972.

Lamb, Martha J., *History of the City of New York: its origin, rise and progress.* New York: A. S. Barnes Co., 1877.

Manna-hatin, *The Story of New York.* New York: The Manhattan Co., 1929. (Planned, prepared and designed under the direction of the Beardley Service Organization: New York, New York.)

Marley, David, *War of the Americas: A Chronology of Armed Conflict in the New World, 1492 to the Present.* ABC, CLIO, Santa Barbara: 1998.

Martin, George Castor, *The Knickerbackers or Knickerbockers.* Philadelphia: Martin & Allardyce, 1912.

McEvedy, Colin, *The New Penguin Atlas of Medieval History.* Penguin Books.

Memorial History of the City of New York and the Hudson Valley (from its first settlement to the year 1892) Vol. I. Edited by James Grant Wilson. New York: New York History Company, 1892.

Pool, David de Sola, Ph.D., "The Mill Street Synagogue (1730–1817) of the Congregation of Shearith Israel." Publication of the American Jewish Historical Society, New York: 1930.

Pool, David de Sola, Ph.D., *Portraits in Stone.* New York: Columbia University Press, 1950.

Pool, David de Sola, Ph.D., and Pool, Tamar de Sola. *An Old Faith in the New World; portrait of Shearith Israel, 1654–1954.* New York: Columbia University Press, 1955.

Preliminary NIS Gazetteer Netherlands. Published by the Central Intelligence Agency, Washington, D.C.: March, 1950.

Reaman, G. Elmore, *The Trail of the Huguenots in Europe, the United States, South Africa and Canada.* Baltimore: Baltimore Genealogical Publishing Company, 1966.

Riker, James, *The Revised History of Harlem, its Origins and Early Annals.* New York: New Harlem Publishing Company, 1904.

Rymer, Russ, "Saving the Music Tree" Smithsonian, April 2004, Volume 35, Number 1.

Shearith Israel, 1654 Congregation of Shearith Israel, Spanish and Portugese Synagogue, http://www.sephardichouse.com/identity/shearithisrael.htm.

Shorto, Russell, *The Island at the Center of the World.* New York: Doubleday, 2004.

Slavery, NOVA Documentary. wwwteachout.org/vna.

Spier, Peter, *The Legend of New Amsterdam.* New York: Doubleday, 1979.

Stokes, I. N. Philip, *The Iconography of Manhattan Island 1498–1909.* New York: Robert H. Dodd, 1916.

Age of the Renaissance. New York: McGraw–Hill, 1968.

The New York Genealogical and Biological Record Vol. XLV, 1914. New York, Genealogical Society and Biographical Society. Volumes XXXIX and XXXX contain information about those who arrived before 1683.

The Vincent Family, Descendants of Adrian Vincent. Millbrook, New York: Millbrook Press, 1959. (Compiled principally by Anne M. Vincent. After her death, it was determined at the 1955 Vincent Family Reunion, that Clifford Buck name a committee to complete her research. They included: Gordon S. V. Andrews, Mrs. Harrie D. Knickerbocker and E. Harold Vincent.)

Thomasson, Clyde Jr., "William Usselinx and his Time," in partial fulfillment of a Master of Arts Degree, University of Houston, Faculty of the Division of Social Services, 1953.

Todd, Charles Burr, *The Story of the City of New York.* New York: G. P. Putnam & Sons, The Knickerbocker Press, 1888.

Valentine, David, *The History of the City of New York.* New York: G. P. Putnam, 1853.

Van Rensselaer, Mrs. John King, *The Goode Vrouw (Good Women) of Manahatta.* New York: Charles Scribner, 1898.

Van Rensselaer, Mrs. Schuyler, *History of the City of New York in the 17th Century Vol. I.* New York: MacMillan, 1909.

Van Winkle, Edward, *Manhattan 1524–1639.* New York: The Knickerbocker Press, G. P. Putnam, 1916.

Viele, General Egbert, "The Knickerbockers of New York" Vol. 54 *Harper & Brothers, New Monthly Magazine* #319, December 1876. New York: Harper & Brothers, Franklin Square.

Viele, Kathryn Knickerbacker, *Sketches of Allied Families: Knickerbacker–Viele Historical and Genealogical Data.* New York: Tobias A. Wright, 1916. (75 copies printed)

Wenkende Wieken in West Vlaanderen 2004 (The Mills of West Flanders 2004) Brochure, Provincie West Vlaanderen, Dienst Cultur, Provinciehuis Boeverhos, Konig Leopold III, 8200 Sint-Andries, Brugge: 2004.

Werner, M. R., *It Happened in New York.* New York: Coward–McCann Inc., 1957.

Wilson, James Grant, *The memorial history of the City of New York, from its first settlement to the year (1600–1775).* New York: New York History Company, 1892–1893.

Windmills of Holland, Kooijman, P.O. Box 179, Koog a/d Zaan. Website: www.woodenshoe.workshop.nl.

Sources

The Knickerbocker Historical Society, c/o General John Hemstreet, USAF Ret., Box 29, Hemstreet Road, Schaghticoke, New York, 12154.

The Holland Society of New York, 122 East 58th Street, New York, New York, 10022.

The Society of the Mary and John, Windsor, Connecticut, 06095.

The Vincent Tin Horn, Newsletter for the Vincent Family, c/o Sheridan Vincent, P.O. Box 15523, Rochester, New York, 14615-0523.

Sephardic House, Institute for Researching and Promoting Sephardic History and Culture. The Spanish and Portugese Synagogue, Central Park West at 70th Street, New York City, New York.

Index

Printed in the United States
202740BV00004B/1-102/P

9 780981 776811